FLOWER ARRANGING STYLE

AN INTERNATIONAL COLLECTION OF IDEAS AND INSPIRATIONS FOR ALL SEASONS

JUDITH BLACKLOCK

A BULFINCH PRESS BOOK
LITTLE, BROWN AND COMPANY
BOSTON • NEW YORK • LONDON

First North American Edition, 1997
Third Printing, 2000
ISBN 0-8212-2386-0

Library of Congress Control Number 96-79047

Bulfinch Press is an imprint of
Little, Brown and Company (Inc.)

Designed and typeset by
Book Creation Services Ltd, London

PRINTED IN HONG KONG

CONTENTS

ARRANGER: JUDITH DERBY

FOREWORD

The language of flowers is universal; this book seeks to extend our understanding and knowledge of a subject which for many of us is an integral part of our lifestyle.

For the beginner it gives a fascinating insight into the joys of arranging a few simple flowers for one's own pleasure and hopefully then encourages further investigation of what the life of the dedicated flower arranger can offer.

With the world getting smaller and the opportunity to discover what our overseas arrangers are producing, the international flavour of this book is of great interest and will challenge the more adventurous to experiment with styles from around the world.

The formation of the National Association of Flower Arrangement Societies (NAFAS) in 1959 led to more people becoming aware of flower clubs in the United Kingdom and in 1981 the World Association of Flower Arrangers (WAFA) was formed. A small group of visionary NAFAS ladies saw the opportunity to widen the horizons and establish that world link through the bond of flowers. This International Book of Flower Arranging will provide information about some of our friends across the sea. The list of flower and garden clubs is a small section which enables the reader to pursue useful contacts, should they wish.

As National Chairman of NAFAS, I am pleased that some of our members have contributed to this book and that Judith saw the potential in providing the information in a clear and informative style. We cross the boundaries of race, language and religion, and flowers with their world-wide appeal can help in a therapeutic way to overcome our differences.

Whether you are an accomplished arranger or a beginner, the pursuit of flower arranging adds quality of life to those who succumb. I hope you find it so, and that this book furthers your enjoyment.

PAULINE COLLINS

NATIONAL CHAIRMAN

Summer 1995

PICTURE ACKNOWLEDGMENTS

Michael Alexander 270, 272, 273
Anna Barbaglia 248, 249, 250, 251 (top & bottom)
Anne Blunt 163 (bottom), 191 (right)
Thierry Dauwe & Bob Niewenhoff 104, 230 (top & bottom), 231 (top & bottom)
Flower Arranger Magazine 202, 225, 227
David Garb 246, 247
Harry Graham 34, 39 (middle), 43, 48, 51 (top & bottom), 57 (right), 87, 110, 114 (top), 116 (top), 120, 122, 131 (bottom), 139 (top & bottom), 146, 158, 162, 166 (bottom), 170 (top & bottom), 178 (2 at bottom), 181, 188, 192 (top), 194, 195, 196, 197, 198, 199, 200, 201 (left), 202, 227, 265
Fotostudio Handel 239 (bottom)
Danny Israel 61, 64–5, 72–3, 76–7, 80–1, 84–5
Kazuyo Kido 274
Daragh McKeon 244, 245
Wilfried Overwater 242
Mike Pannett 39 (top & bottom), 40, 45, 46, 47, 49, 55, 56, 71, 83, 108 (top & bottom), 109, 111 (top & bottom), 112 (top & bottom), 113, 114 (bottom) 115, 116 (bottom), 117, 118 (top & bottom), 119 (top & bottom), 121, 124, 126, 127, 129, 130, 131 (top), 133, 135, 136, 138 (bottom), 140–1, 142, 143 (bottom), 144, 145, 148 (top & bottom), 150, 163 (top), 166 (top), 167, 171, 177 (top), 178 (top), 183, 184 (top), 185, 186, 187, 190, 191 (left), 192 (bottom), 201 (top right & bottom), 218 (left & right), 219, 232, 233 (top & bottom), 258, 259 (top & bottom), 261 (bottom), 263, 266, 268 (right), 269, 293, 298
Tim Saunders 287, 288, 290, 291
Pamela South 260, 261 (top)
Steve Tanner 2, 4–5, 6–7, 8–9, 10–11, 12–13, 14–15, 16–17, 18–19, 20–1, 22–3, 24–5, 26–7, 28–9, 30–1, 32–3, 42, 50, 53, 57 (left), 58, 62–3, 66–7, 68–9, 70, 74–5, 78–9, 82, 86, 88–9, 90–1, 92–3, 107, 123 (top), 134, 138 (top), 143 (top), 147, 152–3, 154–5, 156–7, 160–1, 164–5, 168–9, 172–3, 176, 177 (bottom), 179, 180 (left & right), 182, 184 (bottom), 193, 205, 206, 207, 209, 212, 213, 220, 221, 222, 229, 275
E. Tweedie 210, 214 (top & bottom), 215
Cliff Vincent 149

ACKNOWLEDGMENTS

I MUST THANK ROWENA GAUNT for inviting me to write this book. I first came into contact with Rowena when I was writing my first book, and I was delighted when, after moving to Bloomsbury Publishing, she asked me to write this flower arranging encyclopedia. By doing so, I have joined a number of prestigious authors writing books in this Bloomsbury series.

I have every confidence that the botanical nomenclature in this encyclopedia is accurate and up to date. This is due in its entirety to the professionalism and dedication of Dr Christina Curtis, whose careful study and knowledge of plant names will ensure that this will be a valuable reference source into the next millennium. I have worked with Kate Simunek on other books. How she makes my scribbled sketches look so accurate yet attractive I will never know.

A book of this diversity could only be written with help from many quarters. In the true spirit of flower arranging, so many people were generous with their time and expertise. I would like to mention Norman Allen, Sue Brinton, Judith Butterworth, Pauline Collins, Pamela South and Hilde Woodman and also Yvonne Worth, Sylvie Rabbe and Beatriz Reis at Book Creation Services, and Kate Bouverie, Isabelle Rickard and Diana Rutland at Bloomsbury.

I asked Craig Bullock and Michael Bowyer to contribute to this book because of their creative genius, in-depth knowledge of flower arranging and sparkling sense of humour. A national judge, demonstrator, speaker and teacher, Michael Bowyer regularly designs magnificent floral spectaculars. Salisbury and Canterbury cathedrals are but two venues. Craig Bullock is a brilliant young floral designer, with a love of theatre. He is an innovator and setter of trends. A keen gardener, his garden at Montford Cottage in Lancashire is periodically open to the public under the National Garden Scheme.

I would like to thank the three principal photographers, Harry Graham, Mike Pannett and Steve Tanner, who have given such time and consideration to this encyclopedia. Without them it could not be.

I have had help from many quarters, but without specific help from certain people this book just would not have been possible. First, my family: my parents Cedric and Joan Ward, who allowed me to turn Penington House upside down for photo shots and gave me every support; my husband David, who went through the text and helped me at the word processor; and my wonderful, tolerant children, Charles and Jane.

The Dutch Flower Auctions, Aalsmeer, generously provided most of the glorious cut flowers. I was able to receive these through Cornelius Schrama, from whom Carl Grover of New Covent Garden buys his flowers. Cornelius is one of the most respected buyers in Aalsmeer, known for the high quality of his purchases. He and Carl have a special relationship, based on mutual trust and a desire to deal only with flowers of the highest quality. As Cornelius would say, 'What is in a name – quality, that's all.' These flowers have been a joy to work with.

Hugh Ellis and Carl Grover, together with the Grovers team of Fraser, Lee, Edward and John, give a warm welcome to all flower arrangers. If you go to New Covent Garden be sure to visit them, where you will revel in their vast, exciting range of long-stemmed flowers and receive a warm welcome. Hugh's wife, Pat, is a flower arranger, and perhaps due to this, and to his natural charm and courteous manner, he understands the requirements of flower arrangers and is tolerant of our vagaries.

I would also like to thank Agfa Gavaert for supplying their high-quality film; Leslie Decker of Aujourd'hui for the candles; Just Orchids for their superb orchids and exotic foliage; Ken and Mary Fisher for the loan of their home; Richmond Adult and Community College and Barnes library for the loan of their premises.

• *Chapter 1: Flowers in Season*
For allowing me to help myself from their gardens: Alan and Joyce Meigh, David and Lyn Williams, Rex and Pamela Fernant, Tim and Lorraine Budgen, John and Penny Bayliss, St Paul's School, Juliet Waugh; and Barnes Horticultural and Allotments Society for the magnificent dahlias.

• *Chapter 4: Containers*
Tim Boon at Amalgam, High Street, Barnes, for the use of the inspirational containers on pages 50 and 61; Sandra Rich pots – page 40, 61, 134; Darrel Sherlock – 261; Beverley Beeland – page 63; Susie Lear – page 56; Isobel Dennis Ceramics; Sarah Perry – pages 61 and 123.

• *Chapter 5: Equipment and Accessories*
Triflora for their fresh and dried foam, Triflora ribbon; Wilkinson Sword for the secateurs, Florafix, Seramis, Cowee picks, Flower Dry.

• *Chapter 10: Long-Lasting Flowers*
– *Pressed flowers*: Anne Stringer.
– *Hang-dried flowers*: The Hop Shop and Robson Watley; Charmian Binney and Millenium, High Street, Barnes, for the use of their premises and property.
– *Desiccated flowers*: Moira Clinch, of Flower Dry.
– *Preserved flowers*: Scottish Everlasting; Intermarket Agencies Ltd for the African Everoses.
– *Silk Flowers*: CI Flowers (Blackpool) for their Rhapsody and Dry Image range, and for the sunflowers and fruits in the garland; Floralsilk for other artificial flowers.
– *Parchment flowers*: Vincents.
– *Plastic flowers*: Jenny Tann at Everbloom.

• *Chapter 11: Celebrations and Festivals*
Loan of hat on left: Caroline George at Bazaar, High Street, Barnes; hat on right: Gil Fox for Vincents.

• *Chapter 12: Christmas*
Deran Foliage; Mr & Mrs C.T. Adams for the mistletoe; Just Orchids.

• *Chapter 13: Large-Scale Arranging*
Michael Bowyer; Marion Aaronson.

• *Chapter 14: Wedding and Anniversary Flowers*
Cindy Ang; The Buddhist Society; Betty Cormack; Rosina Dickens for supplying the wedding cake; Victoria Hooton of Lavender Blue florist; Ann Kendrick; Nandini Mane; Marion Motz; and special thanks to Nudrat and Mohammad Sharief.

• *Chapter 15: Show Work*
Craig Bullock.

• *International Section*
– *Australia*: Elva Wass; Mary Mortessen.
– *Belgium*: Elaine Joski; Bérengère Jacques de Dixmude and the Belgian Flower Arranging Society.
– *Canada*: Marisa Berganini; Helen Skinner.
– *China*: Pamela South.
– *Colombia*: Beatriz Alacio de Mejia; Cristina Ospina de Nuttin; Caroline Arrowsmith of New World Translations.
– *Czech Republic*: Jana Zantovska Stirton; Alena Brodska; Claudia Carrington at the Czech Centre, London; Dennis and Jean Geeson.
– *France*: Olga Méneur.
– *Germany*: Wally Klett; Maria Heinemann; Maria Schneider.
– *Holland*: Leo Koolen; Alice ter Haar.
– *Ireland*: Nuala Hegarty.
– *Israel*: Gina Eting.
– *Italy*: Carla Barbaglia; Anna Barbaglia; Rosnella Cajello Fazio.
– *Japan*: Tineke Robertson.
– *Malta*: Mary Mangion.
– *New Zealand*: Anne MacKay.
– *Norway*: Nils Norman Iversen; Rolf Torhaug.
– *Poland*: Barbara Bielecka; Milena Szuniewicz; Rosemary Wetherell.
– *Russia*: Sophie Palmer; Boris and Lylia at the Russian Trade Delegation; Nina Lozovay; Jeff Temple; Pamela South.
– *South Africa*: Rosemary Ladlau; Althea Higham.
– *Spain*: Dori Tiley; Marylin Twyford.
– *Thailand*: Khunying Oranuch; Isarangkun Na Ayuthatya and the 'Support Foundation of Her Majesty Queen Sirikit of Thailand'.
– *USA*: Ruth Crocker, Chairman of the Garden Club of America, Flower Show Committee; Mrs Edward N. Dane, Garden Club of America; Ann Milstead, National Council of State Garden Clubs, Inc., Flower Show Schools Chairman; Mrs Dean Day Smith, third Vice President and Communications Chairman, National Council of State Gardens Clubs, Inc.; Janice Murphy, Past President, Kensington and Chelsea American Women's Club (KCWC).
– *UK*: Mary Law; Sylvia Lewis; Reverend William MacMillan.

INTRODUCTION

What is flower arranging? It is perhaps best described as creating pleasing decorative arrangements, not just with a large bouquet of florist's flowers but also with a few simple flowers, some foliage and a little bit of know-how. If you can arrange flowers, you will be welcome in any part of the world – there is a universal language with flowers that is far easier to understand than Esperanto. Every organization and school has a need for someone who can arrange the flowers for fund-raising events; there are churches, temples and synagogues to beautify; there are flower clubs in most corners of the world, each filled with like-minded people. Have fun, and make friends with flowers.

In this book you will find an enormous range of flower arrangements, both in style and lavishness, and I hope that everyone will find an idea or an arrangement to inspire them. This encyclopedia is equally for those who want ideas for arranging an expensive bouquet and for those who may have only a few snippets from a window-box with which to create a living garden inside their home. Many readers will want traditional arrangements to complement the dêcor of their houses, while others may seek the excitement of trying new styles suggested by flower arrangers in other countries. I hope that this encyclopedia of flower arranging will be all things to many people, and that it will encourage your love of flower arranging. For flowers brighten our lives. Arranging them is relaxing and alleviates stress. Their ephemeral beauty and diversity of colour and form are a wonder of nature.

Flowers transcend all races, cultures and religions. In writing this book I have found that, where flowers are concerned, there are no boundaries – simply a common bond that brings people joy and happiness. On a plane recently I was seated next to a Nigerian, who regaled me with wonderful tales of flowers in his own country – of Bougainvillea, *Hibiscus* and *Nymphaea* (water lily). His face lit up when describing how the children of his country paint with the *Nymphaea* tuber, cut into segments. The dye from the tuber is mixed with other plant dyes to produce colourful, though not colour-fast, nail varnish for the women of Nigeria.

Over the last decade much has been written about giving a 'natural' look to flower arrangements. Since the 1960s experienced flower arrangers have led the way, giving a charming, naturalistic style to their arrangements – a way with flowers that we would all like to emulate. But we all have to start somewhere, and there are very few who arrive at this happy state without a great deal of anguish, practice and hard work. Of the few with a natural talent for creating harmonious flower arrangements – apparently without thinking about it – most have studied art or design in another related subject and consequently have had a head start.

For the rest of us help is needed. This is where classes, clubs and books are useful. Just as the amateur cook needs a basic recipe for white sauce, so the flower arranger needs instructions on how to get started. The artist learns the technique of perspective, the flower arranger the technique of maximizing the potential of the available plant material. This book does not expound rules that must be followed. *I simply want to encourage you to question and explore, so that you will work with a greater understanding of the creative potential of plant material.*

I aim to provide information, instruction and inspiration. In Chapters 2 and 3 you will find information on the elements and principles of design, and on the theory of colour. An understanding of these will enable you to create successful designs with little effort. Chapters 4 and 5 describe the equipment that is available. Chapter 1 the plant material that can easily be grown in the garden and the flowers that can be purchased at the florist's throughout the year; and Chapter 6 the techniques that will enable you to arrange them in the home.

I include information about flower clubs that exist the world over. At these clubs you will find both instruction and inspiration. There is an opportunity to meet people, young and old, who love the same things in life – the beauty of flowers and foliage arranged in the home, to bring temporary or lasting pleasure, sharing the discovery of a new flower variety, dried seedheads from the river bank or a few leaves from the hedgerow; getting excited about the development of a new style of flower arrangement or about receiving a 'Highly Commended' in the club show.

Chapter 7 gives instruction and examples of what I have called 'traditional design classics'. The following chapter explores modern styles which have, I believe, now become classics. Some of these styles originated in Europe and have been adapted to suit local garden plant material. There is presently a tremendous urge among skilled flower arrangers to take the art form of flower arranging to greater heights. They use plant material to create exciting new designs, which are seen – particularly on the show bench – both in Britain and worldwide. Chapter 9 describes those designs that I consider to be 'other design classics'.

Although the flower-arranging movement has countless members worldwide, there are still many people who are unaware of its existence. At the end of the book I have included a list of worldwide contact addresses. The movement is rather like the Rotary Club or the Round Table – there is always a welcome for members, wherever they go.

There are contributions from 25 countries, in which you will find a wealth of information about the different uses of flowers throughout the world. Where we unite is in a universal love of flowers and flower arranging.

And, finally, to inspiration. I know that all readers will be inspired by at least one arrangement in this book. It may be by work shown in the international section. The plant material used may not always be easy to find, but many of the ideas can be adapted to the plant material indigenous to your own country. You may be tempted to try to show work as photographed so dramatically by Craig Bullock. Michael Bowyer's ideas for large-scale arranging may spur you on to start arranging flowers for your place of worship, or to help with a flower festival. After reading about flowers for weddings, you may decide to arrange the flowers for a friend's wedding, or at least be better able to plan what is required.

Whoever you are, whatever your experience, I hope that you will find joy and pleasure in this encyclopedia and gain friendship, knowledge and fun through flowers.

A selection of dried-flower arrangements

FLOWER ARRANGING STYLE

AN INTERNATIONAL COLLECTION OF IDEAS
AND INSPIRATIONS FOR ALL SEASONS

FLOWERS IN SEASON

Every month of the year produces flowers, foliage, nuts, fruit, cones and berries for use by the flower arranger. As the months change there is a gradual shift in the availability of plant material, so that spring, summer, autumn and winter are distinct from each other in their seasonal variations. Far from limited availability being a disadvantage, however, it is the rediscovery of leaves and flowers, as they burst once more into life, that makes gardening and flower arranging so special.

The following pages can give only a rough guide to the flowers and foliage that are available month by month, as geographical location makes a difference, as do climatic variations from one year to the next. However, the pages showing material available from the garden display many plants that are of special interest to the flower arranger, and which are generally available in the period given.

Even the most experienced flower arranger takes time to select and buy flowers for a special design. Often the arranger has only a limited budget and may feel embarrassed at spending half an hour in a florist's shop deliberating over what constitutes a harmonious selection of flowers and foliage. Having a rough idea of the varieties of flowers and foliage available from the florist throughout the year, and of the range of colours in which they are grown, can be of tremendous help when making this decision.

Some flowers are available twelve months of the year, with only a moderate fluctuation in price. These are shown on pages 32 and 33. There are also many useful evergreens that can be planted in the garden to provide foliage all year round. These are shown on pages 30 and 31.

PICKING FROM THE GARDEN
OR FROM THE WILD

The National Association of Flower Arrangement Societies (NAFAS) promotes the conservation of rare and endangered plants and animals. The use of protected plants (as per Schedule 8 of the Wild Life and Countryside Act 1981) from the wild is forbidden. The use of other rare and endangered species, from the wild, in flower arrangements is discouraged.

- Only pick from the wild if there is an abundance, and do not uproot any plant.
- If picking at a distance from home, place your garden material in a plastic bag and blow into it before tying, so that the plant will be cushioned and will have its own contained system.
- Pick from the garden first thing in the morning or late in the evening, when plant material is at its most turgid (firm by distension with water).
- Cut your plant material at an angle and immediately place in a bucket of water, so that a seal does not have time to form over the cut end. Leave in a cool place for several hours before arranging. Remove any leaves that would fall below the water line.

BUYING FROM THE
FLORIST

When buying from the florist the following information will help you choose
good-quality flowers at the right stage of their development.

• Most flowers should be purchased in bud, showing some colour. *Dendranthema*
(chrysanthemum) and gerberas are two of the exceptions. Many spring flowers bought
early in the season should show colour, but later in the season they will develop
even if purchased in tight bud.
• If the flower is a spike, such as *Gladiolus* (sword lily) or *Freesia*,
ensure that the lowest flower is open.
• The flowers on display should always be protected from direct heat,
sunlight and draughts.
• Double flowers usually last longer than their single counterparts.
• There should always be water in the buckets containing the flowers.
• The flowers and foliage should not be diseased or carry insects.

EARLY SPRING

From the Garden

Although the weather can be unpredictable, this is an exciting time of the year in the garden, when bulbs and early flowering shrubs spring into life. The delicate structure of many early flowers makes them ideal for pressing – kerria, buttercups, daisies and forsythia. Foliage that has just acquired leaves will be immature and may well wilt in water, so be sure to condition it well. Float the heads of hellebores in a low dish of water or wait for the fruits to form in the centre, at which point they will last well, once cut.

From top left clockwise:
Camellia cv. pink, white, red
Helleborus foetidus (stinking hellebore) green
Narcissus cv. (daffodil)
Pulmonaria angustifolia (lungwort, Mary and Joseph)
Chaenomeles sp. (quince, japonica) crimson, orange, apricot, deep and pale pink, white
Crocus sp. purple, white, yellow
Anemone blanda (windflower) blue, mauve, pink and white
Arum italicum 'Pictum' leaves
Prunus subhirtella 'Autumnalis' (winter-flowering or higan cherry)
Hedera helix (ivy) with berries
Narcissus 'Tête à Tête' (cyclamineus type) yellow
Vinca major (greater periwinkle)
Helleborus atrorubens (hellebore) plum purple
Sarcococca hookeriana var. *digyna* (Christmas box) flowers
Salix caprea (pussy willow)
Hyacinthus orientalis (hyacinth) pink, purple, blue, apricot
Erica carnea (heather)

Narcissus 'Peeping Tom'
Scilla sp.
Viburnum tinus (laurustinus) cream, pink
Ranunculus sp. (Celandine) yellow
Erica Carnea (heath)
Viola x *wittrockiana* (winter flowering pansy)
Helleborus orientalis sp. abchasicus purple outside and green within
Pulmonaria sp.
Galanthus nivalis (common snowdrop) white
Iris reticulata (bulbous reticulata iris) deep blue-purple with orange blaze

Plant material displayed on a bed of moss, *Bergenia* and *Arum italicum* leaves.

Also available:
Amelanchier sp. (juneberry, serviceberry, shadbush)
Berberis darwinii (Darwin's barberry)
Cornus mas (cornelian cherry)
Daphne mezereum
Forsythia sp.
Hamamelis sp. (witch hazel)
Helleborus orientalis (lenten rose)
Helleborus argustifolius
Leucojum aestivum (snowflake)
Mahonia aquifolium (Oregon grape)
Mahonia japonica and *M. x media*
Muscari armeniacum (grape hyacinth)
Narcissus 'Peeping Tom'
Photinia sp.
Pieris sp.
Prunus sargentii
Rosmarinus officinalis (rosemary)
Salix apoda
Vinca major 'Variegata' (variegated greater periwinkle)

EARLY SPRING

From the Florist

Tulips and daffodils are widely available at every market stall. Do remember to cut the ends of daffodils, and to stand them on their own for 24 hours before mixing them with other plant material. Alternatively, add special cut flower food to the water. Bulb flowers look lovely massed in glass vases.

From top left clockwise
Tulipa sp. (tulip) red, yellow, orange, pink, purple and white as well as bi-coloured
Salix nigricans (black willow)
Crocus sp. (pot grown)
Hyacinthus cv. (hyacinth) mainly white and blue
Narcissus cv. (daffodil) yellow
Chamelaucium uncinatum (wax flower) pink, white
Hedera helix (common ivy)
Iris sp. blue, white, yellow
Tulipa sp. (tulip) red, yellow, orange, pink, purple, white, yellow
Viburnum opulus 'Roseum' (guelder rose, snowball bush) light green, white when flowers open

Anemone coronaria (poppy-flowered anemone) purple, blue, red, white,
pink, yellow
Acacia sp. (mimosa or wattle) yellow
Arachniodes syn. *Rumohra adiantiformis* (leather fern)
Genista sp. yellow, white, pink
Hyacinthus orientalis (hyacinth) mainly white and blue, also pink,
apricot, yellow

Also available:
Ranunculus asiaticus (turban flower)
Narcissus 'Cheerfulness'
Syringa sp. (lilac)
Iris sp.
Trachelium caeruleum (throatwort)
Primula acaulis (potted)
Crocus sp. (potted)
Viburnum tinus (laurustinus)
Rhododendron sp. foliage

Editor's note – All daffodils and narcissi come under
the genus *Narcissus*.

LATE SPRING

From the Garden

Try growing unusual varieties of tulips and daffodils in your garden to complement the more common varieties available at the florist. Yellow, blue and white are probably the colours most prevalent during these spring months. Remove the leaves of *Syringa* (lilac) and *Viburnum opulus* (guelder rose) which greedily drink water, thus preventing it from reaching the flowering heads. *Anthriscus sylvestris* (Queen Anne's lace, cow parsley) grows rampantly by the river, on verges and along hedgerows. Once mature it will last well and is ideal for large arrangements when the budget is tight.

From top left clockwise:

Photinia x fraseri 'Red Robin' red young growth on evergreen

Tellima grandiflora (fringecups) green-yellow flowers

Syringa cv. (lilac) deep lilac, white, pink

Hyacinthoides non-scripta syn. *Scilla non-scriptus* (English bluebell), blue, pink, white

Erysimum cheiri (wallflower) many colours

Viburnum opulus 'Roseum' (snowball bush)

Choisya ternata (Mexican orange blossom) evergreen with white flowers

Genista hispanica (Spanish gorse) yellow

Narcissus cv.

Tulipa sp. (tulip)

Brassica napus (rape) yellow

Euphorbia amygdaloides var. *robbiae* (Mrs Robb's bonnet)

Lunaria annua (honesty) purple, white

Allium schoenoprasum (chives) rose-pink

Wisteria sinensis (Chinese wisteria) violet-blue, pink, white

Malus sylvestris (apple) rosy-white

Anthriscus sylvestris (Queen Anne's lace, cow parsley) creamy-white

Physocarpus opulifolius 'Dart's Gold'

Dicentra spectabilis (Bleeding Heart) white and pink

Rosa cv. (rose) all colours, except blue

Lonicera sp. (honeysuckle) usually creamy-yellow or yellowy pink

Iris germanica (common German flag) purple-blue

Laburnum anagyroides (common laburnum) yellow

Crataegus monogyna (common hawthorn) white
flowers
Cotoneaster, white or pink
Myosotis alpestris (forget-me-not) blue, pink, white
Tulipa sp. (tulip) many colours
Ceanothus thyrsiflorus var. *repens* usually blue

Plant material displayed on a border of *Arum
italicum* 'Pictum', *Bergenia cordifolia* (elephant's
ear), *Fagus sylvatica* (beech) and *Physocarpus*
leaves.

Also available:
Acer platanoides (Norway maple)
Aesculus hippocastanum (horsechestnut)
All fruit trees
Aquilegia sp. (granny's bonnet)
Betula pendula (silver birch)
Chelidonium sp. (greater celandine)
Convallaria majalis (lily-of-the-valley)
Dipelta sp.
Epimedium sp.
Erica sp. (heath)
Euphorbia griffithii 'Fireglow'
Forsythia sp.
Fritillaria meleagris (snakeshead fritillary)

Hosta sp. (funkia, plantain lily)
Kerria sp. (Jew's mallow)
Kniphofia sp. (red-hot poker, torch lily)
Lamium sp. (dead nettle)
Magnolia sp.
Osmanthus delavayi
Paeonia lutea and *P. suffruticosa* (tree peony)
Pieris sp.
Polemonium caeruleum (Jacob's ladder)
Polygonatum x hybridum (Solomon's seal)
Potentilla sp. (shrubby cinquefoil)
Primula sp. (primrose)
Primula auricula (auricula)
Primula veris (cowslip)
Rhododendron sp. (azalea)
Ribes sp. (flowering currant)
Stellaria sp. (stitchwort)
Silene sp. (campion)
Sambucus sp. (elder)
Sorbus aria (whitebeam)
Sorbus aucuparia (rowan)
Taxus baccata 'Aurea' (golden yew) for yellow
new growth
Vibernum carlesii 'Aurora'
Vinca sp. (periwinkle)
Weigela sp.

LATE SPRING

From the Florist

Cheerful spring flowers of blue, yellow, white and pink fill the florist's shops and market stalls. For the cost of a loaf of bread, you can have a bunch of cheerful blooms to brighten up your home. Tulips are widely available, their stems taking on twists and turns as they mature. They continue to grow once cut, so they are ideally suited for arranging in a vase where they will happily do their own thing! A few irises cut at different heights and placed on a pinholder, with a few plain leaves to cover the base, will also give a charming effect.

From top left, clockwise:

Anemone coronaria 'De Caen' (poppy-flowered anemone) purple, red, white, pink, blue

Solidago sp. (golden rod) yellow

Ranunculus asiaticus (turban flower) yellow, pink, red, orange, brown

Xerophyllum sp. (bear grass) green

Tanacetum parthenium (feverfew) white with yellow centre

Leucathemum x superbum white with yellow centre

Craspedia sp. (drumstick) yellow

Gloriosa superba 'Rothschildiana' (glory lily) red petals with yellow edgings

Arachniodes syn. *Rumohra adiantiformis* (leather fern) dark green

Trachelium caeruleum (throatwort) mainly purple, also white, pink

Iris sp. usually blue, also yellow, white

Trachelium sp.

Eustoma grandiflorum (lisianthus, prairie gentian) usually blue or purple, also white, pink

Bupleurum griffithii multi-flowered lime green

Narcissus cv. single flowered stem usually yellow, also white, orange, bi-coloured

Narcissus cv. multi-flowered stem, white, yellow, or white and yellow

Alstroemeria sp. (Peruvian lily) multi-flowered stem multi-coloured, cream, yellow

Syringa vulgaris (lilac) white, cerise, pink, lavender

Primula denticulata (drumstick primula) various colours

Genista sp. usually yellow, also pink and white

Tulipa sp. (tulip) virtually every colour

Asparagus setaceus (asparagus fern)

Campanula persicifolia (bell flower) blue, white

Asparagus virgatus (tree fern)

Dendranthema cv.(chrysanthemum) most colours

Ammi majus (lace flower) white

Triteleia sp. (brodiaea) usually dark blue or violet, sometimes white

Also available:

Primula variabilis (polyanthus)

Viburnum opulus 'Roseum' (snowball tree)

Ixia sp. (corn lily)

Hyacinthus orientalis (hyacinth)

Muscari armeniacum (grape hyacinth)

Phlox sp.

Acacia dealbata and *A. longifolia* (mimosa or wattle)

Viola odorata (sweet violet)

Antirrhinum sp. (snapdragon)

Saintpaulia sp. (African violet)

Gypsophila paniculata (baby's breath)

Calendula officinalis (pot marigold)

Clivia miniata (kaffir lily)

Forsythia sp.

Chamelaucium uncinatum (wax flower)

Tagetes sp. (marigold)

Centaurea cyanus (cornflower)

Cheiranthus cheiri (wallflower)

Convallaria majalis (lily-of-the-valley)

Agapanthus africanus (African lily)

Ceanothus sp.

Cytisus sp. (broom)

Allium sp. (onion)

Campanula sp. (bellflower)

Bellis sp. (potted daisy)

EARLY SUMMER

From the Garden

The long days of these summer months are when many gardens are in their prime, with the flowering of numerous perennials. Pick lavender (*Lavendula* sp.) as the flowers open and dry in a warm room away from direct sun. Glycerine (see page 102) deciduous foliage such as beech (*Fagus sylvatica*), which is mature enough to take up the mixture without wilting. The warmth will enable the mixture to be rapidly absorbed. Glorious garden roses bring colour and fragrance into the home. Lime green Alchemilla mollis lightens the flowerbed and gives grace to any design.

From top left clockwise:
Ligustrum ovalifolium (privet) white flowers

Astrantia sp. (masterwort) white tinged with pink or deep pink
Pelargonium cv. (geranium) white, pink, red, orange
Escallonia sp. pink, red
Liriodendron tulipifera (tulip tree) yellow-green flowers
Euphorbia dulcis 'Chameleon' mahogany leaves yellow-green flowers
Lavendula sp. (lavender) blue, pink, white, green
Allium moly yellow
Geranium 'Johnson's Blue' (cranesbill)
Lavateria olbia 'Rosea' (mallow) pink, wine-red, white
Sisyrinchium striatum creamy yellow
Hosta sp. (funkia, plantain lily) mauve, white
Dianthus barbatus (sweet william) red, pink, white, purple, many bi-coloured
Dimorphotheca sp. (Cape marigold, star of the veldt) many colours
Pelargonium cv. (see above)

Papaver sp. (poppy) seedheads many colours
Heuchera sanguinea (coral flower) all variations of red
Tradescantia x andersoniana (trinity flower) blue, rose-pink, white
Solanum jasminoides (potato vine) white, pale blue
Spartium junceum (Spanish broom) yellow
Paeonia sp. (peony) usually pink, white, red
Lupinus sp. (lupin) many colours
Campanula persicifolia (bell flower) blue, white
Fremontodendron californicum (California glory)
Alchemilla mollis (lady's mantle) lime-green
Mentha sp. (variegated mint) pale purple flowers
Buddleja globosa (butterfly bush) orange-yellow flowers
Calendula officinalis (pot marigold)
Rosa cv. (garden rose) many colours
Sambucus nigra (elder) cream-white flowers
Spiraea japonica 'Goldflame' pink-red
Digitalis purpurea (foxglove) many colours

Various grasses green, pick no later than June for drying
Asparagus officinalis (culinary asparagus) green
Scabiosa caucasica (scabious) lavender, mauve, violet, white

Plant material displayed on a base of limestone slabs and *Alchemilla mollis* (lady's mantle) leaves

Also available:
Antirrhinum sp. (snapdragon)
Astilbe sp.
Coreopsis sp. (tickseed)
Eremurus stenophyllus (foxtail lily)
Galium odoratum (sweet woodruff)
Hesperis matronalis (sweet rocket)
Nigella damascena (love-in-a-mist)
Lathyrus odoratus (sweet pea)
Phlox paniculata (phlox)
Phlomis fruticosa (Jerusalem sage)

EARLY SUMMER

From the Florist

There is a wonderful variety of plant material available from the florist at this time of year. This is the moment to buy inexpensive bunches of peonies, larkspur and roses to hang upside-down to dry, in a warm place with good air circulation. Take advantage of the colours and forms available to create exuberant arrangements.

From top left clockwise:

Tanacetum parthenium (feverfew) white petals surrounding yellow centre or all white

Phlox paniculata (phlox) usually white, purple, pink

Agapanthus sp. (African lily) usually blue, occasionally white

Consolida ambigua syn. *Delphinium consolida* (larkspur) blue, pink and white

Paeonia sp. (peony) usually pink, red or white

Stephanotis floribunda (Madagascar jasmine, wax flower) white

Eustoma grandiflorum (lisianthus, prairie gentian) dark blue, pink, cream, white

Calendula officinalis (pot marigold) bright yellow or orange

Antirrhinum majus (snapdragon) a vast range of colours

Veronica spicata (speedwell) blue, pink, white

Rosa cv. (rose) a vast range of colours all year

Eustoma sp. (see above)

Nigella damascena (love-in-a-mist) pale blue

Astrantia major (masterwort) white, pink, red

Allium aflatunense 'Purple Sensation' usually lilac, purple

Campanula glomerata 'Superba' (clustered bellflower) deep violet, blue

Limonium sinuatum (winged statice) many colours including pink, yellow, blue, apricot

Centaurea cyanus (cornflower) usually blue, but also pink, white, red

Goniolimon tataricum (sea lavender) white

Centaurea sp. red

Dianthus barbatus (sweet william) red, pink, white, purple, many bi-coloured

Matthiola incana (Brompton stock) many colours including white, cream, pink, red

Asclepias tuberosa (butterfly weed) orange

Scabiosa caucasica 'Istafa' (scabious) lavender,
blue, pink, lilac, white
Lilium 'Mid Century Hybrids' (lily) red, orange,
yellow, white
Delphinium elatum (delphinium) usually blue,
purple
Alchemilla mollis (lady's mantle) lime-green
Dianthus allwoodii (modern pink) pink, white

Also available:
Achillea sp. (yarrow)
Ageratum sp. (floss flower)
Alchemilla mollis (lady's mantle)
Allium giganteum
Alstroemeria Ligtu Hybrids (Peruvian lily)
Aruncus dioicus, syn. *A. sylvester*
(goat's beard)
Astilbe sp.
Campanula persicifolia (peach-leaved bellflower)
Cirsium japonicum
Coreopsis sp. (tickseed)
Dianthus sp. (carnation)
Digitalis sp. (foxglove)
Eremurus stenophyllus (foxtail lily)
Euphorbia sp.
Fagus sylvatca (beech)

Galium odoratum (sweet woodruff)
Gladiolus sp. (sword lily)
Gypsophila elegans (baby's breath)
Hesperis matronalis (sweet rocket)
Lathyrus odoratus (sweet pea)
Limonium sp. (sea lavender)
Lupinus sp. (lupin)
Lychnis chalcedonica (Jerusalem cross,
Maltese cross)
Paeonia sp. (peony)
Papaver sp. (poppy)
Pelargonium cv. (geranium)
Rosa cv. (rose)
Spiraea sp.
Stephanotis floribunda (Madagascar
jasmine, wax flower)
Tagetes sp. (marigold)
Trollius sp. (globe flower)
Vaccaria hispanica syn. *Saponaria hispanica*
(soapwort)

LATE SUMMER

From the Garden

Though the land may be parched at this time of year, gardens and hedgerows show their treasures in a rich variety of colours scarlet fuchsias, orange *Pyracanthus* (firethorn) berries, purple *Hebes* (veronica) and yellow dahlias. *Buddleia* (butterfly bush), *Escallonia, Lavendula* (lavender) and many other flowering shrubs give a second flush as the days begin to draw in. Annuals continue to provide flowers for cutting. Foliage is still abundant and long-lasting when cut. The changing colours give an exciting new dimension to flower arrangements.

From top left clockwise:
Rosa cv. (rose) many colours
Abelia grandiflora 'Francis Mason' pale pink
Rudbeckia sp. yellow, orange
Campanula sp. (bellflower) blue
Malus sylvestris (apple) green, red
Lonicera periclymenum (honeysuckle, common woodbine) berries red
Lathyrus odoratus (sweet pea) many colours
Dianthus chinensis (Indian pink) many colours
Coreopsis 'Sun Ray' yellow
Passiflora caerulea (common passion flower) purple, blue, pink, green, white
Tagetes sp. (French marigold) yellow, orange, brown
Erica vulgaris (heather) white, pink, red
Fuchsia sp. red, cream, pink, white, mauve, often combination of colours
Quercus robur (oak) fruits (acorns) green and later brown
Rudbeckia 'Goldsturm' yellow, brown
Antirrhinum majus (snapdragon) many colours
Atriplex hortensis 'Rubra' (red mountain spinach/orach) burgundy, green
Pelargonium cv. (geranium) orange, red, pink, lavender, blue
Acanthus spinosus (bear's breeches), purple, white, green
Viburnum opulus 'Xanthocarpum' yellow
Gerbera hybrid many colours
Pelargonium cv.
Sedum spectabile (ice plant) pink, red
Hydrangea macrophylla (Hortensia hydrangea) pink, red, blue
Aster novi-belgii (Michaelmas daisy) many colours
Celosia argentea 'Plumosa' (Prince of Wales feathers) red, yellow, orange
Sorbus aucuparia (mountain ash, rowan) berries orange-red
Cynara scolymus (globe artichoke) green, purple
Mentha sp. (mint) white, lilac

Lycopersicon lycopersicum (tomato) green turning red
Hebe sp. (veronica) white, pink, red, lavender, purple
Rudbeckia sp.
Rosa cv. (rose) many colours
Eryngium variifolium (Moroccan sea holly) grey-blue
Nicotiana cv. (tobacco flower) many colours
Dendranthema cv. (chrysanthemum) many colours
Echinops ritro (globe thistle) steel-blue
Delphinium elatum (delphinium) blue, white, pink
Humulus lupulus (common hop) green
Crocosmia x crocosmiiflora (montbretia) yellow, orange, red
Rubus fruticosus agg. (blackberry) fruits, red and black

Plant material displayed on a bed of moss and bark.

Also available:
Agapanthus sp. (African lily)
Alnus sp. (alder) with green cones
Amaranthus sp. (love-lies-bleeding)
Ammobium sp.
Anaphalis margaritacea (pearl everlasting)
Anethum graveolens (dill) green-yellow
Anthemis tinctoria

Carthamus tinctorius (safflower)
Clarkia elegans (clarkia)
Cosmos sp. (cosmea)
Dahlia sp.
Dimorphotheca aurantiaca hybrids (Cape marigold, star of the veldt)
Dipsacus fullonum (Teasel)
Eremurus sp. (foxtail lily)
Gaillardia pulchella (blanket flower)
Gladiolus sp. (sword lily)
Helenium autumnale (sneezewort)
Helianthus annuus (sunflower)
Helichrysum bracteatum (straw flower)
Hypericum 'Hidcote' (St John's Wort)
Kniphofia sp. (red hot poker)
Nerine sp.
Persicaria sp. (knotweed)
Platanus sp. (plane tree)
Polygonatum x hybridum (Solomon's seal)
Rosa moyesii (rose) hips
Salvia sp.
Scabiosa sp. (scabious)
Sidalcea malvaeflora (prairie mallow)
Sorbus aucuparia (mountain ash)
Tanacetum parthenium (feverfew)
Thalictrum sp. (meadow rue)
Typhus latifolia (reedmace)
Viburnum lantana (wayfaring tree)
Zinnia sp. (youth and old age)

LATE SUMMER

From the Florist

Garden *Dendranthema* (chrysanthemums), *Aster novi-belgii* (Michaelmas daisies), *Dahlia* (dahlias) and *Gladioli* (sword lilies) fill the market stalls and the florists with their deep rich colours. Flowers are inexpensive at this time of the year. Add a few fruits and vegetables to give form, colour and texture. Do remember that ripening fruit and vegetables give off ethylene gas to which flowers are vulnerable. Ensure that no foliage on your flowering stems lies below the water-line as foliage is particularly susceptible to bacteria. Buy *Limonium* (statice) and *Helichrysum* (straw flower) now and dry them for use in dried floral arrangements in the months to come.

From top left clockwise:
Campanula sp. (bellflower) white and blue
Solidago sp. (golden rod)
Eryngium sp. (sea holly) steel blue
Amaranthus caudatus (love-lies-bleeding) green, burgundy
Celosia argentea 'Plumosa' yellow-red
Achillea millefolium (yarrow) white, cream, yellow, deep orange, brick red
Hypericum x inodorum 'Elstead' green, black, orange, red
Delphinium sp. blue, mauve, white, pink
Gladiolus cv. (sword lily) many colours
Helianthus sp. (sunflower) yellow
Leycesteria formosa (pheasant berry/Himalayan honeysuckle) fruits wine-coloured

Carthamus tinctorius (safflower) yellow

Anethum graveolens (dill) yellow

Sedum spectabile (ice-plant) pink, green

Callistephus chinensis (China aster) purple, white

Echinops ritro (globe thistle)

Phlox sp. pink, mauve, white

Gomphrena globosa (globe amaranth) many colours

Helenium autumnale (sneezewort) yellow, rust

Hydrangea macrophylla (Hortensia hydrangea) white, blue, pink

Dendranthema cv. (chrysanthemum) many colours

Crinum powellii (swamp lily) white

Dahlia cv. (dahlia) many colours

Also available:

Aconitum sp. (monkshood)

Agapanthus sp. (African lily)

Ageratum sp. (floss flower)

Aster novi-belgii (Michaelmas daisy)

Chamelaucium uncinatum (Geraldton waxflower)

Consolida ajacis (larkspur)

Cosmos atrosanguineus (chocolate cosmea)

Eustoma grandiflorum (lisianthus, prairie gentian)

Gypsophila sp. (baby's breath)

Helichrysum bracteatum (straw flower)

Helipterum syn. *Acrolinium* sp. (everlasting flower)

Pelargonium cv. (geranium)

Physostegia virginiana (obedient plant)

AUTUMN

From the Garden

Choisya, Kerria, Escallonia bloom alongside Fuchsia, *Dahlia, Schizostylis* (kaffir lily), *Pelargonium* (geranium). *Dendranthema Sedum* and *Hydrangea* need to be picked for drying. From the hedgerow come *Ligustrum* (privet) berries, hips, *Crataegus* (hawthorn) and *Clematis* seedheads. *Malus* (apple), *Pyrus* (pear), *Rubus* (blackberry), *Cynara* (artichoke) and green *Lycopersicon* (tomato) all have a wonderful affinity with flowers and foliage.

From top left clockwise:
Aster novi-belgii (Michaelmas daisy) blue or pink
Tanacetum parthenium (feverfew) white and yellow
Gaultheria mucronata syn. *Pernettya* berries white, pink and red
Dendranthema cv. (chrysanthemum) many colours
Tropaeolum majus (nasturtium) yellow, orange and red
Schizostylis coccinnea (kaffir lily) pink-red
Dahlia cv. (dahlia) many colours
Ligustrum ovalifolium (privet) berries black
Cyclamen cv. (cyclamen) white and red
Rosa cv. (rose) many colours
Sedum spectabile (ice-plant) pink-red
Rosa cv. (rose) hips green, orange, red
Solidago sp. (golden rod) yellow
Dendranthema cv. (chrysanthemum) see above
Angelica sylvestris (angelica) green
Arbutus unedo (strawberry tree) cream flowers, orange fruit
Nerine bowdenii (nerine) mostly shades of pink
Rosa 'Pink carpet' (rose)
Myrtus communis (common myrtle) blackberries, cream flowers
Tagetes sp. yellow, orange and brown
Tricyrtis formosana (toad lily) spotted purple-pink

Fuchsia sp. shades or combinations of red, pink, purple, white
Chaenomeles japonica (japonica, quince) fruits white, pink, apricot, red
Anemone x hybrida (Japanese anemone) white, pink
Hebe sp. (veronica) usually white, blue, pink
Antirrhinum majus (snapdragon) many colours
Calendula officinalis (pot marigold) yellow, orange, brown, burnt red
Rubus fruticosus agg. (blackberry) fruits red and black
Hedera helix (ivy) flowering seedheads cream
Hydrangea macrophylla (Hortensia hydrangea) white, pink, red, blue
Cotoneaster sp. berries red yellow, orange
Pelargonium cv. (geranium) pink, red, white
Dahlia sp. many colours
Cosmos bipinnatus (cosmea) yellow, orange, pink, red
Heliotrope peruvianum (heliotrope) blue, purple
Sorbus aucuparia (mountain ash, rowan) bright red
Symphoricarpos albus (snowberry) white

Plant material displayed on a bed of moss and bark.

Also available:
Abelia sp.
Callicarpa bodinieri (beauty berry)
Calluna vulgaris (common heather)
Cotoneaster hylmoei berries
Dimorpotheca sp. (star of the veldt)
Erica carnea (winter flowering heath)
Fatsia japonica (Japanese aralia) fruits
Hypericum sp.
Hibiscus sp. (tree hollyhock)
Jasminum nudiflorum (winter jasmine)
Liriope muscari (lilyturf)
Rosa rugosa (Rugosa rose)
Viburnum x bodnantense
Viburnum farreri syn. *fragrans*
Weigela 'Bristol ruby'

AUTUMN

From the Florist

The florist's shop at this season has a host of magical flowers in vibrant colours – glowing yellow *Solidago*, orange marigolds, vibrant pink, red and gold of *Dendranthema*, nerines and dahlias, glorious sprays of *Solidaster* and *Aster novi-belgii*. A wonderful show of colour can be purchased inexpensively, to give joy and pleasure.

From top left clockwise
Hydrangea sp. pink, blue, white, red
Chamelaucium uncinatum (waxflower) white or pink
Dahlia cv. (dahlia) many colours
Carthamus tinctorius (safflower) green with orange or cream centres
Eucalyptus sp. (gum tree) grey, blue, green
Dendranthema cv. (chrysanthemum) many colours except blue
Eustoma grandiflorum (lisianthus, prairie gentian)
Molucella laevis (bells of Ireland) green
Dahlia cv. many colours
Dendranthema cv. (chrysanthemum) many colours
Iris sp. blue, white, yellow
Celastrus orbiculatus (oriental bittersweet, staff vine) red, yellow
Dendranthema cv. (chrysanthemum) blooms lime green, white, bronze, yellow, rust

Limonium platyphyllum (sea lavender) mauve
Sedum spectabile (ice-plant) rusty red
Tulipa sp. (tulip) many colours
Hyacinthus sp. (hyacinth) white, blue, purple, pink, red, yellow
Eryngium x oliverianum (sea holly) steel-blue
Dahlia cv. many colours
Hippeastrum sp. (amaryllis) red, pink, apricot, white
Tulipa sp. (tulip) many colours
Dahlia cv. many colours
Solidago sp. (golden rod) yellow
Ranunculus asiaticus (turban flower) yellow, orange, pink, and
now multi-coloured
Aster novi-belgii (Michaelmas daisy) lilac, white, yellow, pink
Gladiolus cv. (sword lily) every colour except true blue
Calendula officinalis (pot marigold) orange, yellow

Also available:
Aconitum sp. (monkshood)
Asclepias tuberosa (silk weed)
Bouvardia longiflorum
Celosia argentea 'Plumosa'
Dendranthema indicum (chrysanthemum)
Echinops vitro (globe thistle)
Helenium sp. (sneezewort)
Zinnia sp. (youth and old age)

WINTER

From the Garden

For December and the festive season much emphasis is placed on evergreens, and in particular on plain and variegated hollies, ivies and conifers. *Viburnum tinus* (Laurustinus) is an invaluable evergreen shrub which carries pretty white/pink flowers throughout the winter months. All the foliage mentioned on pages 30-31 can of course be used during the winter months, but here you will find those plants that are particularly associated with the depths of winter.

Cyclamen persicum (cyclamen)
Erica x veitchii 'Exeter' (tree heath)
Mahonia aquifolium (Oregan grape)
Cotoneaster salicifolius 'Rothschildianus' berries yellow
Iris sp.
Skimmia japonica 'Veitchii' syn. *Foremanii*
Erica carnea 'King George' (winter heath)
Cotoneaster sternianus syn. *C. franchetii* var. *sternianus* berries orange, red
Hedera sp. (ivy) with berries
Thuja orientalis 'Elegantissima'
Viburnum tinus (laurustinus)

Ilex aquifolium 'Aureo-marginata' (gold-edged holly)
Alnus glutinosa (common alder)
Callicarpa bodinieri var. *giraldii* (beauty berry)
Eucalyptus cv. (gum tree) seed pods
Mahonia x media 'Charity'
Arum italicum 'Pictum' (great cuckoo-pint)
Symphoricarpos albus (snowberry)
Pyracanthus sp. (firethorn)
Abies procera (noble fir)
Picea pungens (blue spruce)
Viburnum farreri syn. *fragrans*
Ligustrum ovalifolium (privet) berries
Cornus alba 'Sibirica' (red-barked dogwood)
stems
Helleborus foetidus (stinking hellebore)
Larix decidua (European larch) cones and lichen-
covered twigs
Cupressus macrocarpa 'Goldcrest'
Ilex x altaclerensis 'Camellifolia' (holly)
Jasminum nudiflorum (winter flowering jasmine)
Cryptomeria japonica 'Cristata' cockscomb-like
faciated growth form
Viburnum davidii
Plant material displayed on a bed of bark.

Also available:
Cotoneaster (other species)
Eucalyptus sp. (gum tree) foliage
Viscum album (mistletoe)
Taxus baccata (yew)
Sarcococca sp. (Christmas box)
Primula sp.
Garrya elliptica (silk tassel bush)
Daphne odora
Ferns
Lonicera x purpusii 'Winter beauty'
Salix udensis 'Sekka' (fasciated willow)
Pachysandra terminalis
Helleborus orientalis (lenten rose)
Hamamelis mollis (Chinese witch hazel)
Helleborus argutifolius syn. *H. lividus* subsp.
corsicus
Helleborus niger (Christmas rose)
Chimonanthus praecox (winter sweet)
Corylus avellana 'Contorta' (corkscrew hazel,
Harry Lauder's walking stick)
Eranthis hyemalis (winter aconite)

WINTER

From the Florist

At Christmas time, *Abies* (fir) and *Picea* (spruce) lie at every florist's door. *Euphorbia pulcherrima* (poinsettia), the Christmas plant, now comes in a range of colours but beware buying those standing outdoors as poinsettias are susceptible to windy draughts. At the same time *Narcissus* (daffodil), *Tulipa* (tulip) and *Hyacinthus* (hyacinth) make their appearance, heralding spring before the New Year is out.

Hippeastrum sp. (amaryllis) peach, red, white, pink
Dendranthema cv. (chrysanthemum) many colours
Prunus laurocerasus (cherry laurel)
Euphorbia fulgens (scarlet plume) orange, pink, salmon, white
Narcissus cv, (daffodil) yellow, white, bi-coloured
Ornithogalum arabicum (Arabian chincherinchee) white
Dianthus sp. (carnation) many colours
Abies procera (noble fir) bluish-green
Anigozanthos flavidus (kangaroo paw) yellow, red, orange
Eucalyptus sp. fruits silver-grey
Euphorbia pulcherrima (poinsettia)
Alstroemeria Ligtu Hybrids (Peruvian lily) many colours

Capsicum annuum (ornamental pepper) bright red, yellow, orange
Hyacinthus sp. (Hyacinth) many colours
Salix caprea (pussy willow)
Polianthes tuberosa (tuberose)
Ilex aquifolium (holly) red or yellow berries on green foliage
Viscum album (mistletoe)
Syringa cv. (lilac) purple, white, pink
Rosa cv. (rose) many colours
Hedera sp. (ivy) berries black
Acacia longifolia (mimosa, Sydney golden wattle)
Dianthus cv. (stem carnation)
Anemone coronaria (poppy-flavoured anemone) purple, red, blue, pink
Chamelaucium uncinatum (waxflower) white, pink
Tulipa sp. (tulip) many colours
Hippeastrum sp. (amaryllis) peach, red, white, pink
Ilex verticillata (winterberry) red
Narcissus sp. (daffodil) white, bi-coloured
Iris sp.
Ranunculus asiaticus (turban flower)
Leucadendron 'Safari sunset'

Also available:
Aster ericoides (September flower)
Rhododendron sp. foliage

ALL YEAR ROUND

From the Garden

Although some deciduous shrubs and trees, such as *Cornus* (dogwood), *Betula pendula* (silver birch) or *Alnus* (alder), are valuable to flower arrangers by virtue of their colourful stems, interesting bark or cones, it is evergreens that provide material for flower arrangers all year round.

From left to right:
Hedera helix 'Oro di Bogliasco' syn. 'Goldheart' (Ivy)
Leucothoe fontanesiana 'Scarletta'
Bergenia sp. (elephant's ear)
Garrya elliptica (silk tassel bush)
Buxus (box)
Griselinia littoralis
Pittosporum tenuifolium 'Purpureum'
Pittosporum tenuifolium 'Irene Patterson'
Corylus avellana 'Contorta' (corkscrew hazel, Harry Lauder's walking stick)
Tellima grandiflora (fringecups) leaves
Choisya ternata (Mexican orange blossom)
Euonymus fortunei 'Emerald Gaiety'
Ballota pseudodictamnus
Cedrus atlantica 'Glauca' (blue atlas cedar)
Leucothoe fontanesiana 'Scarletta'
Elaeagnus pungens 'Maculata'
Brachyglottis 'Sunshine' syn. *Senecio* 'Sunshine'
Rhamnus alaternus 'Argenteovariegata' (buckthorn)

Fatsia japonica (Japanese aralia)
Lonicera nitida 'Baggesen's Gold' (shrubby honeysuckle)
Hebe 'Mrs Winder'
Laurus nobilis (bay laurel)
Sarcococca hookeriana var. *digyna* (Christmas box)
Fatshedera lizei 'Anniemieke'
Vinca major 'Variegata' (variegated greater periwinkle)
Salvia officinalis 'Purpurascens' (purple sage)
Phormium tenax 'Yellow wave'
Skimmia japonica
Euonymus japonica 'Ovatus aureus'
Euonymus japonica 'Aureopictus'
Pittosporum sp.
Eucalyptus gunnii (cider gum)
Heuchera micrantha 'Palace Purple' (purple alum root)
Prunus laurocerasus (cherry laurel)
Mahonia x media 'Charity'
Plant material displayed on a bed of bark.

Also available:
Aucuba japonica (spotted laurel)
Berberis sp. such as *B. darwinii* and *B.* x. *stenophylla*
Ceanothus (evergreen species)
Cotoneaster sp. such as *C. lacteus* and *C. salicifolius*
Escallonia sp.
Ferns such as *Polypodium vulgare* (common polypody), *Asplenium scolopendrium* (Hart's tongue fern) and *Blechnum capense*
Magnolia grandiflora
Phormium cookianum (mountain flax)
Pyracantha sp. (firethorn) such as P. 'Orange Glow' and P. 'Golden Dome'
Rhododendron sp.
Rosmarinus officinalis (rosemary)
Santolina chamaecyparissus (cotton lavender)
Senecio cineraria syn. *S. maritimus*

ALL YEAR ROUND

From the Florist
Modern glasshouse, greenhouses and packaging technology, and improved communications with all parts of the world, mean that many flowers can now be supplied to the florist all year round. The flowers and foliage seen here are those available at florists' shops without enormous fluctuations in price, for most or all of the year.

Gypsophilia sp. (baby's breath)
Dianthus sp. (spray carnation)
Lilium sp.
Lilium longiflorum (Easter lily)
Dianthus sp.
Danae racemosa (Alexandrian laurel)
Trachelium caeruleum (throatwort)
Prunus laurocerasus (cherry laurel)
Alpinia purpurata (red ginger)
Anthurium andreanum (painter's palette)
Camellia sp.
Aster ericoides (September flower)
Eustoma grandiflorum (lisianthus, prairie gentian)
Dendranthema cv. (chrysanthemum)
Rosa cv. (spray rose)
Rosa cv. (hybrid tea rose)
Solidaster luteus (Hybrid *Solidago x Aster*)

Gerbera hybrid (gerbera)
Leucadendron 'Safari sunset'
Xerophyllum sp.
Bixia orellana (rou cou, annatto)
Freesia sp.
Dendrobium sp. (Singapore orchids)
Protea neriifolia
Lilium cv. (oriental hybrid lily)
Zantedeschia sp. (calla lily)

Also available:
All tropical flowers: *Banksia* sp., *Protea* sp. and fruits: *Ananas* sp.
(pineapple)
Alstroemeria Ligtu hybrids (Peruvian lily)
Anigozanthos sp. (kangaroo paw)
Arachniodes syn. Rumohra adiantiformis (leather fern)
Asparagus setaceus (asparagus fern)
Danae racemosa (Alexandrian laurel)
Eucalyptus sp. (gum tree)
Eustoma grandiflorum (lisianthus, prairie gentian)
Galax urceolata (galax)
Gloriosa superba 'Rothschildiana' (glory lily)
Limonium sinuatum (winged statice)
Phalaenopsis sp. (orchid)
Rhododendron sp. foliage
Ruscus hypoglossum
Strelitzia reginae (bird-of-paradise flower)
Zantedeschia aethiopica (arum lily)

ELEMENTS AND PRINCIPLES OF DESIGN

WHAT IS A GOOD DESIGN? A good design is one to which no more can be added and from which nothing can be taken away without causing an impression of incompleteness. Good designs become classics, reflecting the age in which they were created, yet they are comfortable in any period.

Styles do alter, and appreciation of what is aesthetically pleasing changes according to the nature of society, the economic framework and the technology of the day. Compare, for instance, the over-exuberant use of flowers in Victorian times with their more restrained use in Edwardian times. In both periods the style of flower arranging was closely allied to dress, interior design, the economy and general mood. Certain fundamental criteria, however, remain the same and these have been termed the elements and principles of design.

There are four design elements – form, texture, space and colour. Sometimes, in flower arranging, line is referred to as the fifth element of design, but I have included it under form. If you use these four elements in accordance with the six principles of design – balance, scale, proportion, rhythm, dominance and contrast, – the resulting design will be harmonious.

But remember: 'The principles of design are related to the forces of the universe. You feel these forces but they should not be used too obviously. It is only the imperfections and the unexpected that make art what it is' (K.F. Bates, 1960). That is to say, do not be restricted by conforming too rigidly to theory.

But are these design points relevant if we wish simply to place a mass of a single variety of flower in a vase? Yes, because if you wish to maximize the effect of these flowers you will have to choose a vase of the right colour, form, texture and size. The flowers will have to be cut to a length that is compatible with the vase and positioned where their beauty can best be appreciated. With practice you will use all the elements and principles instinctively and well.

An arrangement for the kitchen with the colour of the flowers and fruits repeating the warm colours of the tiles, the wood and the copper accessories.
ARRANGER: PHOEBE TOWERS.

THE ELEMENTS OF DESIGN

Form

Form is the word that describes a three-dimensional object, such as a fresh flower, as opposed to shape, which describes a two-dimensional object, such as a pressed flower. When we talk about form in flower arranging we can be referring to the flower arrangement as a whole or to the individual form of each stem of plant material.

The Form of an Arrangement

The overall form of an arrangement can be classified as being in one of the following categories:

1. Mass

Mass arrangements have their origin in Europe, possibly first coming to light in the great Dutch flower paintings of the sixteenth and seventeenth centuries. We must remember, however, that these were not actual arrangements but the exciting inventions of the artist with his brush. It was perhaps the Victorians who developed the mass arrangement. With the Victorian love of exuberance, little space is evident.

Mass arrangements can best be defined as those that are composed of a lot of plant material, with little or no space between the individual stems. The stems usually radiate from a central point. Examples of mass arrangements are seen in the traditional round and oval designs (pages 132–4), pedestal arrangements (page 104), sculptural mass designs (pages 108–13), tied bunches (page 142–3) and cushion designs (page 148).

2. Line

Line arrangements have their origin in Chinese and Japanese arrangements. They characteristically use a sparsity of plant material, with an emphasis on space within the design. It is the line within the arrangement that is important. Examples are classical Japanese ikebana arrangements (page 275), some free-form designs (page 126), Art Nouveau arrangements, many spatial and most abstract designs.

3. Line mass

A line mass arrangement bridges the gap between the two styles. It might perhaps be described as a marriage between East and West, a compromise. It can be used to describe many of the geometric styles that originated in the 1950s – the crescent, the Hogarth, and any other styles where space exists within the overall form. It is the space that defines the specific form.

The Form of Individual Stems

Flowers and foliage can be loosely categorized as being one of four distinct forms. This knowledge is extremely useful when choosing a mixed selection of flowers and foliage to arrange together. The four forms are line, concealing, focal and spray.

For 'traditional design classics' the four forms are usually combined. In 'other classics' and 'modern design classics' various combinations of form have been used. These are described where appropriate.

1. Line plant material

Line foliage creates the skeleton of your design and is placed in position first. It is later reinforced with line buds or flowers, to take colour through the design to the outer margins. Line foliage can be any straight or gently curved stem or branch of a plant, shrub or tree that provides a linear or gently branching form. In order to create the three-dimensional skeleton, line foliage must have interest down the stem, rather than just at the tip. For smaller arrangements line material could be box (*Buxus*), small-leaved gum (*Eucalyptus*), privet (*Ligustrum*), *Pittosporum* or veronica (*Hebe*). Line material for larger designs could include beech (*Fagus*), *Sorbus*, cherry laurel (*Prunus*), dogwood (*Cornus*) or birch (*Betula*). Examples of line flowers are buds of spray carnations, heather, delphinium, larkspur (*Consolida*), lavender (*Lavendula*) and branches of flowering shrubs such as japonica (*Chaenomeles*) and fruit blossom.

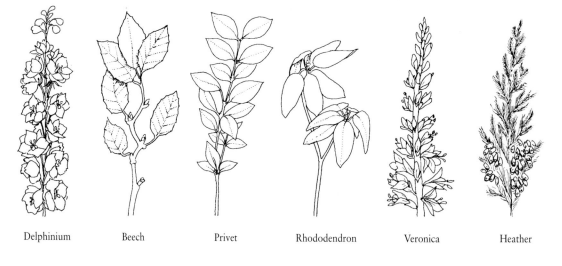

Delphinium   Beech   Privet   Rhododendron   Veronica   Heather

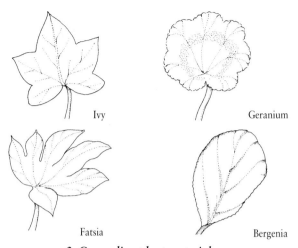

Ivy

Geranium

Fatsia

Bergenia

2. Concealing plant material

Concealing plant material is used to hide large areas of foam quickly and efficiently and to create an area of calm repose, in quiet contrast to the other elements in the arrangement. Concealing leaves need to be round and plain – examples are ivy (*Hedera*), geranium (*Pelargonium*), flowering currant (*Ribes*), *Fatsia* and *Bergenia*. Cherry laurel (*Prunus laurocerasus*) leaves are too ovate to fulfil this function successfully in small designs.

Take care that your concealing leaves are placed at different angles and on different levels, to avoid a static, predictable feel to the arrangement.

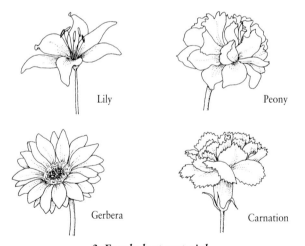

Lily

Peony

Gerbera

Carnation

3. Focal plant material

Focal plant material, sometimes referred to as round or point, is the strongest form in a design. It draws the eye and gives it a focal point on which to rest before moving on to absorb the remainder of the arrangement. Focal material stabilizes. Focal plant material usually comprises flowers, but rosettes of leaves can also have the same effect. Examples are peonies (*Paeonia*), open roses (*Rosa cv.*) and lilies (*Lilium*), gerberas,

chrysanthemums (*Dendranthema*), dahlias (*Dahlia*) and carnations (*Dianthus*).

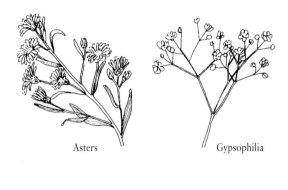

Asters

Gypsophilia

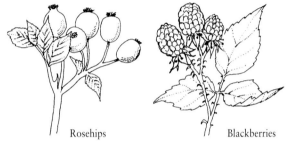

Rosehips

Blackberries

4. Spray plant material

Spray plant material fills the design. It can lighten, soften and give added variation and interest. Examples are Michaelmas daisy (*Aster novi-belgii*), September flower (*Aster ericoides*), baby's breath (*Gypsophila*), spray roses, solidaster, wax flower (*Chamelaucium uncinatum*), hips, sprays of blackberries (*Rubus*) or privet (*Ligustrum*) berries.

Depth

Depth is an important part of form. It makes the difference between a flat and a three-dimensional arrangement, thus heightening interest and giving a more natural feel to the design.

How to create depth

1. The easiest way to create depth is to fill in the back of an arrangement. There is no need to use the best-quality flowers, but foliage and a touch of colour will work well.
2. Gradually use darker or lighter colours, working from the front to the back.
3. Some colours advance, while others recede. Receding colours placed behind advancing colours give greater depth.
4. Turn the flowers or leaves at different angles, particularly at the sides of the arrangement, to lead the eye round to the back of the design.

5. Overlap leaves or half-hide a flower with a leaf.

6. Placing an asymmetrical design at an angle gives a greater impression of depth.

7. Smooth and shiny textures advance, dull and rough recede. Placed next to each other, they will give a greater illusion of depth.

Line

Lines in an arrangement give movement to the design and allow the eye to pass smoothly from one part of the design to the next. Direct line is the term applied to a straight or curved branch. Repetition or radiation of such lines are ways of providing movement.

Indirect lines provide more irregular movement or rhythm. These are created by repeating the form of a flower or leaf throughout the design, so that the eye passes from one to the next. Obviously there can be variation in colour and size – with smaller, paler buds closer to the margins and larger, brighter flowers at the focal area.

Texture

Contrast of texture is vital for good design. Texture is visual as much as real, and it is this visual perception that is so important in flower arranging.

Texture in plant material can be described in so many ways – waxy, spiky, downy, ridged, needled, silky, hairy, to cite but a few.

When more than one texture is being incorporated into the design it is necessary to include a form that is plain and smooth, to give a calm contrast to the other texture(s) in the design. This smooth texture is particularly to be found in:

• leaves such as ivy (*Hedera*), *Fatsia*, *Bergenia* and *Hosta*

• seedheads and berries such as rose, poppy (*Papaver*), Chinese lanterns (*Physalis alkekengi*) and privet (*Ligustrum ovalifolium*)

• many single-petalled flowers, such as the single chrysanthemum, dahlia, *Rudbeckia* and *Cosmos*

• many houseplant leaves, such as *Aspidistra*, croton (*Codiaeum*), *Fatshedera*

• many fruits and vegetables, such as green tomatoes (*Lycopersicon*), apples (*Malus sylvestris*), tangerines (*Citrus reticulata*) and aubergines (*Solanum melongena*).

If you look at the multitude of flowers that constitute Lady's mantle (*Alchemilla mollis*) you will see that the round, plain leaves with their subtle edging perfectly complement the intricate form of the flowering sprays. This happy combination occurs in nature again and again.

Flower arrangements with a monochromatic colour scheme (see page 45) have a need for strong textural contrasts.

Space

Solid is the opposite of space. Without space there is no form. In flower arranging space can be used in the following ways:

1. Beneath the container – this gives a sense of lightness to the design and avoids an arrangement looking rather solid and over-heavy at the base. A smaller base or table mat under a base will raise the arrangement without being seen.

2. Within traditional designs – this often gives a livelier effect. Some areas of the design will require a greater density of material than others. For example, a greater density of solids is needed at the focal areas to hold the eye, but more slender plant material is required at the extremities of the design.

3. Within spatial and abstract designs – these designs utilize space as a major feature, and it is as much a part of the design as solids are. Space can have as much eye-pull as the pierced holes in the sculptures of Barbara Hepworth and Henry Moore. When it is used to balance solid placements, it is often enclosed by manipulation of leaves or loops of cane, raffia, ribbon or plant material such as broom (*Cytisus*). See the arrangement on the opposite page.

4. As an illusion – the eye can be tricked into an illusion of depth, where little or none exists. This adds to the general impression of space. See Depth above.

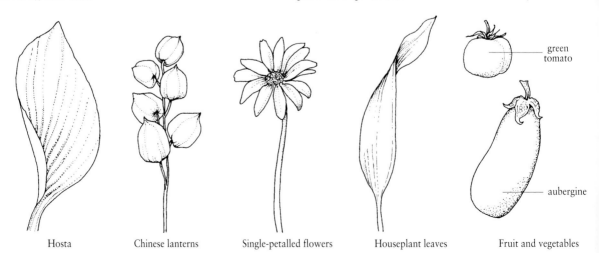

Hosta   Chinese lanterns   Single-petalled flowers   Houseplant leaves   Fruit and vegetables

green tomato

aubergine

△ A fresh topiary tree with a refreshing use of
contrasting textures.
ARRANGER: LINDA ALLUM.

▷ What fantastic balance is achieved through
the use of disparate plant material, careful
placement and the use of enclosed space.
Hold up your finger or pencil, close one eye
and see how this design is beautifully balanced
either side of the central axis, because of the
clever use of space within the design.
ARRANGER: NIKKI LEADSOM.

Space is evident beneath and within
this arrangement.

COLOUR

Colour inspires and is one of the most exciting elements of design. It is emotive and personal; it influences mood and feeling. No-one could be seriously interested in flower arranging and be immune to the power and delight of colour.

There is no definite right and wrong with colour. Any colour scheme that makes an expressive statement is valid.

There are many aspects of colour theory that are easy to understand and there are others that need a little more application. Perhaps two of the easiest ways of choosing flowers that go together are to:

• Choose flowers that all have the same parent, for example pink, red and burgundy or pale blue, blue and dark blue (see monochromatic arrangements page 42);

• Ensure that all the flowers have a link with another variety in the arrangement, for example yellow golden rod (*Solidago*) with blue China asters (*Callistephus*), with a dominant yellow centre and blue veronica (*Hebe*).

The following guidelines will help you use the most effective colours together and place them in the most appropriate setting. But colour theory does not lay down specific combinations that must always be followed. Its aim is to encourage you to question colour and to strengthen your own subjective opinions, so that you can work and design with a greater understanding. I hope that you will try out striking and varying combinations of colour to find those that work.

So how can words help us learn about the visual act of perceiving colour? Until the early twentieth century many civilizations did not have names for colours. In the Bible there are over 400 references to the skies or the heavens, but the colour blue is never mentioned. It was only in 1912 that Albert H. Munsell expounded the excellent system of colour notation that we use today.

Before we talk about the ubiquitous colour wheel, there are three terms that need to be explained:

1. Hue
This is the quality that distinguishes one colour from another – blue, green, red, and so on. It is simply another word for colour.

▷ *Always try to link the colour of the arrangement with that of the room. Here mini-sunflowers (Helianthus) and yellow calla lilies (Zantedeschia) are combined with Mahonia leaves to complement the sumptuous velvet curtains behind.*
ARRANGER: MARY FISHER.

2. Value
This is the quality of lightness or darkness in the colour: the amount of white, black or grey that has been added to the pure hue. When white has been added to the pure hue it is called a tint. Another word for a tint, with which you may be more familiar, is a pastel. If black is added to the pure hue it becomes a shade, and if a mixture of black and white is added it becomes a tone.

3. Chroma
This measures colour intensity. Another way of expressing this is the strength or purity of the colour. A watery colour has a weak chroma. Think of a watercolour seascape with the sea painted a blue-grey colour to which loads of water has been added. This would be a seascape using colours of a weak chroma.

◁ *A monochromatic colour scheme of lilies (Lilium), Astilbe, stocks (Matthiola), fritillary (Fritillaria), dogwood (Cornus) and roses (Rosa) in a lined terracotta plant pot, using tints, tones and shades of red.*

THE COLOUR WHEEL

T HE COLOUR WHEEL is the best guide to colour theory. It contains the colours of the rainbow, curved to form a circle, but only six colours are used, as indigo and violet are combined as purple. The continuum colours of the rainbow – red, orange, yellow, green, blue, indigo and violet – were laid down by Isaac Newton, to whom seven was the perfect number. For the purposes of flower arranging, the three primary colours (red, blue and yellow) and the three secondary colours (orange, green and purple) offer all the combinations that you will need.

The primary colours are so called because they cannot be created by mixing other colours together. They stand alone. Unbroken areas of these primaries can be stimulating and enlivening, but they can also be overwhelming if no green is added to soften the impact. Bright primaries work well in spatial and abstract design, where there are fewer elements to the arrangement.

All other colours can be created by mixing these primary colours together. Thus red and blue create purple; red and yellow create orange; and blue and yellow create green. The greater the number of pure colours used in an arrangement, the more chance there is of them overwhelming each other, unless they are well organized.

Because the colour of flowers is seldom at its full intensity, the colour wheel below has been developed so that you see some of the variety of colours that arise when degrees of black and white are added.

The Diversity of Colour

To get a feel for the diversity of colour take a walk in the country, along a river bank or in a park and observe the different number of greens that you see. Divide them into green-greens, yellow-greens and blue-greens, and the colour wheel will start to make sense. It becomes a delightful yet useful family game and will open your eyes to the intricate detail of nature.

Neutralizing Green

Although black and white are considered neutral, green is nature's neutral colour. Green is the harmonizer. It will bring together flowers of a multitude of forms and colours. Dark green gives depth to pastel colours and light green can bring life and vitality to darker flowers.

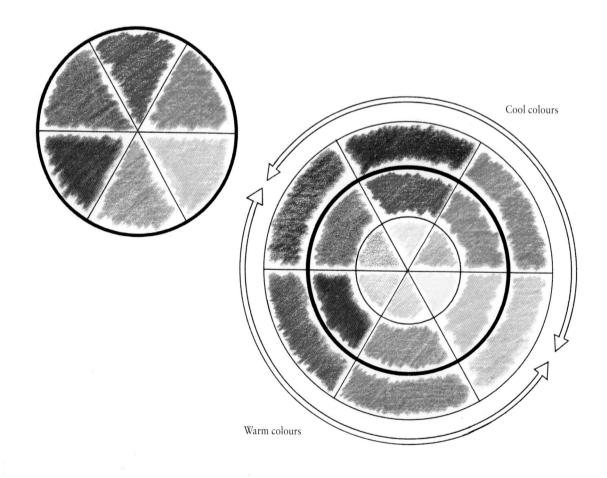

Cool colours

Warm colours

Effective Colour Schemes

So what is a good colour scheme? This is a question that has bemused and intrigued people for countless generations. So much so that in 1349 Florentine artists got together to study this very question. The four following colour harmonies are considered to work, because over the centuries they have been found to be pleasing to many people. Flower arrangers are not actually interested in mixing paints to get a certain colour. They work with existing colours and love to experiment with different colour combinations.

Monochromatic Colour Schemes

Monochromatic colour schemes are safe, and they can be the most effective colour schemes of all, whether you are arranging one or many types of flowers. If you are mixing your flowers, go for extremes in value and chroma and for lots of exciting textural contrasts. There are many monochromatic designs in this book, but all rely on the addition of the flower arranger's neutral colour, green.

Adjacent or Analogous Colour Schemes

An adjacent colour scheme uses up to one-third of a twelve-band colour wheel, the colours all being found next to each other. But it is understood that green may also be included. One example would be green-yellow, yellow, yellow-orange and orange, plus green. See the arrangement above.

This design of orange and yellow poppies (Papaver) with lemons (Citrus limon) uses an adjacent colour scheme. Because the yellow has been arranged with warm rather than cool colours, it takes on a warm rather than a cool aura.
ARRANGER: DOREEN FOX.

Complementary Colour Schemes

Complementary colours lie directly opposite each other on the colour wheel. Each colour heightens the vitality of the other, and they provide the maximum energy and vividness. For example, place purple flowers against a yellow wall, or red flowers against a green wall. A mixture of complementary colours, in equal amounts, produces grey. The most interesting complementary colour schemes are perhaps those which use tints, tones and shades.

Polychromatic Colour Schemes

This is the use of many colours together. An arrangement of this variety is always cheerful and vibrant. To ensure that there is harmony and unity in the design, take care with your choice of form and texture.

Warm and Cool Colours

Warm and cool colours are equally split on the colour wheel. Reds, oranges and strong yellows are warm colours, recalling the hues of fire and the sun. There is a lot of energy in these colours and they can become tiring to the eye. Blues, greens and violets are cool colours – they are calm and easy on the eye.

Warm and cool colours are both used in flower arranging, just as they are in interior design. Warm colours are often used to give vitality to north- and east-facing rooms and cool colours will have the opposite effect in south-facing rooms.

Warm colours brighten under electric light or candlelight but are deadened under fluorescent lighting. For fluorescent lighting blues are best. The coldest colours lie opposite those that are warmest.

Advancing and Receding Colours

Blue, violet and other cool colours recede. This means that they create a feeling of distance. The builders of Gothic cathedrals often painted the ceilings blue to emphasize their lofty height. They also installed blue stained glass to create a feeling of distance. Cool receding colours are best used for camouflage, so if you have ugly pipes or radiators to hide, paint them in blue, mauve, grey or any other receding colour.

The warm colours – orange, strong yellow, red and terracotta – have the opposite effect. They advance or foreshorten.

Just as this colour information is applied to interior design, it can also be applied to flower arranging. Advancing, bright and warm colours are suitable when arranged in a room you wish to make smaller. Conversely, receding and pale colours are suitable for smaller areas. This is called colour movement.

Luminosity

Some colours can be seen more easily than others. Any tint (colours with white in them) can be seen more vividly in dim lighting than those of a pure hue. Conversely, those with black in them can be seen less easily than those of a pure hue. Of the chromatic colours – white and black being neutrals – yellow is the most luminous, followed by orange, yellow-green, red, blue and lastly purple.

For a good example of luminosity turn to page 62, where the creamy yellow tulips and dark blue anemones are an excellent example of colours with high and low luminosity. The tulips have high luminosity and the anemones low.

*A polychromatic colour scheme achieved by using larkspur (*Consolida*). lisianthus (*Eustoma*), spray carnations (*Dianthus*), chrysanthemum (*Dendranthema 'Revert'*), freesia, fuchsia, roses, Himalayan honeysuckle (*Leycesteria formosa*) and Stephanandra tanakae.*
ARRANGER: CHRISTINA WALLIS.

THE EFFECT OF LIGHTING

Fluorescent Lighting

Fluorescent lighting is a flat, cold, bright illumination, which throws little shadow and has a bluish cast. It is most commonly found in shops, offices, factories and kitchens. New technology is now producing fluorescent tubes that produce a light similar to that given by filament lamps. As a consequence, fluorescent lighting can now vary considerably. If your kitchen is decorated in blues and greens and you wish to complement this colour scheme with flowers in the same colours, choose a blue tube; and if decorated in yellows and oranges choose a compatible-coloured tube, as a blue light will muddy the colours of warm-coloured flowers. To get the truest light you could mix tungsten and fluorescent lighting.

Tungsten

The colour spectrum of a tungsten light bulb contains almost no blue, but has a strong red bias. It therefore benefits red, orange and yellow flowers but does nothing for those that are blue.

Candlelight

Yellowish pink or peach-coloured flowers are ideal in candlelight. Receding colours such as blue and violet will disappear. The darker they are, the more they will disappear, so that you appear to be left with holes in your arrangement. Generally speaking, warm pastels will scintillate and cool, dark colours will deaden the overall effect.

THE SIZE OF COLOUR

Dark colours reduce size and light colours increase it. Small rooms look larger, the lighter their colour, in the same way as flower arrangements of light colours maximize the size of a room. As an analogy, dark-coloured clothes are slimming, reducing the apparent size of the wearer, while light colours have the opposite effect. If you wish to use dahlias or a similar large flower in an arrangement, and the other flowers are just too small to be in scale, use dark dahlias rather than those with bright or pale colours, so that they will appear smaller.

The Colour of Your Walls

Grey, blue, soft green or terracotta are the colours that seem to enhance many colour combinations. Grey is the colour against which all colours are truest. Flowers can get lost when placed against a stark white wall. A grey stone wall is far more sympathetic to most colour schemes than a whitewashed wall.

An arrangement of cool colours – sprayed grey-blue poppy seedheads and dragon's claw willow (Salix babylonica var. pekinensis 'Tortuosa') with white lisianthus, dill (Anethum graveolens) and foliage in a blue-grey container.
ARRANGER: ROSIE CRIMES.

An arrangement of freesias and cream and green variegated ivy (Hedera) in a simple glass jug has been placed to complement the china and furnishings.
ARRANGER: LADY REDSHAW.

THE PSYCHOLOGY OF COLOUR

MOST PEOPLE have some reaction to colour, which has been recognized as affecting our physical and mental activity. Religious organizations see colour as an important factor in the expression of life, both in ancient and modern times. And it is important to remember that colours have a completely different symbolism according to race and religion.

Here are some of the connotations that people associate with colours:

Purple – exoticism, aristocracy, senior clergy, royalty.

Black – mystery and power, night, space, nothing, the Grim Reaper, evil, the black market, a symbol of taste. Black Africans wear bright colours because black is associated with death and evil. Arab women wear black according to the Islamic code of decorum.

Red – thought to be the first colour seen by babies. Exposure to red is said to quicken the heartbeat and gives a sense of warmth. Red is the colour of aristocracy, passion, fire, love, the devil, danger, blood. The effect alters when white is added and pink results – in the pink, everything is rosy – giving a sense of well-being. Red and pink foods are associated with flavour. Red is said to be preferred by ten times as many men as women.

Orange – there was no word for orange in the English language until the orange fruit arrived during the tenth and eleventh centuries. If autumn has a colour, then it is orange. It is an exotic colour – the colour of spices, sunsets, autumn leaves, cheerfulness.

Yellow – cheerfulness, caution. Yellow cars are less frequently involved in road accidents (probably because they are the most luminous colour – see page 46). Yellow, particularly a clear yellow, is the colour of spring, the sun, but also illness.

Green – the colour of life. The most restful colour to the eye, representing stability and security, supernatural phenomena, jealousy. Green is the colour that unifies all the elements of a flower design, but green on its own delights the eye.

White – goodness, magic, clinical surroundings, purity.

HELPFUL HINTS

To sum up, if in doubt consider the following:

♦ If you use sufficient green, both flowers and foliage in any colour combination will succeed.

♦ Any mixture of white flowers will be harmonious, especially if the container you use is also white. It is always safe but effective to use any combination of white flowers with green or green-and-white variegated foliage. When you add white to a mixed colour combination the white flowers stand out like dominant blobs, which is not to their advantage.

♦ A design of warm colours, for example terracotta, orange and red, will appear harmonious and comforting and will always work well together.

♦ A mixture of cool-coloured flowers will soothe and calm, and will give the impression of enlarging the room in which they are positioned.

♦ A mixture of flowers with the same colour intensity, for instance blue cornflowers (*Centaurea cyanus*), yellow lilies and red poppies, will sizzle with drama, but if in doubt add the neutralizing ingredient of green.

♦ Try mixing flowers with the same colour parenthood – for example, a monochromatic design that is reliant on the judicious selection of tints, tones and shades.

♦ Arrange the same flowers in a mixture of colours.

♦ If using bi-coloured flowers, such as red daisy chrysanthemums with a yellow centre, the accompanying flowers also need to be red or yellow to provide a colour link. If you introduce another colour, without a link, the result will be discordant. Think of white daisy chrysanthemums with a yellow centre mixed with pink carnations!

♦ A mixture of flowers of one species always looks good.

♦ An arrangement only of tones can look lugubrious and dull. To an arrangement of maroons and crimsons add a touch of pink. This will lift and give life.

♦ An arrangement only of pastels can look calm and gentle, but if you feel it lacks depth add a tone of one variety of flower or foliage to give strength. This will also add to the three-dimensional effect.

*The warm orange and red dahlias, yellow spray chrysanthemums (*Dendranthema*), shocking-pink China asters (*Callistephus chinensis*) and* Houttuynia cordata *'Chameleon' are further enlivened by their placement against a dark background.*

THE PRINCIPLES
OF DESIGN

NOW WE MUST STUDY HOW TO USE these elements – form, texture, space and colour – in flower arranging. The principles of design – balance, scale, proportion, contrast, dominance and rhythm – need to be applied to the four elements. For example, when creating an arrangement, see that you have balance of form, balance of colour, balance of space and balance of texture.

Balance

Good balance is crucial in flower arranging. If there were a scale of importance for the principles, then balance would be high, for without good balance an arrangement cannot be successful. Balance in flower arranging takes two forms – physical and visual. Physical balance means that an object will stay upright and not fall over. Visual balance means that the arrangement does not look as if it might topple over. There are two fundamental types of balance, symmetrical and asymmetrical.

The overall design uses symmetrical and asymmetrical balance. The jug has asymmetrical balance; the form is different each side of the central axis, but the base and lip perfectly balance the rolled handle. The mass of tulips conforms to symmetrical balance.

The asymmetrical triangle is unbalanced by being placed centrally on the symmetrically balanced sideboard.

The asymmetrical triangle is now balanced by being placed to one side on the sideboard and by the addition of ornaments and a figurine on the far side.
ARRANGER: PEARL KNIGHT.

Whatever their style, arrangements need to be balanced vertically and horizontally. To check the vertical balance, close one eye and hold a pencil vertically through the centre of the container and see if the eye is pulled to one side or the other. For horiz-ontal balance, close one eye and hold a pencil or stem two-thirds of the way down the arrangement.

Symmetrical Balance

Western art, architecture and the human body are based on symmetrical balance. It is our heritage from classical Greek and Roman art forms and is the basis of many traditional arrangements, typified perhaps by the symmetrical triangle.

Symmetrical balance means that the weight and outline of the plant material are the same each side of a vertical axis rising from the centre of a symmetrical container. This kind of balance is restful, stately and dignified. In traditional designs, symmetrical balance should be carried through the whole design. For example, a symmetrical arrangement should not have an accessory on just one side. Nor should it be placed against an asymmetrical background.

Asymmetrical Balance

Oriental art is based on asymmetrical balance. From the Chinese and Japanese we have learnt much about asymmetrical or informal balance in painting, landscape design and flower arrangement. Some Oriental teachers believe that the seemingly vacant side of a painting or flower arrangement is a place for the imagination, for meditation and rest.

Asymmetrical balance means that the plant material is not similarly arranged on both sides of an imaginary vertical axis. The two sides may, or may not, have equal amounts of plant material. Asymmetrical balance is subtle, creative, emotional and stimulating. Although more difficult to achieve, it can be more personally satisfying than formal symmetrical balance. Frequently the formal plant material masses do not appear to balance one another, so it is necessary that the voids are significant in order to balance the solids.

Asymmetrical arrangements can be balanced by:

1. Self-balance – in a self-balanced arrangement the lines and masses are so distributed on both sides of a central vertical axis through the centre of the container that, although opposing sides are distinctly different in outline, they have the same visual weight. The result is equilibrium.
2. Balance by placement – this means that an arrangement is not balanced by itself but is heavier on one side than the other. It appears balanced, however, when placed in the right relationship to its base or site. Ornaments or a lamp can be positioned to balance the design or the arrangement can be positioned on the diagonal. Alternatively, an accessory may be incorporated into the actual design.
3. Using longer, lighter plant material to balance shorter, heavier material. Look at the photograph on page 63, where the shorter, heavier nodding pincushion flowers (*Leucospermum cordifolium*) are balanced by the longer, lighter kangaroo paw (*Anigozanthos*).
4. Using space to balance plant material. Enclosed space is visually heavier than open space.

Visual Weight

Whichever type of balance you wish to achieve, the following information on the apparent visual weight and the actual weight of plant material is relevant. This is because you do not wish your arrangement to be top-heavy, bottom-heavy, or side-heavy. The visual weight of plant material increases:

• The further the materials are from the central axis.
• The higher they are in the composition.
• The more solid, rather than airy, the form.
• The stronger they are in colour.
• The darker they are in colour value.
• The warmer they are in hue.
• The more advancing the colours.
• The greater the luminosity of the colour.
• The larger the form.

Also take into account that:

• Focal flowers have more weight than linear ones.
• Shiny surfaces have more weight than dull ones.
• Enclosed space is more compelling than open space.
• Large and shiny plant material is more dominant than rough and small plant material.

Scale

Scale is the relationship between the size of each part of the composition. It is particularly important to consider:

1. The relationship of the arrangement to the room in which it stands. A miniature arrangement would be inappropriate for a sparsely furnished church hall. A large pedestal would be out of scale for a small bedsit, as would a large patterned fabric and huge Victorian furniture. Remember, as you go up in scale, use larger plant material, rather than more plant material.
2. The relationship of the size of the plant material to the container. For a large, heavy vase use tall stems with large flowers. For small containers use more delicate flowers and foliage. If your flowers are too large for the container, add a base.
3. The relationship of the size of the plant material to each other. Very tiny flowers do not sit well with very large ones, unless they are in a tightly massed spray or group. Flowers must relate to the foliage as well as to the other flowers. As a general guide, do not incorporate flowers that are more than twice the size of the ones next to them in size. Ensure that all your plant material is in scale.

a   b   c

Where is Scale Particularly Important?

1. Miniatures and petites

Miniature is the term given to a tiny arrangement no larger than 10 cm (4 in) high, wide or deep. A petite arrangement is no larger than 23 cm (9 in) high, wide or deep. For such small designs even one flower or leaf out of scale will create discord. For photographic purposes, a coin is often placed by the side of a finished arrangement to show its size.

2. Pedestals

If the plant material is not as large as required, use bunches of smaller plant material to create a stronger effect.

3. Landscapes

Scale is particularly important when creating landscape designs. In a realistic landscape design, nature is being copied and reproduced. Other components should be scaled to the natural scale of life. It is easier if you avoid man-made objects and try to create the effect with natural plant material. If a twig is being used to represent a tree, then any figures introduced into the design should be in the same scale relationship as a real man to a real tree.

Proportion

Proportion is the ratio of one area or one part of a structure to another, and to the whole. The Greek mathematician Euclid proposed the formula for perfect proportion around 300 BC. His theory, known as the Golden Section or Golden Mean, has withstood the passage of the centuries. It is the division of a line or area in such a way that the small part is in the same proportion to the greater part as the greater part is to the whole. The formula is based on the proportions of the human body.

AC is to AB as CB is to AC. This theory also applies to areas and volumes.

A   C   B

So how can this be related to flower arranging? It simply means that if the flowers are too wide, too low or too high for the container, or the arrangement too small or big for the background, then the total effect will be lost. If working to the above formula seems too complicated, then apply one of the guidelines overleaf, which are based on the idea of thirds – close enough to Euclid's formula!

As all the components in the design are in scale, it is hard to tell that no dimension of this arrangement is more than 23 cm (9 in).
ARRANGER: MICHIKO YAMADA.

Also remember that:
• Containers that are dark in colour, or constructed of strong material, can support much larger arrangements.
• The weight of plant material affects the proportions. Airy plants may extend much further than strong ones.
• A strong base permits the arrangements to be taller or more volumetric than usual. When the base is larger than the container, the height of the material should be one and a half times the length of the base, rather than the size of the container. Refer to the triangular arrangement on page 74. Here, the amount of flowers in relation to the volume of the container is too great. A base underneath the arrangement would help to correct the proportions.

a   b   c

The flowers in (a) and (b) are in scale with each other.
The flower in (c) is too small to be in scale with the other flowers.

Let your tallest stems be one and a half times the height of a tall container.

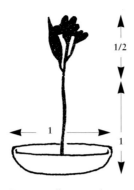

Let your tallest stems be one and a half times the width of a wide container.

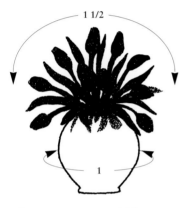

In a mass arrangement, let the volume of plant material be one and a half times that of the container.

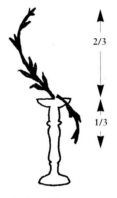

In an S-shaped design, two-thirds of the plant material should be above the rim of the container.

If using a low, flat container cover only two-thirds of the open area with plant material.

The Chinese, however, arrange their flowers so that the container is more dominant than the plant material. You will notice that some of the sculptural containers are more dominant than the flowers. But the proportions still hold true – the proportion of container to plant material is 3:2 rather than 2:3.

Contrast

Contrast is the difference shown when objects are placed next to each other. A good use of contrast is exciting and relieves boredom. There can be contrast between different varieties of flowers and foliage, and contrast within a bowl of flowers of one variety, where the buds and flowers are at differing degrees of development.

With the amount of contrast available to the flower arranger it is careful selection that calls for skill. If the design is intended to be restful, then the amount of contrast should be small but nevertheless present, for without it the design would be lifeless. At the other end of the spectrum, an exciting, startling design demands great contrast in all aspects, especially form and colour, as these are the most apparent. Textural contrasts can be less dramatic but equally effective.

Nature has provided us with unending variety in contrasting textures and forms, which appeal both to the sense of sight and of touch. Put a shiny leaf against a hairy or woolly one, or a leaf of simple, round form against a long, pointed one. Contrast avoids monotony and can be obtained by changing the direction of lines, the length of stems, the size of the material. Vitality is added to any composition by the inclusion of components that contradict the main effect. If a flower arrangement seems too severe, for example, add a softening influence like *Alchemilla mollis*. Well-organized and controlled contrasts make for strong designs.

Contrast in form

This is referred to under form on page 36–7. When using more than one type of plant material in an arrangement, avoid arranging similar flowers, such as larkspur and stocks (*Matthiola*), unless there are other flowers and foliage to keep them apart; otherwise they will create confusion, if too close together.

Contrast in colour

Much can depend on the visual weight and importance of the colours used, and probably no two people see colour in quite the same way. An arrangement of purples, violets and lavenders that could seem too retiring might need the contrast of creamy blooms to bring it to life. Complementary colours make the strongest possible contrasts. Although there should be variation in the quantities of each colour and in the value, one colour should dominate.

Contrast in texture

It is the inclusion of smooth-textured material that is essential to many successful designs. So much plant material has an intricate structure that it is only calm areas of smooth-textured leaves that can show up its full beauty.

Dominance

If a flower arrangement contains two or more equal attractions they will pull the design apart. Without dominance there is a lack of unity. Dominance will provide a sense of order. The following are examples of how you can create the necessary dominance in your arrangement to hold it together. Dominance is often closely linked with proportion.

*A splendid massed arrangement of fluffy orange carnations, smooth shiny aubergines (*Solanum melongena*), frilled soft Celosia and the sinuous strong lines of the tough twisted lengths of bark in a papier mâché container, showing contrast of texture, colour and form. ARRANGER: BARBARA COLLIER.*

Dominant colour

Dominance of either warm or cool colours in an arrangement is far better than equal quantities of each. Dominance of a chosen colour is also necessary for beauty. An arrangement that is half-red and half-green has displeasing competition within itself.

Dominant form

Focal flowers are more dominant than line and spray plant material. Large form is more dominant than small. A greater quantity is more dominant than a lesser quantity.

In a mixed arrangement one kind of flower should dominate in quantity. Without this dominance interest is divided, scattered and quickly lost. In most arrangements the flowers used for a focal area dominate by virtue of their size and colour.

Dominance of container or flowers

In traditional arranging the flowers are dominant, but where the container is of special interest this may well dominate the flowers. What is important is that one should be the key player, rather than having two contenders for the title.

The dominance of flowers over a container or *vice versa* is usually in the ratio of 3:2 (see previous page).

Dominant movement

The emphasis must be chiefly on one kind of movement, in order to have rhythm in an arrangement. A rhythm of radiation is the most common movement in traditional flower arranging. A dominance of parallel lines is the dominant movement in the parallel style.

Dominant texture

Strong dominance of one kind of texture is advisable in most arrangements so that unity in texture results. For example, shiny texture is more dominant than dull. Even when textural contrast is sought, one kind of texture should predominate.

In this arrangement an ornamental cabbage
provides the dominant area.
ARRANGER: DOREEN FOX.

Dominant area

Any planned flower arrangement has one or more areas of
interest. In traditional designs this is usually located near the
place where all the stems of the plant materials converge, because
attention is naturally drawn there. In a good abstract design it
can appear anywhere! The chief function of the area of strongest
interest is to draw together all the separate parts of the design. In
all-round designs there will be several dominant areas distributed
around the arrangement. In front-facing traditional designs the
focal area is found towards the base of the tallest stem.

A dominant focal area can be created by:

• Placing the roundest, brightest, most interesting or largest
flowers in this area.

• Placing the shiniest, largest, roundest leaves in this area.

• Concentrating the flowers at the area(s) selected, even if there is
only one variety of flower in the arrangement.

Rhythm

Rhythm is the beat, the pulse, the movement of the design.
In music it is the build-up of a good rhythm that enthrals the
listener and urges him or her to anticipate with joy the notes that
will follow. In flower arranging good rhythm captures the
viewer's attention and may be predictable or unpredictable. Good
rhythm means that the eye is led through the arrangement from
top to bottom, from side to side and from front to back. An
arrangement without rhythm cannot hold the viewer's attention
for long.So how can rhythm, perhaps the most elusive of design
principles, be harnessed to hold the viewer's attention. It is the
employment of line, form, colour and space in such a way that
the observer achieves the effect of motion, even though the
components are static.

Rhythm is found in all plant material. Flower arrangers should
respect growth habits and arrange their flowers and foliage so
that they follow their natural rhythmic lines, appearing
comfortable rather than awkward.

Some of the ways in which rhythm can successfully be achieved
are by:

Rhythm in line

1. Rhythm can be achieved by radiation of line. The most
important illustration of radiation is when all lines of an
arrangement converge at one place. Nature illustrates radiation in
growing plants. Most flower petals and sepals radiate from a
centre. Palm leaves have flat radiation.
2. Making the top of a traditional arrangement end in one
point only. Do not let two main lines branch off like a Y.
When adding colour to your foliage outline, reinforce the central
stem rather than positioning colour to form this Y either side of
the foliage stem.
3. Repetition of line.

Rhythm in form

1. Repeating the form of a leaf by overlapping leaves of the same
variety to get a patchwork effect. This is often seen in parallel
and sculptural designs, see page 131.
2. Repeating the form of your container in the form of the
arrangement and of your base. For example, create a round
arrangement in a round container on a round rather than
an oval base.

Rhythm in colour

1. Using adjacent colours and placing them in their correct sequence, as on the colour wheel.

2. Using graduations in value, with the darkest values lower down and the lightest values at the top and sides, and medium values inbetween them.

3. Repeating a colour in several places in different amounts, so that the eye flows from one area to another of the same colour.

Different Sorts of Movement that Create Rhythm

1. Ascending or Vertical Movement

This movement is seen in tall arrangements. Tall, slender material such as *Iris* leaves gives effective vertical movement. Additional rhythm results from overlapping such leaves or flowers, with each one shorter than the next, or from placing each one slightly to one side in a sequence of heights. This tends to push the movement up and up. Look at the photograph of bird-of-paradise flowers (*Strelitzia reginae*) in a low bowl on page 123, and the vertical arrangement below.

2. Curvilinear Movement

Circular movement can be found in Hogarth curves (see page 120–1), downward and upward crescents and the gentle curve of cushion arrangements, tied bunches and round designs. It can also be seen where leaves are manipulated, not only to heighten interest but to create new forms in contemporary designs. Round flowers also give curvilinear movement.

3. Horizontal Movement

A calm and restful rhythm. Horizontal plant material in a low container usually repeats the directions of the lines of the table.

4. Diagonal Movement

A strong diagonal action requires a strong horizontal base to support it. An arrangement that features diagonal lines does not usually welcome any straight horizontal or vertical lines within it. It may, however, have a minor rhythm of circular or semi-circular forms at the focal area.

Harmony

Harmony is the compatibility of all the components in a composition. It refers to the absence of any jarring note in the relationship of the elements that make up the arrangement. It is the happy medium between discord and monotony.

Through the good use of the elements and principles of design, harmony will be achieved. Choose plant material of pleasing colours, with interesting variations in texture and a good combination of form. Place the flowers and foliage so that they are balanced. Give dominance and contrast. Ensure that all the components are in scale with each other and are well-proportioned. Get a good rhythm running through the design. Succeed with all these and you will have a harmonious design!

◁ *Rhythm and vitality are given to the arrangement by the repetition of the line material. The wriggly tips of the dried stems echo the movement of the brass detailing.*

△ *A harmonious design using tints, tones and shades of orange positioned where the accessories and polished wood of the chest of drawers adds to the overall effect.*
ARRANGER: MARY FISHER.

CONTAINERS

O<small>N THE FOLLOWING PAGES</small> you will see many containers that are suitable for using with flowers. Some are works of art in their own right. Even so, the addition of living flowers and foliage gives a container life and soul. The word 'container' embraces a vast range of receptacles that can be used to display flowers. But when is a container a vase, a dish or a bowl?

The dictionary defines 'vase' as an ornamental container for flowers (from the Latin *vasum*, meaning a vessel). 'Ornamental' is itself described as detailing used to add beauty or decoration. But perhaps a vase can best be described as a container, created for flowers, that is taller than it is wide.

Conversely, a dish can be described as being a good deal wider than it is tall. The water in a dish is frequently an important feature of the overall design.

A bowl has a round form with curved sides. Bowls are ideally suited to an all-round, massed display of flowers and foliage.

So a container may be a vase, a dish or a bowl.

The list of materials from which containers are made is seemingly endless. There are traditional materials, such as iron, china, tin and clay, and there are those that are new to the twentieth century, starting with Bakelite, which was developed in 1907. It is important to respect the properties of each.

If you love flowers in the home you will want to collect inspirational containers. Craft shops and design studios offer a wonderful range, and the occasional exciting buy can still be made at car-boot sales, jumble sales, bric-à-brac stalls and antique markets, where a chip on the rim or a faded pattern will affect the price, to the flower arranger's benefit. Indeed, the warmth of age can mellow the container's texture and colour to great advantage.

GENERAL GUIDELINES FOR CHOOSING A CONTAINER

- Containers with a wide mouth relative to their base need a generous amount of plant material. Care needs to be taken to ensure good balance.
- Rectangular openings also need a copious amount of plant material, as the stems always seem to fall to one side or into the four corners!
- Shaped vases with a narrow opening need flowing plant material, otherwise the flowers can look stiff and uncomfortable.
- Low dishes should be deep enough to take a pinholder and a covering of water.
- Symmetrically balanced containers (for example, a conventional vase) are generally easier to fill than an asymmetrically balanced container, such as a teapot.
- If ever in doubt, mass one flower, perhaps in different tints and tones, with *Eucalyptus*, fern, or simply on its own.

SCULPTURAL CONTAINERS

Sculptural containers are those with a clean, strong, bold form, usually contemporary in style, which on their own or with the addition of flowers create a dramatic look – non-fussy, direct, dynamic and exciting.

The containers themselves can be outstanding pieces of sculpture in their own right, and the flowers must be carefully chosen to complement their texture, form and colour. It is quite possible for the flowers to be subservient to the container and for the container to dominate the design.

Sculptural containers often lend themselves to exotic plant material, such as *Heliconia*, *Anthurium* and *Strelitzia*. When these are difficult to find, a mass of tulips, roses, carnations or gerberas, or bold leaves such as those of the *Aspidistra* or *Codiaeum* – perhaps twisted or looped – can produce an equally strong effect.

When creating a traditional arrangement in a traditional container, plant material is generally artfully positioned to fall over the rim, but with many sculptural designs the rim can be an integral part of the container and needs to be left exposed. Plant material can be allowed to soar upwards to complement the line and form of the container and to create rhythm, through extension of the upward movement.

The texture of the container is often of great interest, as you can see from the examples on the opposite page. Pitted, woven, embossed, rough, smooth, grainy: the whole gamut of textural variations would appear to be here. Colour is subdued or dramatic, and form can have untold variations. What all have in common is a clear defined form, often angular, never boring. Some of these containers are inexpensive, others are works of art and priced accordingly.

When you are familiar with your container it will be extremely easy to display your flowers quickly and effectively. The boldness of sculptural containers requires flowers of a similar nature, and strong masses of a single flower will always look effective.

An exciting selection of sculptural containers. Some of them are inexpensive and easy-to-find. Others are works of art and priced accordingly.

△ 1950s Wedgwood vase of clean line and bold form.
The texture, form and colour of the vase are repeated in
the waxy cream tulips, which are balanced by a mass of
blue anemones. Dracaena leaves have been manipulated
to create interesting new forms.

◁ Five blue plastic tulips simply placed in a sculptured
blue vase. The tulips complement the container by
repeating its colour and texture without distracting
from its beauty.

⊕ For examples of how other vases are used, see
asymmetrical balance on page 50, rhythm on page 56
and the vertical arrangement on page 123.

◁ *The hint of rusty orange in the surface of this textured vase is repeated in the colour of* Leucospermum cordifolium *and red kangaroo paw (*Anigozanthos rufus)*. The shorter stems of the heavier* Leucospermum *are balanced by the longer stems of the kangaroo paw.*

Clear, opaque, patterned and plain – here just a few from a large range of glass containers.

GLASS CONTAINERS

G~LASS CONTAINERS~ can be found in a vast variety of shapes and sizes, cut and colour. If the glass is clear, rather than opaque or translucent, it is important that the water should always be crystal-clear. When arranging flowers in transparent glass floral foam, chicken wire or pinholders should be avoided, as a means of holding the stems in place, unless they are disguised. This can easily be done by placing an inner container in the centre of the glass container, ideally one that repeats the form of the outer container. The gap between the two containers can then be filled with pot pourri, cinnamon sticks, moss, shells or fir cones.

There are numerous other ways of supporting your flowers in containers. Try twisting tough, long-lasting bear grass (*Xerophyllum*) into rings and then allow these to support your stems. Use pebbles or glass marbles to give extra interest to your vase, but take note – it can be difficult to add your stems if you have too many stones or glass nuggets in your vase. There are also special granules available (one of the trade names being Crystal Earth) which form a translucent gel when water is added. Alternatively, the container can be filled with Seramis ceramic chips – see the pot-et-fleur arrangement on page 146.

Ensure your container is sparkling and clean before you add water. Most water marks can be removed by soaking the containers overnight in warm water and biological detergent.

grid of adhesive tape

◁ △ *The tall spikes of sword lilies (Gladiolus) can look uncomfortable, if made to conform in traditional arrangements. Mass them in a vase of suitable proportion for their majestic height. You can help them to stand happily by creating a grid of adhesive tape across the opening, which can later be disguised with bun moss, if desired.*

▷ *Rectangular containers take a lot of plant material. If you have insufficient stems you will find that they fall into the four corners, leaving the centre bare. If you have insufficient flowers, use plenty of foliage. Ivy (Hedera), gum (Eucalyptus), privet (Ligustrum), myrtle (Myrtus) or Skimmia are all good examples. Place this in position first and then insert the flower stems through the network of foliage stems.*

◁ △ *A quick and easy table centrepiece with a difference, using only one flower. Fix a small pinholder on a plate or dish with florist's fix, then impale one full flower, such as a rose (Rosa cv.) or peony (Paeonia), with a very short stem. It should be smaller than the opening of the goldfish bowl. Add a leaf if necessary to cover the pinholder. Fill the goldfish bowl inside a full basin of water. Lower the flower, upside-down, into the bowl and then invert both plate and bowl. Water pressure will keep the water from leaking from the bowl.*

BASKETS

Bₐₛₖₑₜₛ ʜₐᵥₑ ʙₑₑₙ ₐₛₛₒᶜᵢₐₜₑD with flowers from the earliest times. A Roman mosaic has been discovered that shows a multitude of flowers in a basket. Throughout history the rustic simplicity of baskets as containers has been appreciated,

not only by those wanting an inexpensive and readily available container, but also by the flamboyant court of Louis XVI and by the orderly Flemish burghers of the seventeenth century.

Today the variety of basketware seems limitless. Dried flowers have a natural affinity with baskets. Those below are some of the vast range that is commonly on offer in shops and markets today.

◁ *The short heads of garden roses are massed in a rustic basket with a low handle. So many flowers will need a large amount of water, so ensure that your inner container is able to hold a reservoir. For this fragrant arrangement teeming with colour, take care if you wish to add white blooms, as these will tend to separate out from the other flowers in the arrangement.*

◁ *Reminiscent of the French mille-fleurs tapestries of the early sixteenth century, these delicate flowers rise high in a parallel movement to counterbalance the weight of the basket. Most of the interior of the basket is filled with foam, allowing only sufficient room for water to be added. The foam will stop short of the rim of the basket. Cover the foam with gravel, moss or pebbles.*
ARRANGER:
NORIKO WAKAUMI

even lengths of
stem protruding,
independent of
flowers

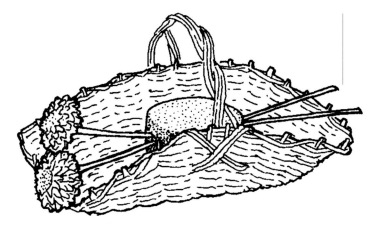

▽ *A basket full of flowers straight from the garden, but not quite! A piece of foam in a dish, placed off-centre in the basket, supports and supplies water to the flower heads. The stems are added separately to balance the plant material and to appear to be a continuation of the flowering stems. 'Love-lies-bleeding' (Amaranthus caudatus) has been laid over the foam to hide the join.*

TRADITIONAL
CONTAINERS

Traditional containers or vases are those that have stood the passage of time. Although they may be of contemporary origin, their style and feel are conventionally old-world – what most people associate with the typically British style of flower arranging. Jugs, bowls, Constance Spry vases, Victorian washbasins, prettily patterned biscuit jars, blue and white ware – all these lend themselves to a profusion of blooms and foliage.

Traditional containers look lovely filled with a mass of flowing blooms, of twigs and berries, of foliage and flowers – perhaps a random selection from the garden, with the addition of a few flowers from the florist.

△ *A profusion of double cream tulips*
complementing the form and texture of a
simple earthenware jug.

◁ *A traditional*
symmetrical
arrangement of late
summer flowers and
foliage. Berries
*(*Atriplex, Hypericum
and Viburnum*),*
*flowers (*Phytostegia,
Phlox, Sedum,
hydrangeas and
chocolate cosmea),
Bergenia *leaves and*
mixed foliage. A base
under the design
would give better
visual balance.

▽ Viburnum opulus 'Roseum', *apple (*Malus sylvestris*), cider gum (*Eucalyptus gunnii*), peonies and 'Queen Anne's lace' (*Ammi majus*), *arranged in chicken wire and lots of deep water.*

METAL
CONTAINERS

Sɪʟᴠᴇʀ, ᴘᴇᴡᴛᴇʀ, ɢᴏʟᴅ, ᴄᴏᴘᴘᴇʀ ᴀɴᴅ ʙʀᴀss are all metals, but their different compositions mean that they enhance different flowers and colours. Mild steel has become very fashionable and is being used to produce a wide variety of containers. As with silver, lead, tin and pewter, its silvery-grey colouring is superb with grey-green or blue-grey foliage and

pink, blue and white flowers. Copper, on the other hand, with its warm pink-orange undertones complements pink, terracotta, peach and burnt orange. Brass lends itself to yellows, golds and browns. Wrought-iron stands can be purchased, which hold glass or terracotta, and the combination is extremely effective.

It is said that metals and alloys are ideal as containers, provided of course they are waterproof, because the metals in some way reduce the build-up of bacteria. This is the reasoning behind the old wives' tale that a penny in the water prolongs the life of plant material.

▷ *Broom and tulips
– two contrasting
masses of differing
forms. The densely
flowering sprays of
broom complement
the firm, waxy
structure of the
tulips, the two
varieties being unified
by their strong yellow
colouring.*

◁*Rhythm and harmony between
plant material and container are
achieved by using the straight stems to
continue the upward movement. The
grey of the pussy willow* (Salix caprea)
*repeats the grey of the metal,
complemented by the pink of the*
Prunus triloba *blossom and the
creamy green of the snowball tree*
(Viburnum opulus 'Roseum').

▷ *The strength of the copper is reflected in the
colour and form of the plant material. Burnt-
orange dahlias, tulips* (Tulipa), *Oriental
bittersweet* (Celastrus orbiculatus), *fruits and sea
holly* (Eryngium) *is combined with foliage from
the strawberry tree* (Arbutus unedo), Photinia
fraseri *'Red Robin' foliage and the three-lobed
Boston ivy* (Parthenocissus tricuspidata) *leaves.*

TERRACOTTA CONTAINERS

TERRRACOTTA today comes in the most amazing range of shapes, sizes and colours, although the colour with which it is naturally associated is a reddish brown. It is particularly lovely with yellows, apricots, peaches and oranges – the warm colours of the spectrum. Terracotta is a porous material and needs to be lined, especially if there is a drainage hole at the bottom; but some terracotta containers have been varnished and there is then no need for a lining.

◁ *A wide variety of terracotta containers are available for flower arranging.*

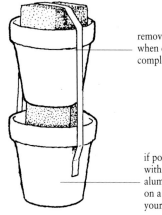

remove florist's fix
when design is
complete

if porous, line pots
with polythene or
aluminium foil. Place
on a base to protect
your surface

▷ *Two terracotta pots, of the same size and form,
filled with foam to rise above the rim of the
container are placed one on top of the other and
filled with gleanings from an autumnal garden.*

△ *A large terracotta planter has beened lined
and given 3 cm (1¼ in) of drainage material in the
form of broken polystyrene chips. This has been
covered with a layer of John Innes no 2. Narcissus
'Tête-à-tête', primroses (Primula acaulis), Ivy
(Hedera), mind your own business/baby's tears
(Soleirolia) and old pots fill the planter. A piece
of wood and some dried mushrooms have been
added for extra textural interest. The method is
the same as for the pot-et-fleur on page 146.*

▷ *A mass of glorious yellow, peach, orange and light
brown turban-flowers (Ranunculus asiaticus) massed in a
terracotta vase. By placing a scaled-down version of the
same vase in front, the proportion of flowers to container
is improved and visual depth added.*

VEGETATIVE CONTAINERS

Vegetative containers can be simple and inexpensive to make and look very effective. They extend the naturalness of the design by taking vegetative material right down to the base. Dried material obviously has lasting powers, but for a special occasion in high summer it is great fun to have your own fresh asparagus container holding your flowers, as you nibble the asparagus from your plate. Think of a tropical party with the flowers spilling out of empty coconut shells. Exciting original containers can easily be created, with a little bit of imagination. Look at the bark container used with amaryllis (*Hippeastrum*) for Christmas, the small tin bound with string on page 53 and the 'container' that Judith Butterworth has created in her arrangement on page 139.

An easy way to cover a straight-sided plastic container is to spray it with spray glue (available from art and craft shops). Next, overlap longlasting, mature leaves, such as *Magnolia grandiflorum*, laurel or ivy around the container and secure with raffia, twine or ribbon.

An array of containers created from such diverse materials as fruit, vegetables, bark and leaves.

◁ Woven plaits of fresh sea grass, purchased
ready-plaited, are wrapped and glued round an
empty tin. Irises cut to different lengths are then
simply placed in the container with some
artificial bulrushes.

▷ Magnolia grandiflora leaves have been glued
onto a plastic bucket. A round baking tin has been
wedged inside the container and filled with 'mind
your own business'/'baby's tears' (Soleirolia syn.
Helxine soleirolii). Salix gracilistyla 'Melanostachys',
Magnolia and the single stem of a Cymbidium
orchid spill out from the centre.

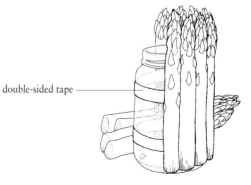

△ ▷ *Double-sided tape has been fixed to the sides of a straight plastic pot or jam jar. Asparagus stems have then been stuck onto the tape and the container filled with nasturtiums (*Tropaeolum*).*

double-sided tape

Knowing the techniques and equipment that make life easier will also make your designs look more effective.

The equipment mentioned here can be found at garden centres, by mail order or from specialist shops. Florist-sundries wholesalers will sometimes sell to flower arrangers, if they purchase sufficiently large quantities.

BEGINNER'S EQUIPMENT

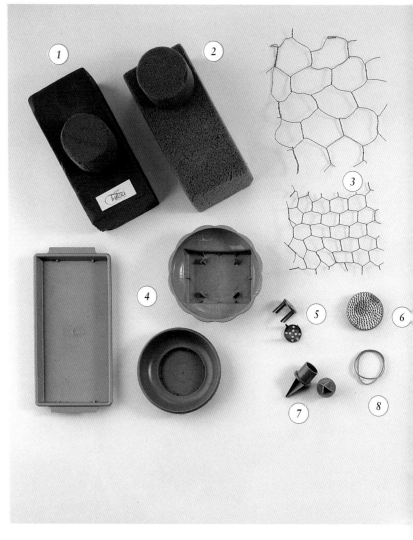

For your entrée into fresh flower arranging you will need only items 1, 4 and 11.

1 Block and cylinder of wet floral foam

Foam that is intended for fresh flowers should be placed in deep water and will slowly sink as it absorbs moisture. Place the foam in the water with the name of the product uppermost so that it retains water most efficiently. A cylinder and a section of a block will take about 60 seconds to sink, an entire block a little longer. If possible, always have a reservoir of water in the dish. Always, add water daily. This foam contains an anti-bacterial substance to prevent a build-up of bacteria. Blocks are now available in a variety of sizes.

2 Block and cylinder of dry floral foam

Dry foam has a harder, firmer consistency than wet foam. It will not retain water, however long it is immersed in water. It is intended for preserved and silk flowers. Avoid rubbing the eyes after hand contact with the dry foam, as it is immensely painful!

3 Chicken wire

Chicken wire, or wire netting as it is sometimes known, can be used:
• As a cap over foam, thus giving extra support, for which a 2.5 cm (1 in) mesh is ideal. A larger mesh can cut into the foam too easily.

• Crumpled into several thicknesses and used on its own as a support, or in conjunction with a pinholder, for which 5 cm (2 in) mesh is ideal. A small mesh when crumpled gives holes too small for easy insertion of the stems.
• As a base for floral rings, topiary rings, swags and garlands, used in conjunction with damp moss or foam – 5 cm (2 in) mesh is the easiest to disguise.

Galvanized chicken wire is inexpensive and is easily hidden when used in conjunction with moss. The green plastic-coated chicken wire is easier on the hands but is usually more expensive, and it can be harder to disguise as the green plastic coating makes it thicker.

4 Plastic dishes

There are three inexpensive plastic dishes widely available, in black, green and white. Green is the best choice, as it is the easiest to disguise. White dishes can be sprayed a less obtrusive colour.
a) A small round dish designed to take a round cylinder of floral foam. Ideal for round table designs.
b) A larger round dish with the inner area moulded to take one-third of a block of floral foam or a mini-brick. Ideal for oval arrangements.
c) A rectangular trough designed to take a complete block of foam, useful for long table centrepieces, to decorate a top table or for a trough design in the parallel style.

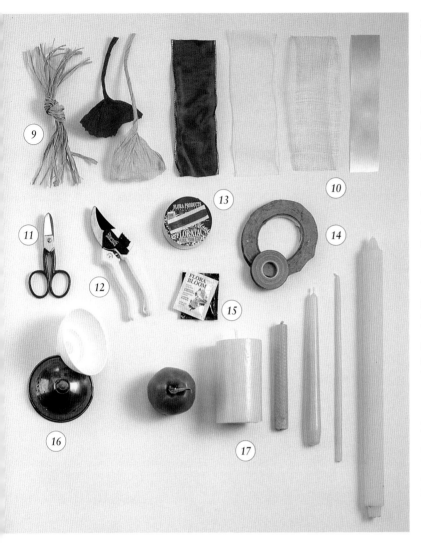

following types of ribbon are commonly available: polypropylene, wired ribbon and paper ribbon.

11 Florist's scissors
Sharp, short-bladed scissors with a serrated cutting edge, which will grip the stems, are ideal. Loop a colourful distinctive tag around the handle, as scissors are so easy to misplace.

12 Secateurs
These are invaluable for cutting thick woody stems. Good-quality secateurs will last you many years. They need to be of a size that fits the hand comfortably.

13 Florist's fix
This is rather like Blu-Tack or chewing gum and is excellent for fixing two dry, clean surfaces together - for example, the bottom of a frog to a container. The fix should be kneaded in the hands, and then a coil or several knobs are fixed to the underside of the frog or pinholder.

14 Florist's tape
A strong tape that can be purchased in varying thicknesses. Unlike Sellotape or Scotch tape, it adheres to wet foam. It is used principally to keep foam securely attached to the container. It is also ideal for many household jobs!

15 Cut flower food
Cut flower food allows the flower to develop fully and last longer. Add it to the water according to the instructions on the packet.

16 Candle-cups
Round dishes with a protrusion from the base, designed for inserting into candle-sticks and bottles in order to create a raised arrangement. An alternative is to glue a cork to the bottom of a round plastic dish.

17 Candles
The range of candles is immense. If candles warp, put them in a bowl of hot water and then roll them. To impale candles on nails, place the end of the candle in a cup of hot water to soften. To make candles secure, see Technique 8 on page 97.

5 Foamholder or Frog
Small, light plastic discs with four prongs. They are ideal for keeping smaller pieces of foam in place, in conjunction with Blu-Tack or florist's fix.

6 Pinholders
Pinholders consist of numerous pins embedded in a lead base. These are ideal for use with hollow and woody stems and in arrangements where the form depends on the minimum use of plant material, such as an upward crescent arrangement (see page 119). Choose one that is heavy, with brass pins close together. For your first purchase select a medium-sized pinholder about 6.25 cm (2.5 in) in diameter.

7 Candle-holders
Specially designed plastic pieces designed to hold a standard candle securely and to create little damage to the foam.

8 Thick rubber bands
Ideal for keeping the foam firmly attached to its container.

9 Raffia
This may be purchased in a natural tone or in a wide range of dyed colours. Raffia can be looped, made into bows, incorporated into 'constructions' or tied round containers and bunches to give a natural look.

10 Ribbon
Like candles, the range is enormous. The

OTHER EQUIPMENT

1 Garland and wreath cages
These cages can be filled with dry or wet foam and linked together to create a wreath or garland. In order to hang these as a garland, ensure that the wire used to hang them is wrapped round the heavier plastic struts of the cage.

2 Stem-tape
This is used to disguise wires that have been added to extend or give support to the stems of fresh and artificial material. Stem-tape is useful when working with dried and silk flowers if the stems need to be lengthened with wire, which would be unsightly if not covered.

3 Bouquet holder (Bridie)
This is the easy way to create wedding bouquets. A fresh foam bridie should be soaked for a short time and the excess water shaken off before use.

4 Mini-decos
These are 5 cm (2 in) diameter half-spheres of wet or dry foam in white plastic trays with self-adhesive pads on the bottom. Dip the wet foam in water, then remove the tape backing to reveal the adhesive. They can be adhered to mirrors, bottles, presents, tables and so on, and can easily be decorated with a few flowers and leaves to great effect.

5 Stem supports
Seramis clay granules and glass nuggets may be used in glass containers to support stems, while also being decorative.

Dry crystals such as Crystal Earth turn to a viscous jelly after water is added. This will support the stems. Food colourant may be added to the water.

6 Glue
For pressed flower work you will need a water-based glue such as UHU or Copydex. When you require a stronger glue, use a special formula glue for flower work, which comes with its own integral brush, or use a glue gun.

7 Glue gun
There are hot glue guns, which heat sticks of glue to a high temperature. These have a strong adhesive quality. Beware of getting glue on the skin, as it does burn. There are also cold glue guns, which heat the glue to a lower temperature. The adhesive quality is not as great, but it does not burn to the same extent. Be sure to buy glue sticks that fit your gun.

8 Spheres of dry and wet foam
These are available in a vast range of sizes. The larger dry-foam balls can be coated with a tough outer crust to make them more resilient. Wet-foam spheres are sometimes made from a stronger, less porous foam, again to make them more resilient. Spheres are ideal for topiary trees (see Technique 12 on page 99) or for hanging arrangements, such as a bridesmaid's hanging floral ball.

9 Bases
A base under an arrangement protects your surface from possible water damage. It can give stronger visual weight to the base of the design and therefore provide stability in a top-heavy arrangement. It can also add colour and textural interest and give added height. A base may be any shape, material, size or colour, but it should always be in keeping with the arrangement – a velvet base, for instance, would be suitable for an

elegant design for a formal dinner, and a wood-cut slice would be appropriate for a naturalistic design. When starting out, cover a 22 cm (8½ in) round cake board with an elasticized mop cap in a neutral, soft green fabric.

10 Picks

These are used to support plant material and fruit. You could use cocktail or kebab sticks, plastic sticks or Cowee picks. The latter are wooden picks, with or without wire attached, which are used to give stability to ribbon loops and soft-stemmed fresh and brittle dried plant material. They can also be used to lengthen short stems or give support to candles.

11 Plastic pan and cages with handle

These plastic dishes are ideal for hanging on a wall or pew-end. Also shown is a more elaborate version with its own cage. If using the former for a fresh flower arrangement, wrap a well-soaked piece of foam in clingfilm and strap it in securely to hold in the moisture. The handle can easily be covered but still used for carrying.

12 Petal Fresh, spray paints and surface sealant

Petal Fresh miraculously lifts the dust from dried and silk plant material.

Spray paints can be used not only to give brightness and glitter at Christmas but to add depth or a change of colour all year round. Sealants are protective sprays, which help prevent moisture re-absorption in dried plant material and enhance colours.

13 Foam pinholder

This is for keeping large pieces of foam in position, in conjunction with Blu-Tack or florist's fix.

14 Wires

Florist's wire is used to support, lengthen and reduce weight. Always use the lightest wire that will achieve your purpose. Florist's wire can be purchased in cut lengths or on a reel. The wires vary in thickness, and in the metric system the thicker the wire, the higher the number. For the flower arranger new to wiring, I would suggest that you acquire three thicknesses or gauges of cut wire, a heavy wire of 1.25 mm or 1.00 mm (18g or 19g) gauge, a medium wire of 0.90 mm or 0.71 mm (20g or 22g) gauge and a light wire of 0.56 mm or 0.46 mm (24g or 26g) gauge. Binding wire comes on a reel and is excellent for binding moss onto a frame. The 0.56 mm gauge is ideal for this purpose.

Reel-wire is available in copper, brass, metallic red, green and other colours. It is used to create decorative effects, particularly in modern work.

German pins, rather like open hairpins, are ideal for pinning moss to foam rings.

15 Dry-foam rings

These are suitable for dried and silk circular arrangements. They can be hung on the wall or placed in the centre of a table. The central ring has a reinforced crust to make it more robust than those produced by many other manufacturers.

16 Dry-foam cones

An easy way to create a cone of dried or silk flowers. Ideally, place the cone on a raised dish to show it off to advantage. As yet, cones are only available in the dry medium. To make a fresh cone, carve a cone from a suitably sized block of wet foam.

17 Wet-foam rings

These should be placed under water for a short time but not over-soaked. They are ideal for a circular arrangement of fresh flowers for the table, see page 192. They can also be hung on a door or wall, but take care that water does not drip and damage your furnishings.

NATURAL ACCESSORIES

1 Bracket fungi and golden mushrooms

Bracket fungi give a rough, lined texture on one side and a smooth texture on the other. They can easily be wired (see Technique 10 on page 98). They can be broken into smaller pieces and, whether large or small, used in wreaths, swags and garlands. Golden mushrooms give the polished texture of turned wood.

2 Cones

Pine (*Pinus*), cedar (*Cedrus*), larch (*Larix*), alder (*Alnus*) and beech (*Fagus*) nut cases give exciting form and texture.

3 Cinnamon sticks

Cinnamon sticks are inexpensive if bought loose from health food shops. They can be wired or tied together to give bundles for adding to wreaths, swags and garlands. Long sticks can be impaled in plaster of Paris to provide the 'trunk' for topiary trees. Their smooth texture is very appealing in dried flower work.

4 Shells and starfish

These are widely available commercially or common shells may be taken from your local beach. Shells and starfish can be easily wired or glued and may be incorporated into swags and wreaths.

5 Wood, bark and cork

Wood, bark and cork from the seashore, woodland or lakeside, is ideal for incorporating into modern and landscape designs. It can give interest, texture and height.

6 Stones and pebbles

These are ideal for covering pinholders in low dishes or for supporting stems in glass vases, giving smooth form and texture. Use in pot-et-fleurs and planted bowls.

7 Lotus seedheads

The dried seedheads from the short-lived lotus (*Nelumbo*) are easily wired and give an exciting addition to dried and fresh flower work.

8 Fresh fruits and gourds

These are easily mixed with flowers. Two wires can be pushed through the fruit at right-angles and then brought down together. This will give a strong, flexible support but will render the fruit inedible. Wooden or plastic sticks can also be inserted into the fruits. Dried gourds can also be wired but a little more effort is required as they will probably need to be drilled.

12 Carpet or flat moss

This is perfect for covering shaped areas of foam, such as spheres and cones, as it covers thinly and neatly. It can be purchased fresh or dried. The dried carpet moss is excellent for covering containers.

13 Terracotta Pots

These are widely available in a broad range of sizes. They give texture, form and interest.

14 Reindeer moss (Cladonia rangiferina)

A soft, spongy moss that has usually been treated with a softening agent such as glycerine and to which a dye is sometimes added. The natural and green colours are to be recommended. They are wonderful for incorporating into wreaths and swags, which they cover quickly and inexpensively, giving a soft texture.

15 Down or grass moss

Grass moss comes from the downs. It comes in layers and binds well, and is therefore the best moss to use for making wreaths, swags and garlands. It is useful for covering dry foam before you insert your dried plant material.

16 Bun moss (Leucobryum glaucum)

Soft mounds of bun moss can often be found growing in shady, damp places on roofs and paving. It can easily be removed with a sharp knife - take some of the soil backing, too. It can easily be dried or may be purchased ready-dried. The colour of the dried moss is more muted. It is ideal for using at the base of topiary trees and in designs where the rounded form will be appreciated.

9 Dried fruit

Cut the fruit or vegetables into thin slices, place on absorbent paper on a baking tray and bake slowly in the oven or micro-wave. Citrus fruits can be slit and baked whole. Pomegranates can be easily emptied of their seeds and dried.

10 Nuts

A wire or stick may be pushed through the soft base of a walnut. Most other nuts will have to be drilled.

11 Sphagnum moss

This comes from boggy areas and can absorb vast amounts of water. In inexperienced hands, binding wire can cut through it easily and it is therefore not entirely suitable for making wreaths, swags and garlands. It is, however, ideal for use in hanging baskets.

TECHNIQUES

Technique 1: Conditioning Plant Material

a) The ends of all stems that have been out of water, however briefly, seal up. In order to allow a supply of water to enter the stem it must be cut cleanly, at a sharp angle, with clean, sharp scissors, secateurs or a knife, ideally under water. Take off 2–5 cm (¾–2 in), according to the length of stem. Any foliage that would lie below the water-line or that might enter the foam should also be removed. The stems should be placed immediately in clean containers with fresh, tepid water.

b) Add plant food to the water, following the instructions on the sachet. Cut flower food allows the flowers to mature fully and last longer. Keep the vase or foam constantly topped up with water. Spraying also helps to keep the plant material fresh. Never hammer the stems, as this encourages rapid bacterial growth.

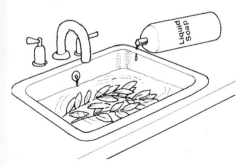

Mature foliage can be left under water for an hour or so. Immature and grey foliage quickly becomes waterlogged and should be treated as in (a). If the foliage is dirty, add a drop of liquid soap but rinse well.

c) Stems such as poppies (*Papaver*) and euphorbias (including poinsettia [*E. pulcherrima*]), which contain a milky sap, need to have the stem end charred. Hold the freshly cut stem end over a candle, gas or lighter flame until the sap bubbles. Place the stem in tepid water and repeat the process if you wish to shorten the stem.

d) Wide, hollow stems, such as amaryllis and delphiniums, can be filled with water with a long-spouted watering can and then plugged with cotton wool, to keep the water in the stem.

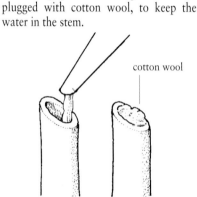

cotton wool

e) Daffodils (*Narcissus*) exude a toxic substance, which is severely detrimental to other flowers and in particular to tulips. Once the daffodils have been conditioned in their own containers or had special food added to the water, they may be used with other cut flowers.

f) The tulip stem will assume whatever shape it has when it absorbs water when conditioned. If you wish your tulips to curve, place them in a low container in relation to their length, with the flowers resting over the rim. To keep them upright, wrap the tulips tightly in news-paper and place in a tall vase or bucket of water

for several hours during the hardening process.

g) Fruit and vegetables emit ethylene gas, which shortens the life of flowers. At a greengrocer's avoid buying flowers that are positioned too close to the vegetables. As a general rule, keep the fruit bowl away from the flowers, unless fruit is being used as part of the design.

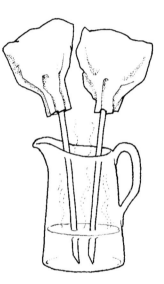

Technique 2: Reviving Wilted Plant Material

a) Blockages usually occur in the bottom 10 per cent of the stem. Remove this amount from the bottom of the stem, with a clean cut at a sharp angle, and then place in 5–10 cm (2–4 in) of very hot water, protecting the flowering head if the stem is short or the flower delicate. If the stem is soft, use water of a lower temperature.

b) Transfer to deep tepid water and leave in a cool place for 12 hours.

Technique 3: Preparing wet foam

a) Cut the piece of foam you require and let it sink under its own weight in deep water. Do not push the block down. This should take approximately 60–90 seconds, depending on the size.

b) When in position, chamfer the edges of the foam. This means removing the angles of the foam with a sharp knife to increase the surface area and soften the outline of the form.

c) Store unused foam that has been wetted in a tied plastic bag. In this way the foam will remain wet and keep for several years. If foam that has been wetted is left in the open air it will dry out and never again retain water with the same efficiency. You can try pouring boiling water, to which a little liquid soap has been added, over used dried foam. The soap reduces the surface tension and helps absorption.

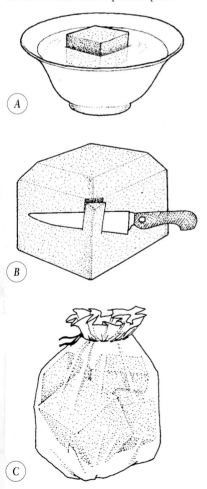

Technique 4: Using Foam

In a Specially Made Container

a) This readily available, inexpensive green plastic dish has been designed to take a cylinder of foam without any extra support.

b) This larger plastic dish takes one-third of a block of foam neatly and securely without any extra support. Ensure that you place the foam with the embossed name uppermost. This enables the capillaries in the foam to absorb the water more efficiently.

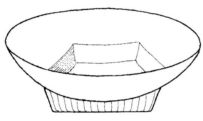

In a Shallow, Heavy Dish

a) For a dish that is not specifically designed to take foam, place fix on the base of a frog, first ensuring that both surfaces are dry and clean. Roll the fix into a longish length with warm, dry hands to make it malleable and to release its adhesive qualities. Place this in a ring around the base of the frog or use four pea-sized blobs. Place the frog firmly in the centre of the dish. Impale your foam on the frog.

b) For larger designs you can use a heavier, lead foam-holder with a circle of widely spaced pins. This will give greater stability. For traditional and many other designs it is vital that the foam rises above the level of the dish, so that stems can be inserted at an angle when desired.

c) For additional support, bind florist's-tape around the foam and down the sides, or use a *thick* rubber band, which if too noticeable can be cut, once the arrangement is complete and in position.

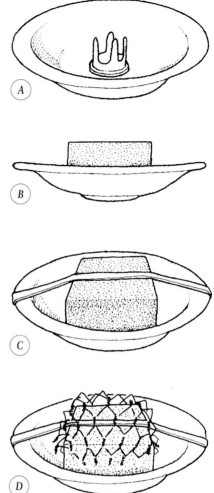

A thin rubber band would slice through the foam.

d) If you wish to give extra support for heavier or more numerous stems, create a cap of 2.5 cm (1 in) chicken wire to fit over the foam. Use a rubber band over the netting to keep it in place, or take a length of tape from one side of the netting under or round the container and attach it to the other side of the netting.

In a Vase

a) Place an exact-fitting plastic plant pot, plant-pot holder or small dish in the opening of the vase. Place a little fix or Blu-Tack round the rim of the vase to secure the container. Place foam inside the inner container.

b) Place a tall piece of foam on top of one you have first inserted horizontally. As a very rough rule of thumb, the foam should rise approximately one-fifth to a quarter of the

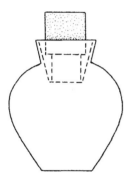

plant pot

height of the vase above the rim. Secure a wire netting cap over the foam for extra support if desired, as shown in the technique for a shallow, heavy dish.

Preparing a Pedestal Arrangement
a) Use a bowl that will fit into the pedestal bowl or that will rest securely on a pedestal top. For an average-sized bowl use one block of wetted foam upright, on a frog, at the back and two-thirds of a second block horizontally at the front. Avoid filling the bowl so full that there is no gap for watering. Fill the bowl with a reservoir of water, as adding water will be more difficult once the flowers and foliage are in place.
b) Use florist's tape to secure the foam. Avoid using too much tape, as this will cover too much of the foam. Use a cap of 2.5 cm (1 in) chicken wire with tape or wire, over the foam, to give added support for heavy stems. Before you attach the bowl to the pedestal too firmly, consider whether the arrangement without the pedestal may need to be moved.
(c) If you need added height, use specially

manufactured cones, which will raise the height of the plant material. If your cone does not have an integral pick, attach a length of garden stick to the cone with florist's tape. If you pack the cone with wetted foam it will also support short, heavy, multi-flowered stems, such as those of Casablanca lily (*Lilium* 'Casa Blanca').

Technique 5: Using a Pinholder

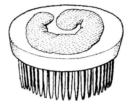

a) Place a coil of fix or four pea-sized blobs on the base of the pinholder and position it firmly in the dish. Alternatively, cut a piece of rubber, or the packing that is placed under packaged meats from the supermarket, to fit under the pinholder.

b) Cut stems at a sharp angle. For woody stems make one short slit up from the base. The angled cut of the stem should face away from the direction in which the branch is to lean. Tie thin-stemmed material, such as freesias, together with wool before placing on the pins.

Technique 6: Other Mechanics

a) Use pebbles, stones, Seramis or glass nuggets in a clear vase. Insert only a few before placing your stems. Add the others later, as it is difficult to position the stems once the stones are in place.
b) Put a jar inside your glass container and

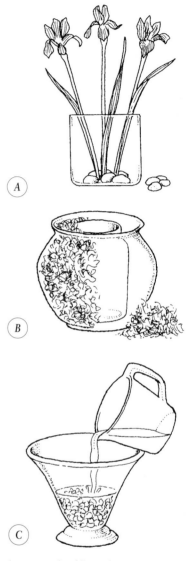

disguise it by filling the gap between the two with moss, shells, fruit or pot pourri. Place your plant material in the inner container.
c) Take specially formulated granules, such as Crystal Earth, which expand to a jelly-like substance when water is added – rather like frogspawn. Allow the solution to stand until full expansion of the granules has taken place. Colour dyes may be added to the solution if desired.
d) Create a grid of adhesive tape across the opening of a vase. This works particularly well if you have only a few stems of plant material and do not wish them to fall into the corners of a rectangular or square container.

Technique 7: Using a Candle-Cup

a) Choose a candle-cup that matches your candlestick or bottle, or spray one to match. Wrap a coil of fix or Blu-Tack around the protrusion and insert into the opening. Not all bottles have an opening large enough.

b) A do-it-yourself candle-cup can be made by gluing a cork to the bottom of a small plastic dish.

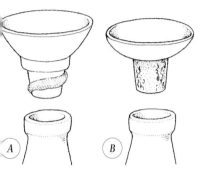

c) If your container is metallic, silver or brass, for example, it could be marked by the fix. To prevent this, place a ring of plastic tape in the opening so that the fix will not mark the actual container.

d) Place a frog with fix on its base in the candle-cup and secure with florist's tape or a thick rubber band.

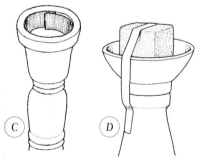

Technique 8: Securing Candles

a) Use a specially manufactured candle-holder, which is widely available and suitable for standard table candles. If your candle is a little wide, shave off a small amount with a warm knife.

b) Secure your candle in the foam by placing three, four or five cocktail sticks or Cowee picks on a piece of florist's tape.

Wrap this tightly around and insert the ends of the sticks or picks in the foam. Slim taper candles can be inserted in the foam without further support.

c) If you wish to have candles at different heights, you can lower the height of an area of foam by cutting it out with a knife.

d) For thicker candles you can heat the ends of three heavy-gauge wires and then ease them into the base of the candle. The heat will soften the wax and allow easy insertion.

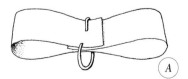

Technique 9: Making Bows

Figure-of-eight Wired Bow

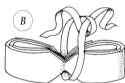

a) Take a length of wired ribbon. Find the central point and bring the ends over across the centre. Take a length of medium-gauge wire and wrap it around the

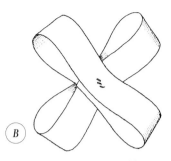

central area. Because the ribbon is wired and has volume, it can be manipulated so that the wire will not be seen.

b) Secondary loops can be added by sewing a length of ribbon into a circle, the same size as the two original loops, and incorporating them into the bow with wire.

Inexpensive Polyethylene Ribbon Bow

a) Take a long length of ribbon – about 1.5 m (5 ft). Make a coil of ribbon about 10 cm (4 in) long if extended. Take a second length about 30 cm (12 in) long. It needs to be only about 1 cm (⅓ in) wide, so tear a strip off and use the wider piece to create another bow.

b) Flatten the coil very slightly. Find the central point, make a slight indentation to mark the spot and cut an open V into each side.

c) Wrap the second length around the narrow part of the ribbon and tie.

d) Pull the loops out from the centre, one from each side, giving a half-twist as you do so.

Technique 10: Wiring

Wiring a Small Cone

a) Take a medium-gauge wire and thread the centre of the wire round the scales of the cone at the lowest possible point.

b) Bend the wire round, pulling it tight, then twist and take under to the central base of the cone.

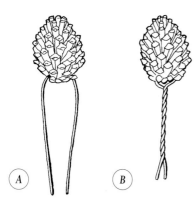

Wiring a Large Cone

a) Take two medium-gauge wires and thread each halfway round the circumference of the scales.

b) Twist the wires together at each side and bring them down under the base of the cone.

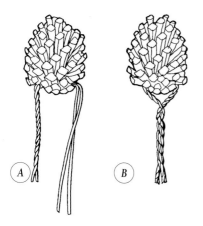

Wiring Lotus Seedheads

Push a wire through the underside of the lotus seedhead, so that it projects through one of the 'holes' in the head. Make a small hook and pull the wire back down into the 'hole' so that it cannot be seen. Alternatively, glue the wire to the side of the seedhead.

Wiring Walnuts

Walnuts have a soft spot in their base. Take a wire and simply push it through the soft spot into the centre of the nut. Add a drop of glue for extra security, if desired.

Wiring a Mini-terracotta Pot

a) Take a medium- or heavy-gauge wire (depending on the size of the pot) through the hole in the base, up over the rim, and then twist so that the wire ends protrude from the top or the bottom, depending on which end of the pot you wish to show.

b) Alternatively, use a glue gun to stick the wire to the side of the pot.

Wiring a Dried Mushroom

Take a piece of dried mushroom and decide if you wish the smooth or the ridged side to show. Place a dab of strong glue at the base of the side to be hidden. Place a wire on the glue and leave until it sets.

Drying and Wiring Fruit Slices

a) Choose fruits that have a firm flesh and only a few, or no, pips. Slice as thinly as possible. Place on kitchen towelling on a baking tray and cook in a slow oven – the bottom of an Aga or kitchen range is ideal – turning occasionally until the slices are firm. They can be varnished with a clear varnish, but this is not necessary if all the flesh is firm.

b) To wire single slices or bundles of slices, take a medium-gauge wire through the slice, as close to the pith as possible, bend over and twist as close to the fruit as you can. If desired, spray with gloss varnish.

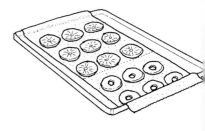

Wiring Fresh Fruits

a) Take a medium- or heavy-gauge wire through the fruit and out the far side, about one-third of the way up the fruit. Repeat with a second wire at right-angles to the first. Bring the wires down and twist together.

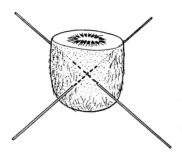

b) Alternatively, insert wooden or plastic sticks or Cowee picks into the fruit. The advantage of not using wires is that you can eat the fruit afterwards.

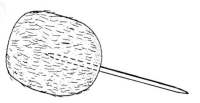

Extending a Stem with a Single-leg Mount

Take a medium-gauge wire and bend approximately one-fifth of the way along the wire. Place the bent wire against the stem you wish extended, so that the short leg extends to the end of the stem. Wrap the longer wire around the shorter wire and the stem, leaving one wire end free for inserting in your foam.

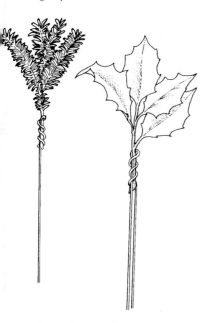

Extending a Stem with a Double-leg Mount

For heavier stems, use a medium- or heavy-gauge wire and bend it one-third of the way along. Place the wire so that both ends project well beyond the stem end. Wrap the longer wire around the shorter wire and the stem, so that both wires project the same length beyond the stem.

Technique 11: *Making a Buttonhole*

a) Take one carnation, one medium-gauge wire, three small sprays of asparagus fern, silver wire and stem-tape. Cut off most of the carnation stem and insert the medium-gauge wire up through the flower. Do not wire onto the natural stem. Make a small hook in one end and then pull down into the flower. Cover the protruding end with stem-tape.

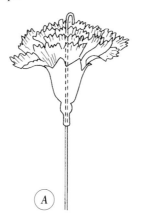

b) Using silver wire, give each spray of asparagus fern a single-leg mount. Cover with half-width stem-tape. Arrange the fern around the carnation and tape it. Add a pin and keep well sprayed.

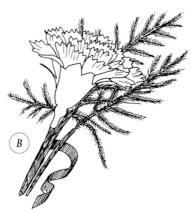

c) If using rose or ivy leaves, wire each leaf by threading fine wire through the main stem of the leaf, about one-third of the way from the top of the leaf. Hold your finger on the threaded wire, bend the wire down centrally and twist.

Technique 12: *Making a Topiary Tree*

a) You will need plaster of Paris, a plastic plant pot, a trunk of several branches, twigs or cinnamon sticks or a single thick branch, and a sphere or cylinder of foam.

b) Place some stones in the bottom of the pot to stop the plaster of Paris oozing out, to give stability and to save on the amount of plaster needed. Mix the plaster of Paris with water in a glass or disposable bowl, using a disposable stick. Fill the plastic pot about two-thirds full with the plaster of Paris mix.

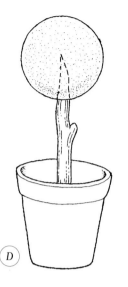

b) Tease out the moss, removing any stones or twigs. Fix the twine or reel-wire to the frame where its structure is strongest. Form a tight ball of moss, so that it is packed hard, and place on the ring, close to the tying point.

c) Wrap the string or wire tightly round

with a neat ring of cherry laurel (*Prunus laurocerasus*) leaves, or a strip of black bin-liner, kept in place with medium- or heavy-gauge wire bent into hairpins, or with German pins.

e) For Christmas, blue spruce (*Picea*

c) Impale the branch(es), twig(s) or cinnamon stick(s) into the centre of the plaster of Paris and hold until the plaster begins to set. This will take 2–5 minutes.

d) When completely set, place the ball of foam firmly on the free end of your stick(s) and decorate. If desired, place a blob of glue into the hole in the foam sphere and replace it on the trunk, for extra security.

Technique 13: Making a Wire and Moss Wreath

a) You will need a special wire frame or a coat-hanger bent into a circle, a bag of moss and a roll of reel-wire or garden twine. Sphagnum moss will do fine if you cannot acquire down moss (see page 93).

the moss at approximately 2 cm (¾ in) intervals. Push another tight ball of moss close up against the first ball and repeat. Continue until the ring is evenly covered.

d) If desired, cover the back of the ring

Pungens) or noble fir (*Abies procera*) is ideal for creating a luxuriant wreath. Take a spray and cut all the pieces off the main stem. Wire small, less attractive pieces to the inner and outer edges, keeping the best pieces to cover the more dominant central area. Add baubles, fruit and ribbon as desired.

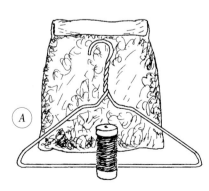

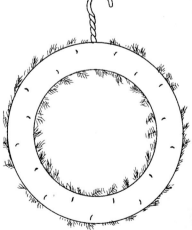

Technique 14: Making a Garland

Method A
You will need rectangles of foam, a length of thin plastic (such as that used by dry cleaners) and fine-gauge wire. Place the rectangles of foam on a long length of the plastic. Wrap the foam with as little double layering of plastic as possible, so that insertion of the stems will be easier, then pass a warm iron over to make a seal. Alternatively, sew the plastic. Tie between the foam with plastic ties or fine-gauge wire.

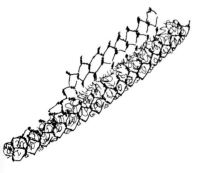

Method B
You will need a long length of 2.5 or 5 cm (1 or 2 in) gauge wire netting and a large amount of grass or down moss. Place tight, hard bundles of moss on the chicken wire to make a continuous length. Roll the chicken wire into a sausage over the moss and secure. The length of chicken wire will elongate as it becomes heavier when decorated.

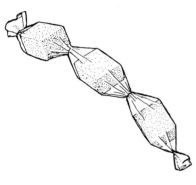

Method C
Use the 2.5 or 5 cm (1 or 2 in) gauge chicken wire and place rectangles of foam at intervals along it. Catch the two sides of the chicken wire together so that the foam is securely in position, twisting extra lengths of stub-wire through the chicken wire if necessary. Use lengths of stub- or reel-wire to divide the pieces of foam.

Method D
Use plastic cages called 'Simply Garlands'. Cut a block of foam into 12 rectangles and place a rectangle in each of the cages. Attach wire, for hanging, to the part of the cage that will bear the weight.

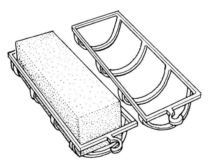

Method E
For a large garland, for which you have masses of long-lasting fresh foliage, take a long, thick rope (which can be purchased from a ship's chandler) and bind bundles of foliage onto the rope. Decorate with gourds, fruits, baubles or flowers.

All fresh garlands are heavy and you need to ensure that they are well supported before you start. Put the structure in place before you start decorating, as it turns if it is moved. Decorated garlands need a large amount of plant material, as you are using mainly

the heads of flowers rather than the stems, and there is generally little space within the design.

Technique 15: Making a Swag

Method A
Take a thin rectangle of pegboard of the desired size and glue narrow rectangles of foam onto the board. Create a hanging loop by passing wire through one of the central holes.

Method B
Take a length of carpet grip and firmly strap rectangles of foam onto the larger nails with florist's tape. Attach a hanging wire round one of the larger nails left exposed.

Method C
Place a rectangle of foam on 2.5 cm (1 in) gauge chicken wire. Cover lightly with grass or down moss and wrap the chicken wire firmly around it. Create a loop attached to the chicken wire for hanging. Cover the back of the swag with a piece of black bin-liner, using hairpins of wire or German pins to secure.

Technique 16: Preserving Plant Material by the Glycerine Method

a) Mix two parts boiling water with one part glycerine and combine well in a jam jar or other container warmed to prevent breakage. A plastic container is rather light and may fall over easily. If using anti-freeze, use equal parts anti-freeze and boiling water. If you wish to add dye, add this to the mixture according to the instructions on the bottle.

b) Trim your chosen stems to a good shape, removing any damaged leaves. Cut the stem ends on the slant to aid absorption of the glycerine mixture and place in water for several hours to become turgid.

c) Place your stems in the glycerine, ensuring that no leaves remain below the level of the mixture. You may wish to place your container in a larger outer container so that there is less likelihood of it toppling over. Place in a warm, dry place for quickest absorption. Mould may form if it is left in a damp location. Pass any remaining mixture through muslin or a sieve and re-use.

Technique 17: Preserving Plant Material by Desiccant

Desiccant
a) Cover the bottom of a cardboard or plastic container, which has an airtight lid, with a good layer of dry desiccant.

b) Cut short the stems of dry, unblemished flowers. If the stems are hollow, dry them separately. If you are not using a

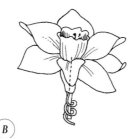

microwave you can wire the flowers for easier use after the drying process. Take the lightest wire that will support your flower and insert it up the remaining

length of stem so that it becomes firm. Coil the extruding wire so that it takes up less space. As the drying process proceeds, the stem shrinks and grips the wire.

c) Place the flowers upright in the desiccant, so that every space and every petal can be filled with desiccant but without the flowers touching.

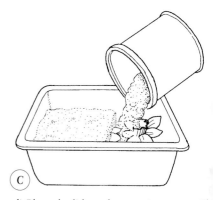

d) Place the lid on the container to avoid absorption of moisture from the atmosphere. Position in a warm, dry place. Many items take only five to ten days to be preserved. If they are ready they will feel dry and light to the touch.

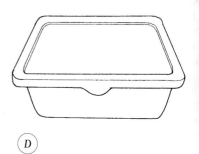

e) Empty the box through a sieve so that the desiccant falls into another container.

f) Use a paintbrush to remove any residual desiccant from the petals. Follow the instructions on the box as to how to re-dry your desiccant before re-use.

Warning: do not use where food is prepared.

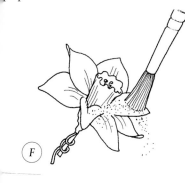

Desiccant and Microwave

a) If using a microwave, do not wire the plant material. Space the flowers widely in the desiccant. Cover with desiccant and a lid. Aim to reach a temperature of 60–70°C/140-60°F. This usually means one and a half to two minutes on full power for 500 g (1.1 lb) of desiccant, but this will vary according to the microwave. Keep checking the temperature with a thermometer.
b) Allow the desiccant to cool before removing. Seal all desiccated material with artist's spray fixative, Floraseal, nail varnish or hair spray. For double-petalled flowers with thick stems try melting white candles and dipping the flowers in the wax for a magical effect. Shake off any residue.

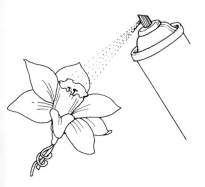

Technique 18: Preserving Plant Material by Pressing

a) Take an old telephone directory, as these have absorbent pages. Starting at the back, place one variety of flower or foliage (for a uniform thickness) on each page, avoiding the margins.

b) Turn a few pages and repeat. Label with variety and date.
c) Store in a warm, dry place, with weights on the directory, for at least one week under optimum conditions; otherwise for several weeks. Placing the directories on night-storage heaters speeds up the process for more robust specimens.

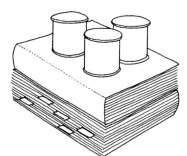

Technique 19: Preserving Plant Material by Hang-drying

a) Take small bunches of material to be dried and remove any heavy foliage. The plant material should be dry and at the peak of perfection – perhaps just short but never over, as the petals will eventually drop.

b) Place elastic bands round the bunches or use strips of nylon tights or stockings. Delphiniums should be attached singly or in pairs, lavender perhaps in bunches of 30–50 stems. Attach directly to your support. If using elastic bands, attach to butcher's hooks or lengths of strong wire, bending each free end into a hook.
c) Hang in a warm, dry location. The warmer and drier the location, with good air circulation, the quicker the drying process will be, and the brighter the colour. A boiler room is ideal, or an attic. A basement may well be too damp. An unheated garage will certainly be too damp.

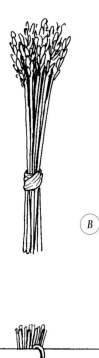

TRADITIONAL DESIGN CLASSICS

T<small>HE STYLE THAT TYPIFIES</small> the traditional design classic is one of "ordered and stylized loveliness" (Iris Webb, 1979). Traditional designs have changed little since their creation in the 1950s and are still happily in tune with the interiors of many homes today.
Traditional 'stylized' arrangements have been criticized by some in recent years for conforming to the criteria of a conventional form. But to be a style *per se* requires conformity to certain criteria.

Such traditional design classics are known in Europe as *Le style Anglais* and are seen as being quintessentially English. I, along with many others, believe that there will always be an appreciation of these delightful classics, which make the most of the great diversity of plant material available in the garden.

I have listed overleaf the points that all traditional classics have in common. This will enable you to recognize them and help you to re-create them in your own home. Remember, there are no rules in flower arranging, only guidelines to get you going.

In this glorious pedestal of summer flowers, foxgloves (Digitalis), delphiniums and peonies (Paeonia) are complemented by the bold blue-green plantain lily (Hosta sieboldiana) leaves. All the elements in the design are in scale.
A<small>RRANGER:</small> F<small>RANÇOISE</small> V<small>ANDERHAEGHEN</small>.

CHARACTERISTICS

- The different designs are all loosely based on a geometric form or shape.
- Each design incorporates line, concealing, focal and spray plant material.
- In each design every stem, without exception, radiates or appears to radiate from a central point. This is most important if you wish to create a successful traditional design.
- There are no strong surprises or contrasts. Variation is soft and gradual.
- The designs are often dependent on garden plant material, using buds, half-open and full-blown flowers, with curving branches of foliage.
- There is a more dominant area at the base of the tallest stem, approximately two-thirds of the way down the design. This can be achieved with larger forms, stronger colour or the use of a different texture.
- There is a certain amount of space between each element of plant material to show each to advantage. Avoid the temptation to overfill the arrangement in an attempt to hide every minute bit of foam. Space and rhythmic movement are more important in this style of design.
- The plant material is usually woven through the design. Rhythm is created by making flowing lines, through the judicious use of colour and the repetition or graduation of form. Sometimes the plant material is grouped, as in the symmetrical triangle on page 46.
- Some of the plant material should be gently recessed (that is, placed on shorter stems) to build up depth and heighten interest.
- Visual and actual balance is achieved by the following:

a) the use of containers that are as dark as the flowers or leaves.

b) keeping dark colours relatively low in the arrangement.

c) making the two sides equally heavy, by symmetry, placement or the use of an accessory.

d) using smaller forms for the outer edges of the arrangement.

e) correcting a top-heavy arrangement by placing a base beneath the container.

f) keeping the centre of interest low and around the vertical axis.

g) angling some plant material to hide part of the container rim, and to allow the plant material and container to belong to each other and appear stable.

Important

Do not think in terms of specific plant material. Think in terms of the four different forms you will need – line, concealing, floral and spray plant material – for all traditional design classics of fresh flowers and foliage. You can then take any basic design and develop your own personality around it, according to your garden, your purse and seasonal availability. These forms are described in depth on pages 36 and 37 but to emphasize the point, refer to the line drawing below.

Some of the photographs show variations on these traditional design classics, conforming to the form but not always to the criteria described later.

Canterbury bells (Campanula), turban flowers (Ranunculus asiaticus),
rape (Brassica napus), lisianthus/prairie gentian (Eustoma),
lady's mantle (Alchemilla mollis), cornflower (Centaurea cyanus),
throatwart (Trachelium caeruleum) and mixed foliage arranged
in an antique soup tureen on a slate base.

ROUND ARRANGEMENTS

Low, Round Table Arrangement

This is a highly popular style of arrangement, perhaps because it can be adapted to purse and occasion. An all-round arrangement is easy to create and looks charming, whatever the shape or size of the table, although a round table is ideal. Do remember that a larger table will need a larger design and the plant material should be correspondingly in scale.

For more experienced arrangers size has no limits. Exactly the same method is followed and the scale of plant material and container can be increased to correspond to the overall size of the arrangement.

A traditional, colourful all-round table arrangement placed on a slatted wooden table.

*Ivy (*Hedera*), amaryllis (*Hippeastrum*) and dragon's claw willow (*Salix babylonica var. pekinensis*) arranged in a round basket.*

GUIDELINES

1. Use a small plastic dish and cylinder of foam (see page 95). The key to a successful design is to cut all your line material to the same length. Keep it quite short, for your first attempts. Create a regular framework by seemingly radiating all the stems from the central area of the foam. Angle the stems in the lower part of the foam over the rim of the container. The number you need will depend on the size of the leaves. Use sufficient in the lower part so that the leaves closest to the foam touch, or nearly touch.

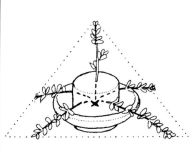

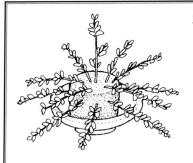

2. Place your concealing leaves throughout the design. Avoid creating a frill by using stems of different lengths and placing them at different angles. Keep within the framework created in (1).

3. Take line flowers out to the outer framework of the design. Add focal flowers – you may wish to recess some of these to give added interest.

4. Fill in with spray flowers and additional foliage if necessary, until you have an arrangement that pleases. Avoid a compulsion to hide every last bit of foam. You may forgo space, which is an important element in traditional design.

A variation on the round classic arrangement, a round pottery bowl filled with moss balls and pomanders is placed in a larger, low glass bowl. Michaelmas daisies (Aster novi-belgii), golden rod (Solidago) and poppy-flowered anemones (Anemone coronaria) splay out, repeating the rhythm of the container.

ROUND ARRANGEMENT
IN A TALL CONTAINER

THIS IS A LOVELY FREE-FLOWING design. It follows the same principles as those for the low, round arrangement. Hotels often have a large-scale version of this design in their foyers. For the appropriate impact it is essential to have a strong framework of foliage and open, focal flowers such as gerberas (*Gerbera* hybrids), lilies (*Lilium*), chrysanthemums (*Dendranthema*) or dahlias (*Dahlia*). There is less recession than in other traditional designs.

*A copper container holds gerberas, lilies (*Lilium), golden rod (Solidago), roses (Rosa cv.), purple pansies (Viola)*
*petunias (*petunia x. hybrida) and Bergenia leaves*

GUIDELINES

1. Strap a small dish and foam to the vase opening with florist's tape. For a larger arrangement, wedge or insert a larger piece of foam in the opening and fill the vase with a reservoir of water (see page 96).
2. Place the first stem centrally in the foam. This should be the same length as, or slightly shorter than, the height of the vase. Your other stems will be approximately the same length as this first stem. Angle stems down over the rim of the container and fill in the overall form of the arrangement to create a loosely spherical shape. Radiate all the stems from the central area.

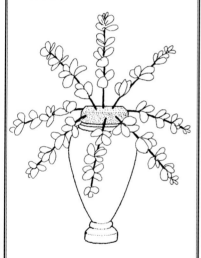

3. Add your concealing leaves, line flowers, focal flowers and fill in with spray flowers and extra foliage, using a judicious mixture of colour, form and texture.

▷ *Hawthorn* (Crataegus) *berries create the skeleton, Boston ivy* (Parthenocissus tricuspidata) *provides concealing leaves, China asters* (Callistephus chinensis) *and dahlias the focal flowers, and sprays of heather and mixed foliage complete the design.*

△ *Late garden roses* (Rosa sp.) *combined with smoke tree* (Cotinus coggyria *syn.* Rhus. cotinus) *in a glass vase with a wooden base.*

OVAL ARRANGEMENTS

Oval Table Arrangements

An oval arrangement looks lovely on an oval or rectangular table. Its size will depend on the size of the dish and foam that you use. If you wish to create a large design – perhaps for a table that will seat 12 – it is wise to select a heavier pottery dish, which will be more stable and hold more water.

*This traditional table arrangement uses love-lies-bleeding (*Amaranthus caudatus*), *Brachyglottis monroi, Brachyglottis 'Sunshine', berries of snowberry (*Symphoricarpos albus*), 'Constance Spry', 'Silver Jubilee' and 'Carol' roses, Cosmos bipinnatus and common ivy (*Hedera helix*).*
ARRANGER: LYNDA M. BROWN.*

An alternative way of displaying flowers on an oval or rectangular table.
ARRANGER: LYNDA M. BROWN.*

GUIDELINES

1. Use the larger round plastic dish with a rectangular recess and insert one-third of a block of foam in the recess. Establish the height of the arrangement. Try about 20 cm (8 in) for your first attempt. Create the overall length of your finished arrangement by placing a stem in each end of the foam. If you wish to use a candle, place this in position (see Technique 8 on page 97).

2. Create an oval shape by placing shorter lengths of stem in the longer sides of the foam on both sides, to create a smooth oval outline. Create an ovoid form by filling in between the base outline and the central placement.

3. Add your concealer leaves and line flowers. Check that you have an ovoid form. Check that areas (a) in the diagram are not too sparsely filled.
4. Add your focal flowers. Lastly, fill in the design with spray and other flowers that you have available.
5. Hold the arrangement up to eye level periodically, to check that you have colour low enough down in the design to give good balance.

An oval arrangement of asters, solidaster, berries and mixed foliage.

TRIANGULAR ARRANGEMENTS

The Symmetrical Triangle

The symmetrical triangle is a graceful way of presenting a mass of plant material. Each flower and leaf can show its individual beauty, and there is the combined appeal of the arrangement when viewed as a whole. Although the symmetrical triangle is to a certain extent stylized, this does not mean that it has to be stiff or awkward. The more it is practised, the more relaxed the design will become.

A symmetrical triangle with a difference. △
ARRANGER: NOREEN FISHBURN.

▷ *A symmetrical triangle. The outline of this miniature uses* Dianthus *(pink) leaves. Focal flowers are a miniature rose* (Rosa 'Simple Simon'). *Variegated ivy leaves conceal the mechanics and give weight to the base of the design.* Calluna vulgaris *'Silver Knight',* Chamaecyparis lawsoniana *'Pembury Blue', mini-chrysanthemums and tiny tendrils of gilded passion flower* (Passiflora caerulea) *fill in the design.*
ARRANGER: DR CHRISTINA CURTIS.

GUIDELINES

1. You will need a container that is raised, as you want the plant material to flow downwards. Place a stem or branch of line material centrally, two-thirds of the way back in the foam. This stem (a) should be approximately the height of the container plus the foam.

2. Insert two more line stems to create a triangle ABC. As a very rough guide, these two stems (b) should be two-thirds the length of the first placement and should be angled downwards out of the foam. If it is available, choose plant material that has a natural curve in the direction in which you wish it to flow. The remainder of the line material, which you use to complete the skeleton, will keep within the triangle ABC that you have now created.

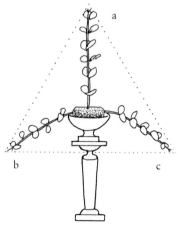

3. Place two stems (c) half the length of (b) over the front rim of the container and repeat at the back. Remember that all stems should appear to radiate from the centre of the foam (see page 106).

4. Place stems (d) in position. It is important that these stems radiate from the centre and fill in the triangle ABC. As a rough guide, they should be approximately half the length of (a).

5. Fill in the shape you have created with more line material to give it form. Add your concealing leaves.

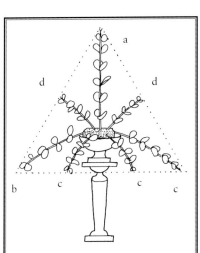

6. Add your line flowers, focal flowers and spray flowers to get a pleasingly full arrangement. Ensure that the weight is equally distributed each side of the central axis. The bottom half of the design will be visually heavier than the top half, but it should not be too obvious and there should be no large gaps between the stems of plant material, although there will be more space towards the extremities of the design. Check that you have plant material flowing downwards at the back and that your arrangement is not flat. Filling in the back gives depth and adds interest. Create your focal area close to where stem (a) enters the foam. The more experienced you become in creating the symmetrical triangle, the more relaxed the design will look and the more you will successfully break these guidelines, without destroying the overall triangular form.

▷ *A traditional arrangement using tints and shades of the complimentary colours blue and orange.*
Arranger: Sei Trevellick.

The symmetrical triangle can be scaled down to provide a miniature, or scaled up to give a pedestal arrangement suitable for the grandest occasions. The principles are exactly the same, only the scale changes.

Pillars, wrought-iron stands, plinths and columns are all suitable for raising the arrangement. Alternatively, it can be placed close to the edge of a piece of furniture, so that the plant material flows down over the front of the furniture.

Where to Place a Symmetrical Triangle

Symmetrical triangles need to be placed centrally, on a chest of drawers, chest or table, rather than to one side. The balance and outline of the arrangement are equal each side of the central axis and this balance needs to be repeated in the arrangement's setting.

For show work a miniature arrangement is one that is no more than 10 cm (4 in) in any dimension – height, depth or width. For enjoyment in the home these dimensions need not be respected. Use side shoots of flowers, miniature roses or single flowers from multiple heads, such as hydrangeas, chincherinchees (*Ornithogalum thyrsoides*), brodiaea (*Triteleia*) and African lily (*Agapanthus*). Small alpine flowers are perfect for miniatures, as many have fine wiry stems, which are easily inserted into foam. For containers you could use a thimble, doll's house furniture, a pill box or even a bottle top. Instead of a frog, use a drawing pin. Handle the plant material as little as possible, as hot hands will cause the material to dry out rapidly. You can handle the stems with tweezers. Embroidery scissors are ideal for cutting.

The Asymmetrical Triangle

A good asymmetrical triangle is difficult to achieve, but immensely satisfying when it works. It is often used in competition work as it is most suitable for the incorporation of accessories. It is also ideal for positioning on a piece of furniture, where it will complement and balance a lamp, picture frames or a favourite ornament.

Asymmetrical balance occurs where the weight and outline each side of the central axis are different. So why does it not appear unbalanced? In a good asymmetrical design sound balance is achieved by scooping out the longer side of the triangle to make it less dominant and:

a) judicious placement, or

b) incorporation of an accessory.

The design may be positioned to the side of the piece of furniture on which it is arranged, and balanced by a lamp or ornaments. Alternatively, an accessory can be placed on the lighter side and its additional weight will give visual balance.

This asymmetrical arrangement is balanced firstly by the incorporation of the lamp into the design and secondly by its placement – its weight being offset by the placement of the preserving pan and china on the right.
ARRANGER: JOAN WARD.

Cut ornamental cabbage (Brassica oleracea) and Bergenia (elephant's ear) leaves create the heavier side, and lisianthus the lighter side. Other materials used are tulips (Tulipa), dill (Anethum graveolens) and Alexandrian laurel (Danae racemosa).
ARRANGER: JOAN WARD.

GUIDELINES

1. You will need a low container. You could use the larger plastic dish with one-third of a block of foam. Alternatively, use a container on a short stem. Chamfer the edges of the foam (see page 95).

2. Your tallest stem (a) should be linear with a gentle curve. It should be placed towards the back of the foam, two-thirds over to one side.

3. Your second stem (b) should be about one-third the length of (a), angled slightly towards the viewer. The third stem (c) should be about two-thirds of (a), also placed towards the viewer. These three stems will create the triangle abc. Ideally stems (b) and (c) should also be gently curved.

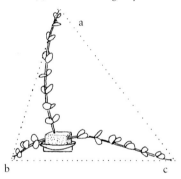

4. Place your heavier concealing leaves in the short side of the triangle and your lighter material in the longer side.

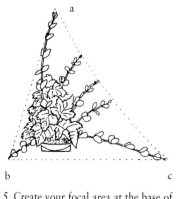

5. Create your focal area at the base of the tallest stem (a).

6. Fill in with spray material and any other suitable plant material.

Nodding pincushion protea (Leucospermum), Leucadendrons and rolled aspidistra leaves create
the heavier side of the arrangement, and the freesias and calla lilies the lighter side.
ARRANGER: JOAN WARD.

CRESCENT ARRANGEMENTS

Downward Crescent

This is a graceful design using a small amount of plant material, so that it looks most effective. It is essential that a tall container is used and that you have curved line plant material to create your downward sweep.

A downward crescent arrangement with a candle.
ARRANGER: GLADYS BETTISON.

Eucalyptus and Euphorbia create the outline of this crescent design. Galax urceolata act as the concealing leaves and opened tulips as the focal flowers.

GUIDELINES

1. If you are using a tall container without an integral dish, fix a candle-cup to the container and then add your foam. A cylinder of foam is appropriate for most candle-cups (see Technique 7 on page 97).
2. If using a candle, place this in position.
3. Place stem (a) centrally to repeat the line of the candle. It should be no more than half the height of the candle. Insert curved plant material from each side of the foam so that it flows gently downwards. These stems should be approximately twice the length of stem (a) or about the height of the container, if they were straightened. Avoid positioning the stems so that they appear to be falling out of the foam. Place two short stems (c) over the rim of the container at the back and front. Place stems out of the top (d) to fill in the triangle ABC. Ensure that all stems radiate from the central area. You will be using only a small amount of plant material and it is important that the geometric form is not lost at this stage.

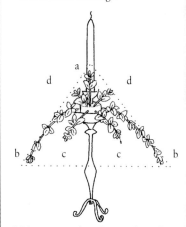

4. Place concealing leaves throughout the design. Add line flowers, focal flowers and fill with your spray plant material.

A contemporary variation of the downward crescent – a piece of driftwood, a couple of Japanese aralia (Fatsia) leaves, a few carnations and the effect is stunning.
ARRANGER: GLADYS BETTISON.

<table>
<tr><td>

GUIDELINES

1. If you are using a plate or another accessory, place this in position first. Insert two stems on the pinholder to create a curve. Allow the tips of the stems to rise to different heights. Often the best effect is achieved if the line of the curve established by the two stems forms part of an uncompleted circle.
2. Graduate further material to fill out the design, so that the area at the base is fullest and at the tips lightest. Create your focal or strongest area slightly off-centre, towards the longer length of outline material. Because this design uses minimal plant material the focal area may well consist of only one or two flowers.

</td></tr>
</table>

Upward Crescent

An upward crescent is a stylized design with plenty of charm. It is particularly appealing when used to complement a special plate, as the shape repeats that of the arrangement. It creates an effective design with a minimal amount of plant material. As a mechanic, foam is rarely as successful as a pinholder, for it often fails to hold the stems in position. They tend to twist round just when they seem firmly in place.

You will therefore need a pinholder and curving plant material, such as broom (*Cytisus*), rosemary (*Rosmarinus*) or branches with or without blossom. If you do not have these, try another design.

An elegant upward crescent with plant material chosen to complement the colour and mood of the plate. Marion Rivenell has used broom for her outline and has combined Iris and carnations with exotic dried plant material.

*An upward crescent in a glass candle-holder. Three stems of chincherinchee (*Ornithogalum thyrsoides*) are arranged with three Galax leaves, a lily bud and flower.*

THE S-CURVE

AN S-SHAPED ARRANGEMENT IS CALLED A 'HOGARTH', named after the great eighteenth-century artist who considered this the most beautiful form of art. If you create an upward Hogarth, you need to consider the fundamentals of good proportion so that you have approximately three-fifths of the arrangement above the centre of the foam and two-fifths beneath. Alternatively, choose a horizontal Hogarth – a delightful design for the dining table.

Vertical

GUIDELINES

1. A raised container and curved plant material are essential for this design. If a bottle or a candlestick is being used, add a candle-cup containing the minimum amount of foam that will hold your stems in position. Place one curved stem (a) towards the back of the foam, so that the tip is in line with the stem of the candlestick. This needs to be about one and a half times the height of the container without the height of the foam. Add a second stem (b) about two-thirds the length of the first stem (a). This should come forward towards the viewer and curve towards the stem of the container. Alternatively, position the stems as in line drawing below. But as you use a symmetrical raised container for this design, good balance is more easily achieved if the first method described is used, as it distributes the weight equally each side of the central axis.

A vertical Hogarth.
ARRANGER: JOAN WARD.

b

2. Concealing leaves should be added around the central area.
3. Graduate your flowers from the centre outwards, towards the tips of your line material, placing the most dominant flowers centrally.
4. Add other plant material to fill in the form so that there is a smooth flow from top to bottom.

Horizontal

GUIDELINES

1. For this arrangement you will need:
– a foam ring sawn in two and placed to form an S, or
– rectangles of foam wrapped in clingfilm or thin polythene. For the second method you can reinforce the part that will be making contact with the table with strips of thick black bin-liner.
2. Use a mixture of foliage to cover your foam. Keep your stems short and be sure to angle some down over the rim of the ring. You can extend the length of the S by using longer-stemmed plant material at the extremities, but be sure to follow the curve of the S. Remember to include some smooth-textured plant material.
3. Place your focal flowers throughout the design. Keep them reasonably central but avoid positioning them in too regular a line. They are the most visually dominant part of the design and if you place them in the outer limits you will disturb the smooth flow of the S. Fill in with your other plant material.

A horizontal Hogarth
ARRANGER: MARY LAW.

△ *A vertical arrangement in a terracotta container.*

In a Tall Container

GUIDELINES

1. Fix a small dish containing foam to the top of the container or wedge foam into the opening. Place your tallest stem centrally. This should be approximately one and a half to two times the height of the container. Place your focal flowers at angles coming down towards the rim of the container, reserving the brightest or largest flower for the bottom. The bottom placement should be in line with your tallest stem.

2. Fill in the design with foliage, ensuring that there is a leaf underneath the bottom flower, otherwise it can give the impression of falling out. Keep the overall form narrow, repeating the upward movement of the container.

In a Low Container

GUIDELINES

1. You will need only a few flowers, but to give contrast they should be in varying stages of development. Place a pinholder in the centre of your bowl and arrange your flowers at different heights and at different angles. If you are using five to seven stems, place the tallest leaning slightly backwards and add the others at different heights. Your tightest bud should be at the top of the design and your fullest bloom reserved for the bottom placement. If you are using lilies you may need only two or three stems.

2. Add large plain leaves, flat stones or glass chunks at the bottom of the stems to give textural contrast and to hide your pinholder.

The subtle colouring and muted form of this low dish is ideal for the addition of a few bold flowers. Here five bird-of-paradise flowers (*Strelitzia reginae*) have been positioned at different height to show off the detail of their amazing heads and long stems. Flat stones have been placed low at the base to cover the pinholder. Alternatively, you could use pebbles, glass chunks or a few bold leaves. Bearded irises, lilies or gerberas could also be used effectively. Ensure that your pinholder is heavy and large enough to take the weight of such heavy stems. Use florist's fix under the pinholder to give extra stability, if required.

VERTICAL ARRANGEMENTS

A VERTICAL ARRANGEMENT IS SIMPLE and often economical to create. It is an ideal arrangement when space is at a premium and you want a bold, simple statement of flowers. Depending on your home, it could be the perfect arrangement for an entrance hall, porch or niche. A vertical in a low container is ideal for showing off the lofty stems of irises, sword lilies (*Gladiolus*) and amaryllis (*Hippeastrum*). A tall, slender container is ideal for shorter straight stems.

△ *A vertical with a difference. In this arrangement the dominant vertical movement of the snake grass (*Equisetum hyemale*) and bamboo is softened by the curvilinear placement of the asparagus fern (*A. setaceus*).*

◁ *Five bird-of-paradise flowers (*Strelitzia reginae*) positioned at different heights to reveal the detail of their heads and long stems.*

MODERN DESIGN CLASSICS

MODERN DESIGN CLASSICS INDICATE styles that have broken with tradition and represent a new age. I have endeavoured to place in this chapter styles that have developed from the 1950s to the present day. It is anticipated that they will have a lasting value. Such styles have their roots in different cultures and different countries, and have been created both by florists and flower arrangers.

In traditional designs certain factors are common to all the arrangements. In this chapter, however, nothing works quite so neatly. What is common to all the arrangements, both traditional and modern, is the good use of the elements of design – colour, form, space and texture – as well as the principles: scale, proportion, contrast, dominance, rhythm, balance and harmony.

A mass sculptural design, showing a French influence, using internal space and repetition of form, texture and colour. The two New Zealand flax leaves are curled and fixed together, and to the container, with heavy-duty double-sided sticky tape. The ends are wired to fix into the foam. Three painter's palette/flamingo flower (Anthurium andreanum) leaves are rolled and glued to achieve a very strong textural effect. Two green arum/calla (Zantedeschia 'Green Goddess') flowers are placed looking into the space created by the Phormium loops.
ARRANGER: MARGARET MACSHEEY.

FREE-FORM DESIGNS

FREE-FORM OR FREESTYLE DESIGNS first appeared in the 1950s and were influenced by the modern, rather than the traditional, Ikebana (the Japanese art of flower arranging) and by new trends in home decoration. They should not, however, be confused with modern Japanese freestyle. Free-form can be defined as free and imaginative designs inspired by nature's growth patterns. They are designed with a more restrained amount of plant material than that used for traditional arrangements.

Good examples of free-form design are always harnessed to the elements and principles of good design. Think of free-form as being free from traditional patterns. Just as Picasso was able to paint beautifully in a naturalistic way, so the best free-form designers are able to create traditional masterpieces.

SPATIAL DESIGNS

SPATIAL OR 'MODERN' designs, as they are often still called, developed from free-form designs. The title 'modern' could now be considered an anachronism, as other styles, such as sculptural and parallel, have evolved that do not bear the same characteristics. I have therefore referred to this style as 'spatial', which will relate to flower arrangements that show a restrained use of plant material and emphasize the use of space.

So how do spatial designs differ from free-form? Perhaps it can be best summed up that spatial designs have a more structured and controlled form, and that in the main they use less plant material.

Like free-form design before it, spatial design came into being to keep in line with the ever-changing styles of architecture and home decorating, and with the increasing economy of time and money. It was called modern because at that time it was new, fresh and entirely different.

CHARACTERISTICS – FREE-FORM

♦ The shape is determined by the nature of the plant material used and cannot be reduced to any sort of discipline or control.
♦ The designs break completely with the semi-stylized triangles, crescents, and so on.
♦ There should be an emphasis on space.
♦ There is lots of flowing movement.
♦ There is a unified plan, which is asymmetrical.
♦ Depth is extremely important.
♦ There is always a feeling of enjoyment and exuberance.
♦ A wide diversity of containers may be used – they could be ultra-modern, rather unusual, but generally they are unsophisticated.

For an example of a free-form design look at the photograph on page 249.

Two containers of similar design have been used, one in front of the other. Good design has been achieved through the use of enclosed space and the choice of colour, form and texture.
ARRANGER: MARY GWYTHER

CHARACTERISTICS – SPATIAL

♦ It makes restrained use of plant material, in quantity and/or variety, with emphasis on form, texture, colour and space, often with dramatic contrasts.

♦ Space is not equally distributed throughout the design, as in traditional classics.

♦ Space is often used to balance a heavy solid and becomes even more emphatic when enclosed.

♦ Each component is appreciated for its own merits and for its contribution to the design as a whole.

♦ Anything can be used as a container – a bottle lid hidden by a piece of wood, pottery (but not traditional) vases – for example, an urn.

♦ Depth is vital.

♦ Textural contrasts are extremely important.

♦ There is a lack of transition.

♦ Good balance is absolutely essential. It is not apparent in the same way as it is in traditional design classics but it is always evident.

*The purity and form of the Easter lilies (*Lilium longiflorum*) contrast with, yet complement, the rough-textured wood to give a simple and tranquil design.*
ARRANGER: ELIZABETH WAITE.

ABSTRACT DESIGNS

THE TERM 'ABSTRACT' REFERS to an arrangement in which the plant material is used only for its colour, form or texture. The emphasis is on design. There is no attempt to place plant material so that it appears to be growing naturally. Abstract design uses the form, colour and texture of plant material to create a design, rather than a flower arrangement per se. Thus a flowering onion (*Allium*) is used because its colour and form give a purple sphere; the form of an open lily (*Lilium*) gives a trumpet; bulrushes (*Typha*) give lines; a teasel (*Dipsacus fullonum*) prickles. A good abstract flower arrangement can only be created by someone with a developed sense of design. Just as the greatest artists and sculptors were, and are, capable of creating both representational and abstract design, only experienced flower arrangers can create the powerful images portrayed by an award-winning abstract design.

It is said that abstract flower arranging will never have the same following as traditional work. Why not? Perhaps because it is bold and dramatic, rather than pretty, and therefore needs a plain dramatic background to reinforce the drama of the design. Dramatic backgrounds are not found in every home. Another factor could be that many abstract designs rely on plant material that is not often found in the garden.

A good abstract design relies on hard work, inspiration and the right materials. Such designs may not always appeal, and readers may not wish to move in this direction, but abstracts should always be respected, as they reflect the innermost thoughts of their creator. For the creator of abstracts a successful design brings immense satisfaction.

CHARACTERISTICS

♦ Interest is distributed throughout the design rather than in just one area.

♦ There should always be strong rhythm throughout the design, achieved by the judicious placing of every element to create a strong pattern.

♦ Space is integral to the design and should be considered part of it. Enclosed space has a powerful impact and can be used to balance the weight of solid objects. It also connects one side of the design with the other, making it immediately more three-dimensional.

♦ Plant material is used non-vegetatively – there is no pretence of presenting it so that it appears to be growing. It is chosen for its texture, colour or form alone.

♦ There are no unnecessary additions to the design, which is pruned to its bare essentials.

♦ Balance is absolutely vital. The focal area may be one of many and placed in unconventional areas of the design. As Julia Berrall says in her History of Flower Arranging (1969), 'Successful contemporary creations call for a basic knowledge of design used with acute sensibility to the demands of perfect balance.'

♦ Contrasts are usually dramatic, and there is little transition.

♦ Containers are usually hidden or vegetative.

♦ Plant material is usually bold and arresting. Evergreen leaves such as New Zealand flax (*Phormium tenax*), Japanese aralia (*Fatsia japonica*) and cast iron plant (*Aspidistra elatior*) can easily be manipulated to give exciting new forms. In their own right they give bold form and strong line. Exotic dried material also gives the required form.

'Crinkum-Crankum' is the title of this abstract design – a word applied to all things crooked, anything full of twists – an interpretation of a title using simplified forms, extracting the essence and eliminating all unnecessary detail. Good use of design elements with an emphasis on space as an integral part of the design.
ARRANGER: MARY GWYTHER.

THE PARALLEL STYLE

THIS STYLE IS SOMETIMES KNOWN as continental design, but its style is distinctive. Such designs have long been created by Dutch florists, but it was only in the late 1980s and 1990s that they became generally popular and practised in Great Britain. The style has been adapted to the plant material available in the typical British garden, to which it is ideally suited. The principal difference between this and any other design is that there is little or no radiation. The rationale is to make plant material look as natural and unstylized as possible, following its natural growth pattern.

A ring of spring flowers using an assembly of forms, colours and textures from a flower arranger's garden.
ARRANGER: JEAN STICHBURY.

CHARACTERISTICS

♦ Flowers are usually grouped, rather than scattered throughout the design.

♦ There is great emphasis on texture and form. It is sometimes viewed as a patchwork design, creating areas of contrasting texture and form.

♦ The container can be round, rectangular or oval, although many find the rectangular or round shape easiest to start with. You could use a casserole, a foam ring, a 1950s log container, even a shallow plastic foam tray designed to take a block of foam. A plastic foam tray, cut in two lengthways, will give a narrower, rectangular shape to the arrangement. Simply slot one length over the other and then glue the join. However, if the container is too shallow or devoid of interest then a good design can be more difficult to accomplish.

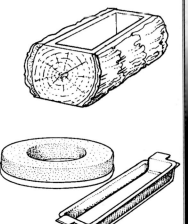

♦ The design can be achieved with garden material or flowers from the florist, or with a mixture of the two.

GUIDELINES

1. The foam should rise above the rim of the container but not too high. If the foam rises more than 5 cm (2 in) above the rim, for a medium-sized design, then the arrangement tends to become bottom-heavy and rather leaden.

2. Chamfer the foam (see page 95).

3. To give interest you will need placements at various heights. You could establish the tallest placements first, with line plant material, but avoid having these all at the same height. If you have a circular container try three taller groups, and if you have a small rectangular container two groups. Sometimes the plant material in one of the taller placements is positioned so that each tip rises to the same height. In this instance the stems may be bare and can be bound with raffia, twine or wool. This is called 'bunching'. If the binding is decorative and/or intricate, it is referred to as 'bundling'. When using garden plant material it is more usual to give a softer look with graduated heights of plant material, but still keeping within a roughly linear framework. Some minor radiation may be evident.

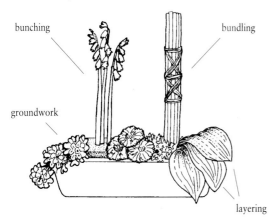

4. You will then need to cover your foam with plant material. This is kept short and used in blocks of contrasting form, texture and colour. It is often referred to as 'ground work'. 'Layering' is the term used to described a mass of overlapping leaves which extend beyond the front and sides of a container. There is little or no space between the leaves which are angled downwards.

5. Rather than working your way systematically around or along the container, ensure good balance by moving from one area to another.

6. Contrast your forms and textures, placing smooth, plain leaves such as ivy (*Hedera*) next to more intricate plant material, such as veronica (*Hebe*).

7. Fruits, vegetables, lichen, moss, Spanish moss (*Tillandsia usneoides*), seedheads and fungi all look good incorporated into the design. They give contrasting forms and textures and can fill the design quickly and inexpensively.

A parallel design in a rectangular container, of an exciting array of garden plant material including a branch of a lichen-covered apple tree. ARRANGER: DOROTHY BYE.

ARRANGER: NOREEN FISHBURN.

MASS SCULPTURAL DESIGNS

A MASS SCULPTURAL ARRANGEMENT CAN perhaps best be described as a controlled design in which the plant material is chosen and displayed to create a dried or living sculpture. The sculpture is created partly through the massive blocking of plant material to create bold, strong areas of colour, form and texture, and partly by the manipulation of foliage to create new forms and to liberate space.

This style of arranging has evolved from work that originated in France and Italy in the 1980s and 1990s, influenced by the Grand Japanese Master Houn Ohara. In Britain we have taken the basic concept and adapted it to the plant material that we have more readily available and given it a British touch. I hope that the instigators of these styles will approve of our adaptations.

Leaf Manipulation

Leaf manipulation is possible with tough, bold, long-lasting, evergreen leaves, such as those of the cast iron plant, *Aspidistra elatior*, cherry laurel (*Prunus laurocerasus*), New Zealand flax, Japanese aralia, *Galax urceolata*, palm, elephant's ear (*Bergenia*) and ivy. It is a particular feature of designs inspired by the French who, with the Italians, have helped lift flower arranging to a fine art.

Twisting

Staple the tips of two strong leaves such as *Aspidistra* together, then twist the stems to entwine the two leaves.

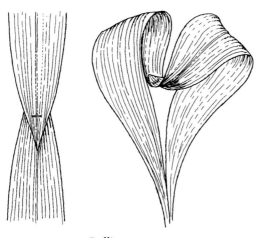

Rolling

a) Take a *Galax* or *Bergenia* leaf and roll it into a cone shape.
b) Alternatively, roll the leaf upon itself horizontally.

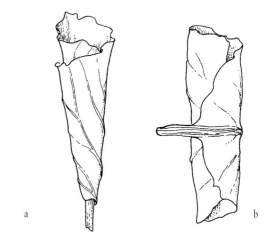

Folding and Pleating

Take a large ivy or *Bergenia* leaf. Pleat the tip down and bunch in the two sides. Take a wire and thread it through the pleats of the leaf, then twist around the stem to secure.

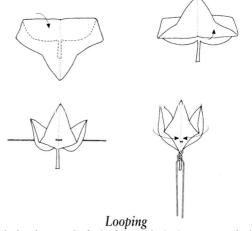

Looping

a) Push the sharp end of a leaf through the lower part of a linear leaf, where it will stay happily in place if the hole made is not too big. *Iris*, tulip (*Tulipa*) and *Aspidistra* leaves are ideal.
b) Loop the tip of the leaf down to meet the top of the stem and tie with a short length of wire.

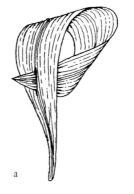

CHARACTERISTICS

Sculptured designs contain a restricted number of different types of plant material.

♦ Foliage and flowers can be blocked, excluding space to give strong, bold images.

♦ Balance is asymmetrical, as symmetrical designs are considered more static.

♦ Good proportions are important.

♦ Containers are bold, strong and upright, with a simple structure, so that they form a happy marriage with the bulky plant material that is such an important part of the sculptural style. In Britain, Habitat, the Reject Shop and other chain stores have suitable containers at all prices. Lined terracotta pots also make good containers.

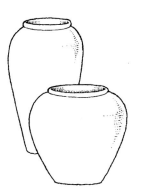

♦ In designs inspired by the Italian style there is often a central pivot of linear plant material, placed vertically. Examples are bamboo, gay feather (*Liatris*) and bulrushes (*Typha*).

♦ The foam must rise well above the container and this can be achieved by:

a) first inserting a plastic plant pot of exactly the right dimensions into the opening of the vase. This is then filled with foam and secured with florist's tape.

b) standing a block or piece of foam upright. If it is insufficiently tall, stand it on a second piece and fill the vase with water.

c) in small designs a small plastic dish can be strapped onto the vase opening.

♦ The plant material is positioned so that it covers the rim of the container.

Clipping
Cut the tip of linear leaves, such as iris and flax, to give them a stronger form.

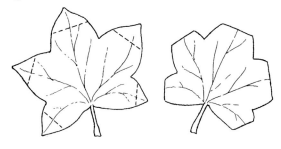

Shredding
Cut vertically with knife along surface of leaf keeping outside form of leaf intact.

An arrangement inspired by the Italian style, using glorious flowers of late summer – sunflowers (Helianthus), sword lilies (Gladiolus), carnations (Dianthus) and roses (Rosa), with loops and separate tails of New Zealand flax.
ARRANGER: ANN KENDRICK.

Plaiting

a) Take a *Phormium* or *Cordyline* leaf and split. Bring one section across the other section at a 90° angle. Take second section across the first. Repeat to last 10 cm and tie the two loose ends together.

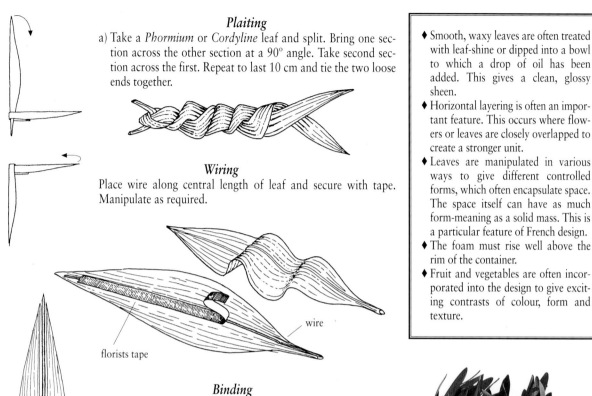

Wiring

Place wire along central length of leaf and secure with tape. Manipulate as required.

florists tape

wire

Binding

Tie the tip of a *Phormium* or *Cordyline* leaf to the top of a piece of long bamboo. Tightly bind the *Phormium* leaves around the bamboo, tying them at the base. Soak overnight and allow to dry. Then remove the bamboo.

- ♦ Smooth, waxy leaves are often treated with leaf-shine or dipped into a bowl to which a drop of oil has been added. This gives a clean, glossy sheen.
- ♦ Horizontal layering is often an important feature. This occurs where flowers or leaves are closely overlapped to create a stronger unit.
- ♦ Leaves are manipulated in various ways to give different controlled forms, which often encapsulate space. The space itself can have as much form-meaning as a solid mass. This is a particular feature of French design.
- ♦ The foam must rise well above the rim of the container.
- ♦ Fruit and vegetables are often incorporated into the design to give exciting contrasts of colour, form and texture.

The leaves and flowers have been chosen and positioned to complement the colour, texture and form of the deep cherry-red vase. A cork of wet foam has been wedged into the opening and firmly strapped in place with florist's tape. The two large roses are made of polyester silk and have been teamed with rolled Aspidistra, cordyline, leucadendron leaves and deep cherry-red tulips, which have been arched down over the vase to repeat the line. The use of houseplant foliage makes this an easy design for those without a garden.
ARRANGERS: JOAN WARD AND JUDITH BLACKLOCK.

WATERFALL OR CASCADE

A STYLE INTRODUCED TO BRITAIN by the great German designer, Gregor Lersch, this has great panache and impact but is not practical for every home, as it requires a large amount of plant material of varying forms and textures, and careful positioning to show it off to advantage.

The objective is to build up an arrangement composed of many levels, which is cohesive despite the numerous varieties of plant material and the many contrasts of texture.

A delightful cascade
ARRANGER: AVRIL BRISSENDEN.

*This cascade has a flowing silhouette using plant
material, that falls vertically from within. Susie has used
tuberose (Polianthes), Bianca rose (Rosa 'Bianca'),
cast iron plant, white arum and trailing ivy. Her hanging
trails are of Gomphrena fructicosa and chunks of glass,
wrapped and linked with copper wire. Similar pieces
of glass are tucked into the openings of the arums.*
ARRANGER: SUSIE EDWARDS.

GUIDELINES

This is just one of the methods for creating a waterfall, but the result is most effective.

1. Set up your mechanics so that they are secure and well balanced. The foam can be shaped into a cheese wedge to help establish the overall form.

2. The first layer can consist of large leaves with some mixed foliage added to give variation, for instance ivy (*Hedera*), alum root (*Heuchera*) or privet (*Ligustrum*). This layer should loosely cover the foam.

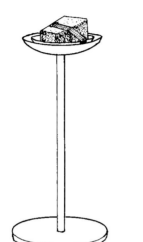

3. The second layer establishes the form. For this you will need a selection of long, light, flowing plant material, such as periwinkle (*Vinca*), *Asparagus densiflorus* or indeed any of the ferns, honeysuckle (*Lonicera*), gum tree (*Eucalyptus*), *Rubus tricolor* or Alexandrian laurel (*Danae racemosa*). You will also need a few long, bold leaves, such as cast iron plant, New Zealand flax, crotons or *Dracaena* or perhaps painter's palette (*Arthurium andreanum*), to give strength, if you are working on a large design. If these leaves appear too heavy, split them. The short side of the wedge will bear shorter, heavier stems and the shaped side will take the long, flowing stems.

4. The third layer consists of line flowers such as spray carnations, sweet peas (*Lathyrus odoratus*), freesias or lisianthus (*Eustoma*) which will take colour out to the perimeters of the design. The stems should be flexible, rather than the rigid stems of, say, chrysanthemums.

5. The fourth layer is of larger, bold, round flowers, such as peonies, hydrangeas, gerberas, full roses, open lilies. You will need about five or seven. The larger, more dominant flowers will graduate to a certain extent to the periphery.

6. The fifth or final layer is ethereal to create an extra dimension, so giving greater depth and heightening interest, without obscuring the layers you have already built up. It can be woven into the design or looped. The material can be kept low and in position by tying down the tips with coloured reel-wire or raffia. It can be the same material used in (3) if sufficiently light, for example asparagus fern or bear grass. Alternatively, you can use baby's breath, sea lavender (*Limonium ferulaceum* 'Karel de Groot'), *Rubus tricolor* or split New Zealand flax leaves.

7. You may wish to add a vertical hanging element. If you want to use coloured reel-wire, wrap this securely round each component, leaving a gap of the same or varying lengths between each one. Attach the end of the reel-wire to a heavier wire and insert this in the foam, tucking it underneath the plant material already in place. Alternatively, you may wish to position this at an earlier point in the making of your design.

8. If your foam is not in a container you can add water by placing ice cubes on the foam and allowing them to melt.

CONSTRUCTIONS

CONSTRUCTIONS ARE CREATED WITH PLIABLE, smooth stems, such as dogwood (*Cornus*) or willow (*Salix*). Perhaps the greatest influence on this style of arranging comes from Germany and the Netherlands, where constructions are incorporated into simple gifts, tied bunches and wedding bouquets. For your first construction try creating one in a low bowl.

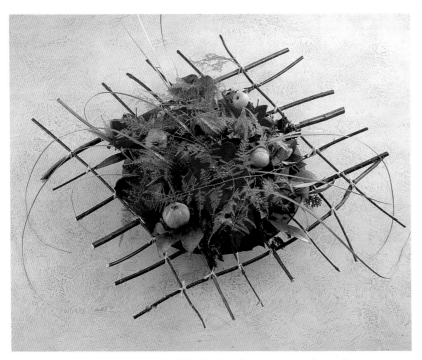

A construction containing Skimmia, *single heads taken from two stems of amaryllis* (Hippeastrum), *japonica/quince* (Chaenomeles), *chinese lanterns* (Physalis alkekengi var. francheti) *and assorted foliage.*

This hand-tied design incorporates a willow construction made from basket willow (Salix viminalis) tied with raffia. All the fresh flower materials are woven and layered throughout the construction to form a landscape design. All stems are parallel and tightly bound. Start with very fine material at the outer edges, adding the focal flowers and then filling in with cascading material, such as grasses, ferns and split New Zealand flax leaves. This hand-tied design holds 'Leonardis' roses (Rosa 'Leonardis'), x Solidaster luteus, Love-lies-bleeding (Amaranthus caudatus) and (A. hypochondriacus), stem carnations (Dianthus), sword fern (Nephrolepis exaltata), asparagus fern, gum tree, Dracaena leaves, bear grass and ferns.
ARRANGER: JUDITH DERBY.

CHARACTERISTICS

The basis of the design is a construction of stems secured with raffia, or wire and raffia. Pliable stems can be tied into a shape that they will readily take on. If the stems are soaked prior to manipulation they will take on the shape even more readily. The form of the construction can vary.

- The plant material is built up through the construction using a contrast of colour, form and texture.
- Use is frequently made of light, feathery asparagus fern, ming fern (*Asparagus umbellatus*), bulrush (*Typha*) or bear grass or the stronger steel grass to give a final extra dimension to the design. This can be woven through the design or tied down with reel-wire or raffia.
- Interest can be enhanced by adding moss balls, which can be bound with coloured reel-wire. These can then be hung from the design with coloured reel-wire.

GUIDELINES FOR A CONSTRUCTION IN A LOW BOWL

1. Choose a low bowl and place foam within it so that it rises just above the level of the container and fills about one-third to half the area of the opening. You will be restricted to a certain extent by the flat bottom of your bowl.
2. You want your grid to extend beyond the perimeter of the bowl. It is part of the design and you want it to be seen and not hidden. You should take the dimensions of the bowl into account when making your grid. Make the actual grid larger than your bowl, with the free ends extending well beyond it.

3. To make your grid, cut a number of stems to the same length and ensure they are stripped clean. Lay them on a flat surface in a grid formation, so that each of the squares formed is approximately equal in size.

4. Take lengths of raffia and tie the stems at the joints, making sure that they are securely held. This is a time-consuming task but quite enjoyable.

5. Lower your grid onto the foam. Thread your plant material through the grid, using a mixture of forms and textures. Start with your foliage, keep the stems short, but angle some in the foam so that the opening of the bowl is filled. Use some bold forms to give focal enrichment to the design.

6. Add more bold focal flowers and other plant material - flowers, fruits or berries - to give additional interest if necessary.

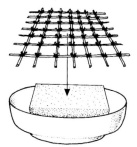

7. Finish your design by placing light and airy material over the whole to build up a final layer. Asparagus fern and strands of bear grass are ideal. Plant material can be tied down to the construction with raffia or coloured reel-wire. Incorporate mossed balls or coloured reel-wire, if desired.

THE WAY FORWARD

THE WORLD OF FLOWERS IS SUCH that there will always be excitement in what is to come. There have been so many movements in recent times that no-one need worry that flower arranging will ever become stale or boring. There are influences from all over the world that can be adapted to the plant material available to you.

One trend is to create designs that have characteristics of both naturalistic and abstract designs. These are perhaps best termed semi-abstract. Their main features are:

Plant material is, to a certain extent, used naturally.
• More plant material is used than in an 'abstract' design.
• Much bold material is used, but delicate trailing and cascading plant material can also be incorporated into the design. Bare stems can be manipulated to give space within the arrangement.
• Plant material can be grouped to give greater impact and/or built up in layers. This can happen in a bowl or spherical container that is part of the overall design. Vegetative containers are often used.
• Good design is essential. Colour is often used in bold splashes.

The two designs below are Judith Butterworth's vision of what could lie ahead. Will she be right?

A design using asparagus fern, Lilium 'Star Gazer' carnations and giant Elephant's ear (Alocasia macrorrhiza).
ARRANGER: JUDITH BUTTERWORTH.

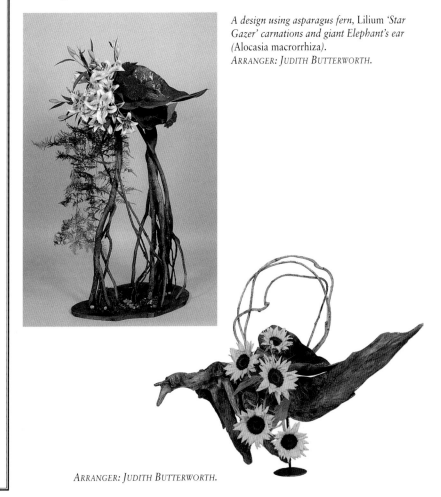

ARRANGER: JUDITH BUTTERWORTH.

OTHER DESIGN
CLASSICS

THE DESIGNS IN THIS CHAPTER ARE NOT BASED on geometric form
and in other ways do not conform to the criteria
for traditional design classics.
On the other hand, they do not have their origin
in the recent past and cannot be labelled 'modern'.
They are therefore described as
other design classics.

A *tied bunch of cream roses and gerberas, purple lisianthus (*Eustoma grandiflorum), *snowberry*
(*Symphoricarpos albus*) *and variegated buckthorn (*Rhamnus alaternus *'Argenteovariegata').*

TIED BUNCHES

TIED BUNCHES, OFTEN REFERRED to on the European continent as hand-ties, have their origin in the tussie-mussies of the Middle Ages. These were sweet-smelling bunches of herbs that detracted from the ugly odours of an age without effective sanitation. Today tied bunches have undergone a revival, although European florists have long found tied bunches a popular item.

There are several ways of making a tied bunch and two methods are described below. A third type of tied bunch – often termed 'a constructed hand tie' – is described on page 239. This intricate method is much practised in Germany and the Netherlands and gives an exciting design with a difference. Whatever the style, it is the choice of plant material that will make your arrangement successful.

*A tied bunch of garden annuals with pink spray roses. The annuals include clary (*Salvia viridis*), S. farinacea and Verbena.*

CHOOSING THE PLANT MATERIAL

1. Your tied bunch will need to have immediate impact. Flowers in bud would not have the required effect, even though the bunch would last longer. You need at least one variety of flowers with large open blooms.

2. The stems of the finished bunch will all be the same length, so do not choose a combination of short-stemmed flowers, such as grape hyacinths (*Muscari*), and long-stemmed flowers, such as sword lilies (*Gladiolus*).

3. Avoid stems on which the flowers branch off low down the stem. You will be tying the string or raffia half way down the stem and any flowers below this line will need to be removed.

4. You will need at least 15 stems. The longer their length, the more flowers you will need. I like to use about 20-36 stems for an average-length tied bunch.

5. Soft stems, such as daffodils (*Narcissus*), can get squashed when you tie the bunch, so avoid these for your first attempts.

6. The addition of bear grass (*Xerophyllum*) or ferns gives a soft, natural look to the design.

7. Aim to keep the stems short. If they are too long you will detract from the impact of the flowers. As a rough rule of thumb, the width of all the flowering heads needs to be about one or one and a half times the final cut length of the stems.

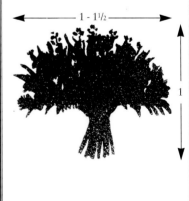

METHOD 1

1. Decide on the height of the tied bunch and remove any obvious excess from the end of the stems. This will make the bunch lighter to hold when assembling.
2. Remove foliage from the bottom half of your stems.
3. Have a length of raffia or string and a pair of scissors to hand.
4. Create a spiral of stems by:
a) Holding the first stem upright across the palm of your hand, using the thumb to keep it in position. Cross a second stem over the first.
b) Take a third stem and repeat the action in the same direction.
c) Continue adding stems – all in the same direction. You can also add stems behind, but ensure that you do not cross any.
d) When you have placed the majority of the stems you may wish to insert a certain colour or round, dominant flower close to the centre. At this point just push the requisite stem through the bunch where required.

5. Holding the bunch very tightly, tie string, ribbon or raffia round it in a bow. Cut the stems neatly and try standing the bouquet on a flat surface.
6. For left-handed people this method can prove difficult. They may find it easier to follow method 2.

METHOD 2

1. Prepare your plant material as above. Put your thumb and forefinger together to form a hole.
2. Place five pieces of leather leaf or other strong plant material of a similar form through this hole, so that the stems interlock and form a circular framework of crossed stems.
3. Start to weave your flowers and other foliage into the design. Keep your fingers loose all the time in order to obtain a relaxed design. Try standing in front of a mirror so that you can see the shape developing.
4. When you have finished, tie off with string, cord or raffia, cut the stems to the same length and finish with a simple bow. This is suitable for a wedding bouquet.

If you wish to give the bouquet with a reservoir of water, take a square of cellophane and place the bouquet centrally on the cellophane. Pull the four corners up to the centre, *making absolutely sure that the stem ends remain in contact with the cellophane.* Gripping the cellophane against the stems very lightly, so that the ends continue to remain in contact with it, allow a gap to open into which you pour a jug of water or hold under a running tap until it fills sufficiently. Pull up the slack cellophane and tie firmly. You may need help from a friend the first time you attempt this. If you do not need a reservoir of water, wrap a scrunched-up sheet of a colour-co-ordinated paper around your bunch before using the cellophane. This has a strong inpact and can make the flowers appear to go further.

A tussie mussie – herbs, foliage and fragrant flowers have been bound to give a slightly rounded shape with an informal , unpretentious look. Tussie mussies were created for many occasions in Medieval and Tudor times. They were the forerunner of today's tied bunch.

LANDSCAPE DESIGNS

A LANDSCAPE IS A NATURALISTIC DESIGN. It captures the essence of a lakeside, wood, seashore, mountain or moorland scene that has been imagined or actually viewed. The judicious use of scale is vital for an effective design, for you are taking a particular scene and reducing it in size so that it can be appreciated in the home.

For the flower arranger the landscape design is one that can give great pleasure at minimal cost. To quote Jean Taylor in *Creative Flower Arrangement* (1973), 'The secret of composing a good landscape lies in the use of restraint, for one or two brown leaves suggest autumn, a trickle of sand – the beach, a little moss – woodland.'

Enjoy your landscape design. For your first attempt you could ignore all the good advice and just have a go. Re-create your own experience of nature with pleasure and abandon. Visualize the surging life of damp woodlands, the beauty of a wild coastline, the stillness and calm of a deserted lakeland tarn, and delight in the beauties of nature.

A truly magnificent landscape design with two herons carved drinking from a pool. The plant material includes the seedheads of large cuckoo pict (Arum italicum pictum), love-lies-bleeding (Amaranthus), fern, Sempervivum and umbrella plant (Cyperus involucratus). The effect succeeds through its restraint and judicious selection of appropriate material – all of it in scale.
ARRANGER: ILONA BARNEY.

CHARACTERISTICS

♦ Containers are rarely, if ever, seen – for when would you see a container in nature? Water often plays an important part in a landscape design, and where this is evident the container should be of lead, pottery, or any other material that is in harmony. It is rarely left totally 'exposed' for the rim is usually softened with moss, stones or other natural material.

♦ Plant material must be chosen with care. If you wish to depict a seascape, the flowers need not be entirely those that thrive by the sea, but they should be of a colour and compatibility with those that do. A hedgerow scene could include old man's beard (*Clematis vitalba*), hips, haws, ferns and berries, and a moorland scene heather (*Calluna vulgaris*), common cottongrass (*Eriophorum angustifolium*), gorse (*Ulex europeus*) and moss.

♦ Accessories should be in keeping. If you wish to add birds or animals to complete the scene, do try and use those with a matt rather than a shiny finish and endeavour to keep them in scale. Scale is important in all aspects of the design. And too many accessories will spoil the effect.

♦ Although you are dealing with an illusion of scale, do try to avoid creating a scene where the branch representing your tree is the same height as your flowers.

♦ For landscape designs a base is important, to unite the different elements that will constitute your design. Perhaps you are using a dish for your water, some pebbles and moss, two hidden dishes containing your plant material and a bird or woodland animal. Without the unifying base these various elements could well appear disparate, rather than a well-planned microcosm of an inspiring scene. Avoid over-basing the design, with too wide or thick a base or too many levels of base as shown below.

Bluetits carved in a beautifully harmonious design, using grey weathered wood and foliage to complement the colour and texture, and elements of European design with the grouping of plant material. ARRANGER: ILONA BARNEY.

GUIDELINES

1. If you select a pleasing combination of pot plants, then your pot-et-fleur will be a success. You can either choose a selection of different plants, each complementing the others, or you can create a massed effect using several of the same variety. If you are choosing different plants consider the following:

a) Your plants will be living together in close proximity. They should therefore thrive under similar, rather than contrasting, conditions: that is to say, do not plant a cactus in the same bowl as a plant that needs copious amounts of water.

b) You can start your selection with a pot plant that you already have in your home and choose others to complement it. Alternatively, take your basket or bowl to the garden centre and try out a combination in situ. Make sure that you do not pay for your container on the way out!

c) You will need contrast of form and texture. If you are mixing your pot plants in a traditional design you should consider buying at least one of each of the following.

♦ a tall plant for the back, such as weeping fig (*Ficus Benjamina*) or one of the palms (such as parlour palm (*Chamaedorea elegans*) or areca palm (*Chrysalidocarpus lutescens*).

♦ a trailing plant, such as an ivy (*Hedera*) or trailing Cape grape (*Rhoicissus capensis*)

♦ a more compact or bushy plant, such as a begonia

♦ and one plant should have a smooth, plain leaf.

A traditional pot-et-fleur design created with a variety of pot plants and three cut stems of 'Star Gazer' lilies.
ARRANGER: JOAN WARD.

d) For a pot-et-fleur be careful how many flowering pot plants you use, as they may detract from the cut flowers. Take care also that you do not include too many variegated plants as they can create a fussy effect.

2. Choose a container of a suitable size. If it is porous or of basketry, line it with a piece of thick black bin-liner.

3. Place a thin layer of broken pots or small pieces of expanded polystyrene chips in the bottom of your container.

4. Scatter some powdered charcoal over the crocks or polystyrene. This will keep the pot-et-fleur smelling sweet.

5. If you are taking the plants out of their pots, pour a layer of Super Natural Multi-purpose Houseplant Compost or John Innes no.2 – both of which are available from many good garden centres – over the charcoal. If they are to remain in their pots, simply place these on the charcoal. This compost can also be used to raise the level of pots that are not as deep as others. Place your plants in a pleasing composition, leaving space into which you can position the jar or pot that will contain the cut flowers.

6. Position your flowers in a narrow-necked jar or on a pinholder placed in a container. You will need only a few bold flowers to complete your pot-et-fleur.

POT-ET-FLEUR

A POT-ET-FLEUR IS A DELIGHTFUL NAME for a planted bowl of houseplants and cut flowers. The pot plants create a long-lasting framework and the flowers give colour, form and variation. You can alter your designs each week simply by changing the flowers. A plants and flowers design could include extra cut foliage but a pot-et-fleur would not include any additional foliage. You can choose plants that would not survive outside, which give a wonderful range of exotic leaves for gentle snipping. There are two ways in which you can create the framework for your pot-et-fleur. You can arrange your pots directly in a basket or bowl, so that they can easily be changed, or you can try the following method.

*Ornamental kale or cabbage (*Brassica oleracea*) have been removed from their pots and placed in a glass bowl filled with* Seramis, *an alternative growing medium to which liquid food and water should be added. A well pinholder has been placed in the centre of the bowl and a bunch of bear grass has been impaled on the pins. The cut bear grass means that this design cannot strictly be termed* **Pot et Fleur***.*

CUSHION DESIGNS

CUSHION DESIGNS HAVE THEIR ORIGIN in Victorian times, when the spirit of the age was to cram as much material as possible into as small a space as possible! Constance Spry also used this style of arranging in the 1940s and 1950s and it is presently undergoing a fashionable revival. Delightful though these designs are, they do necessitate a greater abundance of plant material, because no space is incorporated into the design and it relies strongly on focal plant material.

CHARACTERISTICS

♦ These are compact, massed designs, with no space between the individual heads of the plant material.
♦ The absence of space means that the emphasis is on the focal head of the plant material, of which you will need a large amount.
♦ The effect relies on the juxtaposition of colour, form and texture.
♦ The stems are positioned so that they appear to radiate from the same area of origin.
♦ The container may be low or raised.

An autumnal medley of flowers and foliage.
ARRANGER: BERYL BOOTH.

A simple cushion arrangement of orange tulips
(Tulipa), mauve rhododendrons
(Rhododendron) and pine (Pinus) needles.

STILL LIFE

A STILL LIFE IS WHERE PLANT MATERIALS, either fresh or dried, are grouped with inanimate objects. Its characteristics are use of rhythmic forms, texture, colour and excellence of overall design. In many parts of the world, plant material does not necessarily have to predominate in a still-life study.

Still lifes in painting originated in Europe, in particular in the Low Countries and in Spain, during the fifteenth and sixteenth centuries, although they took as their example the frescos and mosaics of ancient times. Although they were considered at that time a lesser form of art – after the more prestigious portraiture and landscape painting – 'still lifes' have proved extremely popular over the centuries. Today exhibitions draw millions of viewers to revel in the almost photographic representations of vegetables, flowers, fruit and game, often with the theme of the Vanitas – the symbolic tokens of the transience of human existence on Earth.

In flower arranging today creating compositions with flowers, fruit, vegetables and inanimate objects is simple yet effective. Objects can now form up to 50% visually in a still life (see *New Schedule Definitions* 9th edition 1996).

*A traditional still life, using grape (*Vitis vinifera *'Purpurea'), crimson glory vine (*Vitis coignetiae*) and* Ampelopsis *brevipendunculata* var. *maximowiczii syn.* A. *heterophylla with its wonderful berries, which range from deep violet through turquoise to the marble colour of the containers. Here the* Ampelopsis *richly deserves its common name of 'porcelain berry or vine'.*
ARRANGER: *DIANA HOLMAN.*

LONG-LASTING PLANT MATERIAL

Flowers have been pressed, dried with a desiccant, or simply hung up to dry from the earliest recorded times. The discovery of glycerine has introduced yet another method of preservation. And recent developments in the manufacture of silk and parchment flowers have produced natural-looking flowers that can be used alone or mixed with fresh or preserved plant material with impunity. Natural flowers that have been preserved must be considered as long-lasting and not ever-lasting. This is because the colours fade and the arrangements become tired and dusty.

Parallel designs arranged on a dresser.

PRESSED PLANT
MATERIAL

Alchemilla conjuncta, *sweet alyssum* (Lobularia maritima), *scarlet pimpernel* (Anagallis arvensis), *windflower* (Anemone blanda), *Queen Anne's lace/cow parsley* (Anthriscus sylvestris), *masterwort* (Astrantia major), *blazing star* (Mentizelia *sp. syn.* Bartonia), *daisy* (Bellis perennis), *cosmea* (Cosmos sulphureus), Crocus chrysanthus *'Cream Beauty'*, *delphinium* (Delphinium elatum), *larkspur* (Consolida ajacis *'Frosted Skies'*), *pink larkspur* (Consolida ajacis *'Giant Imperial'*), *blue larkspur* (Consolida ajacis), *meadowsweet* (Filipendula vulgaris), *lady's eardrops* (Fuchsia magellanica *'Alba'*), *snowdrop* (Galanthus nivalis), *bloody cranesbill* (Geranium sanguineum), Gaura lindheimeri, *ivy* (Hedera helix *'Glacier'*), *royal flower* (Heuchera sanguinea, Heucherella *'Bridget Bloom'*, Hypericum x inodorum *'Elstead'*), *loosestrife* (Lysimachia clethroides), *lobelia* (Lobelia erinus), *mallow* (Malva *'Ice Cool'*), *baby blue eyes* (Nemophila menziesii), *tobacco plant* (Nicotiana langsdorfii), *love-in-a-mist* (Nigella damascena), *field poppy* (Papaver rhoeas), *ivy-leaved geranium* (Pelargonium *sp.*), *Russian vine* (Fallopia *syn.* Polygonum baldschuanica), *shrubby cinquefoil* (Potentilla fruticosa), Potentilla nepalensis *'Miss Wilmott'*, *cowslip* (Primula veris), *purple cherry plum* (Prunus cerasifera *'Nigra'*), Tanacetum *'Silver Feather'*, *meadow buttercup* (Ranunculus acris), *lesser celandine* (Ranunculus ficaria), *dog rose* (Rosa canina), Rosa *'Eye Paint'*, Rosa *'Red Blanket'*, Verbena hybrida, *speedwell* (Veronica spicata), *grape vine leaf* (Vitis vinifera), Viola *'Sorbet'* and *heartease* (Viola *'Tricolor'*).

Flowers lose their form, but not their shape, when pressed. They are ideal for making into cards and pictures of many different kinds. These can range in complexity from a single study of one flower to detailed landscape scenes.

It is extremely easy to press flowers and you do not need a flower press – simply an old telephone directory (see Technique 18 on page 103 for the method).

Colour

The colour of plant material can change with the pressing process. The following information reveals the changes that may occur.

• Some white flowers remain true, while others turn deep cream. It usually depends on the purity of white in the flower, when fresh. If there is any moisture on the flower when it is pressed, it is likely to turn brown.
• Yellow flowers usually remain true.
• Bright blue flowers retain their colour well.
• Silver foliage is excellent.
• Pinks are generally good, but a very pale colour may brown.
• Reds can darken.

Making Cards

Making pressed-flower cards is immensely satisfying. They are inexpensive, easy to produce and it is unlikely that the recipient will ever want to throw them away! The secret to immediate success is to keep the card simple and small. Do not rush into trying to press large wedding bouquets behind glass. Start with a single perfect flower or leaf. Progress to a card that is a collage of pressed material. This is wonderfully stimulating to create, and you will find that your enthusiasm for the craft will lead you into creating pressed-flower pictures of greater complexity, place mats, paper weights, jewellry, boxes and even fire screens.

Stylish and original cards can be made by adding a few brush strokes, some embroidery or tapestry stitches, or by incorporating tissue paper or hand-made paper. Here are some guidelines:

1. Collect only the best flower specimens for your cards. Their colour will be richest just after the petals have unfurled. Pick on a dry day – a sunny afternoon, when the dew has evaporated, is best.

On the right is the pressed boss of a daisy on a background of different layers of tissue paper. The garland is composed of sunflower (Helianthus) *heads, bundles of cinnamon* (Cinnamomum zeylanicum) *sticks, dried chilli peppers* (Capsicum annuum acuminatum) *and bay leaves* (Laurus nobilis) *threaded onto a strong length of wire.*

2. For the card itself, fold a piece of deckel-edged writing paper or a piece of hand-crafted paper in two. Hand-crafted paper can be torn to size by defining the size on a larger sheet with a paint brush and water. Tear whilst the paper is still wet. Alternatively, buy special cards from a craft shop or mail-order company.

3. Play around with the design in a draught-free environment until you are satisfied. Three easy methods of creating cards are:

a) If you are using hand-made or interesting paper, you can simply place a smaller piece of a different-coloured paper onto the card and then glue a single leaf or flower, or even a thin slice of dried fruit, onto this. Gold foil, sweet papers, scraps of photocopied old manuscripts and frayed strips of fabric could also be used.

b) Cut out a square frame from the card and machine-stitch two pieces of light muslin with a zigzag stitch either side of the cut-out, fixing the leaf, fruit or flower inside the two layers of muslin with a dab of glue. This simple formula produces magical cards.

c) Press larger leaves to cover your card completely. These can be cut into smaller areas if necessary. Start with your background and then add the detailing. Round, focal flowers, such as roses, pansies, *Nigella* and *Astrantia*, are ideal for this type of collage. You can place finer, branching plant material over these to create depth and interest without obscuring the beauty of the flowers.

4. Use a glue that will dry clear. A latex adhesive is ideal and you can use a cocktail stick to put dabs of it on the back of your flowers. Place the glue, if possible, on thicker parts of the plant material, such as the central boss of a daisy or the stem.

5. Use tweezers to place and move your plant material. Use a soft painting brush to smooth out any petals.

6. Protect the finished design with special clear, self-adhesive covering film, cut to fit. This can be purchased from large stationers.

7. If you do not have an appropriate envelope, take a suitably sized envelope, dismantle and use this as a template. Cut this out of the same paper you have used for the card and glue together. Use sealing wax to seal the envelope.

The card on the left is made from a skeletonized ivy leaf. Glue has been applied sparingly and the n sprinkled with gold powder and glitter. The leaf was then mounted on a three-page card, using blue flock paper, and carefully bordered with fine jap gold.
ARRANGER: LIZ DEWEY.

HANG-DRIED PLANT MATERIAL

HANG-DRYING IS THE MOST COMMON METHOD of preserving plant material. It is extremely easy to get good results this way and is suitable for a wide range of plant material. Material dried by this method is ideal for creating dried flower arrangements, swags and floral rings.

Round Plant Material
Artichoke (Cynara scolymus), *Love-in-a-mist* (Nigella damascena) *(above)*, *safflower* (Carthamus tinctorius), *alpine thistle* (Carlina acaulis), *rose* (Rosa), *poppy* (Papaver), *seedheads, hydrangea, sunflowers, globe thistle* (Echinops), *peonies* (Paeonia), *strawflower* (Helichrysum) *(in left*

Line Plant Material

Wheat (Triticum), lavender (Lavendula), oats (Avena), larkspur (Consolida),
reed grass/canary grass (Phalaris), Love-lies-bleeding (Amaranthus), gayfeather (Liatris).

Branching Plant Material

Sea lavender (Limonium) (in left corner), honesty (Lunaria), golden rod (Solidago),
winged statice (Limonium sinuatum), lady's mantle (Alchemilla mollis), baby's breath
(Gypsophila), linseed (Linum usitatissimum), marjoram (Origanum), lonas (Nigella
orientalis).

The secret to successful drying is to pick and choose flowers and foliage that are at
the right stage of development and to dry them under optimum conditions, so that
the process is carried out in the minimum possible time. This will mean that the
colours remain truest and the flowers do not soon drop. The following guidelines
should help you.

METHOD FOR DRYING

The technique for hang-drying plant material is explained on page 103, but here are a few extra tips:

1. Hang the material out of direct sunlight, as this will bleach the colour from the plant material.

2. Colours that remain truest are those that are closest in colour to the pure hue, when fresh (for example, bright red roses, blue delphiniums, yellow sunflowers). Dark-coloured flowers will dry darker and pale-coloured flowers will usually dry paler.

3. Foliage such as *Eucalyptus*, *Magnolia grandiflora*, box (*Buxus*), cherry laurel (*Prunus laurocerasus*) and *Camellia* will all dry well, keeping a healthy green colour for some time. Culinary herbs, such as rosemary and sage, dry well but become very brittle, so they are easily damaged. For this reason it is probably better to dry these yourself rather than buy them already dried.

4. Flowers with woody stems, such as poppy seedheads and hydrangeas, will dry if left upright in a jar or vase, rather than hung upside-down. Place hydrangea stems in a little water so that the drying process takes place more slowly, resulting in a smoother texture. Hydrangeas should be picked for drying when their colour has changed to a more subtle tone, just before the first heavy frosts.

5. Experiment with all the flowers to which you have access. You will have some failures but you will learn a lot and be delighted with most of your efforts. Perhaps the least successful dried material is that which had a volumetric form, such as lilies, tulips and daffodils, although the small-trumpeted *Narcissus* 'Tête-à-Tête' dries remarkably successfully.

6. All dried flowers will eventually fade. Strong light causes more rapid fading. It is obvious that dried flowers will last longer than fresh flowers, but do remember that they will need revamping or changing at least once at year to keep good colour in your arrangement. Sunflowers, larkspur, delphinium, yellow *Achillea*, strawflowers and winged statice keep their strong colour extremely well.

7. If you need the hanging area for more flowers once the plant material is dry, store it in boxes containing a little desiccant, for this will combat any moisture in the atmosphere that may cause the plant material to become limp or mildewed. Store the boxes in a dry place. Some plant material, such as peony (*Paeonia*), is particularly susceptible to moth infestation. Take the necessary precautions against moths or check your boxes on a regular basis.

*A wreath of silk and parchment roses mixed with artificial plums, moss and dried poppy (*Papaver*) seedheads.*

ARRANGING DRIED PLANT MATERIAL

To arrange dried flowers consider the following:

- Do not underestimate the amount of dried flowers you will require. Arrangements can be deceptive in the amount of material they require to look effective. This is because there is frequently less foliage to bulk out the designs, not all foliage being suitable for this method of preservation.
- For those of you wishing to purchase flowers for traditional arrangements, you will need a variety of different forms. For traditional designs incorporating space you will need at least one or two varieties of each. For parallel designs you may need only one form, such as the linear form of lavender or wheat.
- To increase the size of a multi-petalled flower, such as a rose or peony, hold the head in the steam of a kettle for 30-60 seconds.
- Arranging dried flowers makes a mess. Put a tablecloth or sheet on the floor or resign yourself to clearing up afterwards.
- For the majority of plant material it is the heads of the flowers that provide the volume. The leaves shrivel and often drop and you are left with bare stems, which can be difficult to disguise if the stems are left long. Therefore, if you have limited plant material or for your first attempt, keep your arrangement small.
- Naturally preserved glycerined foliage, or pressed ferns and bracken (*Pteridium aquilinum*), is ideal for creating the skeleton of your larger designs.
- When flowers dry, their texture coarsens and becomes fussier. This is fine when you are working with only one flower, but when you are mixing your flowers you need the complement of a smoother texture in every design. This can be found in exotic plant material like poppy seedheads, in Chinese lantern (*Physalis alkekengi* var. *franchetii*), *Nigella orientalis* and cinnamon sticks. Non-plant material, such as terracotta pots, can also provide this smooth texture.
- If stems are delicate or broken, if there is little space to insert them into the design or if you wish to bunch them together for greater impact, you will need to wire the flowers in bunches. See Technique 10 on page 99, on single- and double-leg mounts.

With a few pointers it is possible to re-create any design that you see and admire, incorporating your personal touches.

METHOD

Parallel Designs

If you use dried flowers in a massed parallel design it is very easy to achieve a professional effect. This design is an excellent way to start working with dried flowers and building up confidence.

1. Choose your container – it could be a basket or terracotta pot. A basket can have side handles but avoid choosing one with a central handle. Place foam in the container so that it fills most of the interior and rises to just level with the rim.
2. You will need several bunches of wheat or lavender. Place one stem in the foam to establish the right height – usually about one and a half times the height of the container. Cut all the other stems to the same height and place them upright, en masse, in the foam to create a block of form and colour.
3. Finish the design by pinning a little moss round the base of the stems to hide the foam and/or by adding a ring or line of roses, as in the photograph opposite. You could also tie raffia or ribbon around the container.

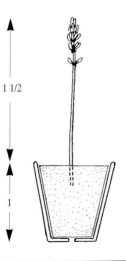

1 1/2

1

Traditional Designs

Traditional designs follow much the same criteria as for fresh flower arranging but differ in the following respects.

For traditional arrangements incorporating space you need a variety of different forms. Three different forms of dried plant material can be loosely categorized. Refer to the border on page 156–7 and you will see that the artichoke (centre top), and the flowers that continue up to the peonies, have a round form. The wheat around the love-lies-bleeding has a linear form. The remainder of the plant material has a branching or spray form. For traditional designs that radiate from a central area you need at least one or two varieties of each form.

- In fresh designs, foliage covers the foam easily. If you do not have preserved foliage, cover the foam with moss before you start. Use sphagnum moss, where most of it will be hidden, or reindeer moss (*Cladonia rangiferina*) where more will be exposed, and fix in place with wire hairpins.
- Just as in traditional fresh designs, radiate all your stems from the central area of foam.
- Be aware that your plant material should be approximately one and a half times the height or width of the container – whichever is the greater – or one and a half times the volume of the container.

DESICCATED
PLANT MATERIAL

THE FOLLOWING HAVE ALL BEEN DESICCATED in Flower Dry. The timings for desiccating in silica gel or borax may be slightly different.

From top left, clockwise:
*Orchid (*Phalaenopsis *sp.) – 4 days*
*Ivy leaf(*Hedera helix *'Adam') – 2 minutes on high in the microwave or 3 days*
*Singapore orchid (*Dendrobium *sp.) – 7 days*
*Orchid (*Cymbidium *sp.) – 2 minutes on high in the microwave and then transfer to desiccant*
*Boston ivy (*Parthenocissus tricuspidata*) – 2 minutes on high or 3 days*
Freesia sp. – 5 days for a spray with buds

Sage (Salvia officinalis 'Purpurascens') – 2 minutes on high or 3 days
Passion flower (Passiflora caerulea) – 3 to 4 days
Ladder fern (Nephrolepsis cordifolia) – 2 minutes on high or 3 days
China aster (Callistephus chinensis) – 5 days
Spray carnation (Dianthus sp.) – 3 days
Rose (Rosa cv.) 4–5 days
Hellebore (Helleborus sp.) – 3 days
Peony (Paeonia sp.) – 5 days
Oak (Quercus sp.) – for a spray 3 minutes on high, or 4 days
Marguerite (Argyranthemum sp.) – 4 days
Stargazer lily (Lilium 'Star Gazer') – 4–5 days
Granny's bonnet foliage (Aquilegia sp.) – 2 minutes on high, or 3 days
Tulip (Tulipa sp.) – 4 days
Carnation – 3 days
Rose – as above
Wisteria sp. – 4 days
Carnations – as above

If you use a desiccant you preserve your plant material by dehydration. It was the ancient Egyptians who were among the first to discover that plant material could be preserved, by immersing it in sand. Today sand is rarely used, as other materials are quicker and probably more effective. If you use sand, ensure that it is scrupulously clean. Desiccation by sand usually takes longer than using silica gel, clay pellets (Flower Dry) or borax.

Preserving with a desiccant is particularly suitable for volumetric flowers, when you wish to keep their form and colour. Desiccated flowers can then be made into arrangements, jewellry,

used to create a cone or picture. It is important to remember that desiccated flowers retain their shape because all their moisture has been removed. But moisture can quickly be re-absorbed by the desiccated plant material, which would destroy the form you have carefully preserved. You must spray with a sealant to prevent the re-absorption of moisture and keep the finished item or arrangement under airtight glass. Sealant can be obtained from an art shop, from Flora Products or from Moira Clinch (see address on page 306). Ensure that any desiccant you have used is dried out before re-use.

A simple hanging arrangement of poppy seedheads,
wheat, grasses and Eucalyptus.
ARRANGER: SALLY HART.

I am going to mention in detail here two desiccants that I believe are reliable and not too difficult to find. The first is silica gel. The plant material decorating the wooden church window in the photograph below has been preserved in silica gel, which is available from many chemists or from Flora Products. If buying from the chemist, ensure that the grain of the gel is small and fine.

The plant material on pages 160–1 has all been preserved in Flower Dry, which is composed of small clay pellets which, like silica gel, absorb the moisture from the plant material. Flower Dry is available from many garden centres and specialist shops. Alternatively it may be purchased directly from Moira Clinch – distance is no problem in supplying this form of desiccant.

Follow the technique on page 102–3 for successful results.

Colours

Strong reds, yellows, oranges and purples retain their colours well, though they can darken slightly. Pale colours are not quite as reliable. Once your plant material has been preserved, keep it out of strong sunlight and prevent moisture re-entering it by spraying with a special sealant designed to prevent this occurring.

Preserving with a Microwave

For those of you with a microwave, preservation with a desiccant becomes even simpler. Remember – do not wire any plant material and make sure you remove the stamens from lilies.

With silica gel:

1. Aim to reach a temperature of 60-70°C (140-60°F). Depending on the microwave, this will take between one and a half and two minutes for approximately 500 g (1.1 lb) of desiccant. Once the microwave has been used it will hold residual heat and consequent heatings will take less time. Check the temperature with a meat thermometer.
2. Allow the desiccant to cool to 40° C (104° F) or lower, before you remove the plant material from the desiccant. Fleshy or large items of plant material should be left in the desiccant for several hours in a warm place.

With Flower Dry:

1. Place a layer of Flower Dry in a pottery or Pyrex bowl. Place your plant material on this and cover it with more Flower Dry. Do not place a lid on the container.
2. Place in a 650 microwave on high for two minutes. If your microwave is more powerful, adjust the timing accordingly.
3. If the plant material is not completely preserved, leave in the desiccant until cool.
4. Foliage is preserved particularly well, with good colour retention.

Whichever desiccant you choose to use, remember to keep the desiccated plant material out of strong sunlight and to spray with a sealant. Keep sealed either in a box, a tin or behind glass.

Dried, pressed and glycerined foliage in a cream vase.

A simple church window enhanced with the addition of beautifully preserved plant material. The plant material includes flossflower (Ageratum), montbretia (Crocosmia), coral flower (Heuchera sanguinea), rose (Rosa cv.), golden rod (Solidago), marigold (Tagetes), Euphorbia and grape (Vitis vinifera 'Purpurea').
ARRANGER: ANNE BLUNT.

GLYCERINED
PLANT MATERIAL

From top left, clockwise;
*Beech (*Fagus sylvatica*), cider gum (*Eucalyptus gunnii*), New Zealand
flax (*Phormium tenax*), maple (*Acer palmatum*), Alexandrian laurel
(*Danae racemosa*), Escallonia, strawberry tree (*Arbutus unedo*),
lady's mantle (*Alchemilla mollis*), juniper (*Juniperus sp.*),*

*mexican orange blossom (*Choisya ternata*), *camellia* (Camellia sp.),
Elaeagnus pungens 'maculata', *bracken (*Pteridium aquilinum*),
Pittosporum sp., *cherry laurel (*Prunus laurocerasus*),
*flowering currant (*Ribes sanguineum*), *tree ivy (*Hedera helix*),
*Japanese spindle (*Euonymus japonica 'Aureopictus'*), *date palm*
(*Phoenix dactylifera*), *yew (*Taxus baccata*), Fatshedera lizei,
*Italian buckthorn (*Rhamnus alaternus 'Argenteovariegata'*),
Magnolia grandiflora, *silver-margined holly (*Ilex aquifolium 'Argenta
marginata'*), Mahonia xmedia 'Charity'.

*A collage of Vincent Van Gogh, made from glycerined bird-of-paradise flower (*Strelitzia reginae)*, lily-of-the-valley (*Convallana majalis) *and plantain lily (*Hosta*) leaves, with assorted seeds and bleached dried leaves,* ARRANGER: MARY GWYTHER.

The great advantage of preserving foliage in glycerine or anti-freeze is that it becomes flexible, water-resistant and can last a lifetime. Another advantage is that the textural surface of the leaf is unchanged, therefore giving a smooth texture, which gives greater volume and a delightful contrast to the busier, more intricate texture of hang-dried plant material. One part glycerine is mixed with two parts boiling water and thoroughly stirred. The mixture is allowed to cool before the stem ends are inserted. For further information refer to page 102.

Glycerined material looks lovely mixed with dried and silk flowers, or used on its own to create designs in a colour range from creamy white, browns, blacks and dark greens. Viscous glycerine takes the place of water in the cell structure. It is first mixed with water to enable its uptake into the stems.

Suitable Plant Material

This method of preservation is much more suitable for foliage than for flowers, because foliage is stronger and the inevitable change of colour is more suited to green leaves than colourful flowers. Foliage that is particularly suitable includes smooth-textured leaves, long-lasting evergreens and, perhaps best of all, beech, tree ivy and eucalyptus. Heather is one of the few flowers that takes up the glycerine solution without changing the colour of its flowers.

The plant material will change colour – slightly or dramatically, depending on the type of foliage you are preserving – and all colours will be more subdued than their fresh counterparts. If you wish to add colour you should include the requisite amount of dye in the solution. Special dyes are sold by Carters of Blackburn (for address see page 306). Full details on how to use their dyes are included. Glycerine may be purchased from most chemists. Buying the largest available container represents the best value.

The stems of two bunches of glycerined eucalyptus, dried flowers and seedheads and a few artificial flowers and berries have been crossed, and the join hidden by a sumptuous wired ribbon bow. ARRANGER: SALLY HART.

Try glycerining fresh plant material in wet foam to which the glycerined mixture has been added. Keep topping up with this mixture until the plant material is preserved. And if you do not have the time or patience to carry out this process yourself, you can now buy preserved plant material that has been commercially glycerined and dyed. The range of plant material preserved by companies such as Verdissimo is vast and includes ferns, conifers, statice (*Limonium*), lavender (*Lavendula*) and safflower (*Carthamus*).

There is also a brand-new range of preserved foliage created by Scottish Everlasting, who have discovered the process that stabilizes chlorophyll. No dyes are used, but the foliage retains its colour and flexibility. It will last for about one year. This product will be appearing under various names, one of which is 'Grandeur'. The photograph below shows a variety of foliage preserved in this way.

An arrangement of mixed foliage preserved without the use of dye by Scottish Everlasting, together with roses preserved in desiccant by African Everose. This arrangement should last at least a year if kept out of direct sunlight.

ARTIFICIAL PLANT MATERIAL

Different Types of Artificial Plant Material:

Foliage

Artificial foliage can vary in quality. Often matt, rather than shiny, foliage is reproduced most effectively (for example Eucalyptus, rather than Camellia). Sprays or picks of large leaves can be taken apart and used individually.

Polyester silk flowers

The vast majority of 'silk' flowers are in fact made from polyester blends. Good-quality 'silk' flowers are extremely realistic, and in some cases almost indistinguishable from their natural counterpart.

Parchment flowers

These are created from natural fibres matted onto paper sheet, dried and bleached in the sun. They are hand-painted and then twisted and shaped. They are particularly effective when decorating hats.

Fruits and berries

These give the bold form and smooth texture often needed in arrangements. They can be used on the stem or split into individual units.

Dried-look flowers ('Dry Image')

A different finishing process produces flowers that bear more of a resemblance to dried than fresh flowers. They are therefore extremely suitable for mixing with dried flowers, to give added bulk and focal interest.

Plastic flowers

These are great fun and, if imitating flowers that are naturally waxy, such as Anthurium, Strelitzia and Tulipa, can be amazingly realistic.

A swag of 'silk' hydrangeas, roses and Ranunculus, with artificial plums and apples.

TIPS FOR ARRANGING ARTIFICIAL PLANT MATERIAL

ARTIFICIAL FLOWERS HAVE COME A LONG WAY in the last few years. Some appear so naturalistic that, if used with flair and style, they can be almost indistinguishable from the real thing.

- When you start to arrange artificial flowers you have to make a certain investment. One or two flowers in a vase is not particularly effective. You are probably better off buying seven to ten of the same variety and massing them in an arrangement, or mixing them with dried or fresh flowers and foliage. Then you can add to the display or to your collection by buying other varieties.
- Artificial flowers look wonderful mixed with fresh foliage. In the garland on page 172 silk sunflowers have been mixed with a few fresh sunflowers (*Helianthus*) in a wreath of fresh cherry laurel (*Prunus laurocerarus*). For churches, use silk flowers to make the budget go further. Artificial flowers are useful whenever the fresh alternative would prove costly or short-lived. Consider using poppies in November, or Christmas roses in December.
- Decorating hats is extremely satisfying. It is simple yet effective. Sew a few flowers, with short stems, onto a plain hat so they are pleasingly grouped. See photograph on page 182.
- Dry Image polyester flowers are superb when mixed with dried flowers.
- If you wish to make swags or garlands, you will not need long stems. You could therefore purchase dry-look polyester flower heads on short wire stems which are less expensive.

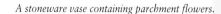

A stoneware vase containing parchment flowers.

A large, exuberant massed design of dried and silk flowers. Some of the hydrangeas are silk and others are dried.

SWAGS, WREATHS
AND GARLANDS

Here I mention some points that are particularly applicable to working with dried flowers and fruits.

- The plant material that you will be using requires only short stalks and is ideal for dried material with short or broken stems.
- Any item of material that is visually heavy must not be placed close to the outline of

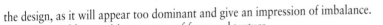

the design, as it will appear too dominant and give an impression of imbalance.

- Dried fruits add an exciting contrast of form and texture.
- Use moss to cover large areas quickly and easily, using German pins or hairpins of wire to keep it in place, especially for areas on the extremities, which need to look understated.
- Running a length of material or ribbon through the swag, garland or wreath will cover a large area quickly and inexpensively and create an exciting contrast of form and texture.
- Garlands need copious amounts of dried plant material. If you wish to make a full, generous garland of plant material ensure that you have a big budget or a good supply of bold-headed plant material from the garden such as hydrangeas, peonies or Achillea, and consider adding some silk or Dry Image flowers.

CELEBRATIONS AND FESTIVALS

Homes are decorated with flowers for many weeks of the year, but there are occasions when flowers have a special significance, symbolism or are displayed to add traditional festivity. Flowers have always been an important part of many festivals throughout the world. We associate spring festivals with the gathering of blossoming boughs and the wearing of garlands, wreaths and circlets. Scattering flowers at the feet of heroes and nobility has long been an established custom. Flowers are also an essential part of many Hindu and Buddhist festivals. In this chapter some of our most well-known special days or events are described, with ideas about how to celebrate them florally.

Four terracotta pots filled with violets have been wired to a flower-filled basket.

CANDLEMAS

CANDLEMAS, ON 2 FEBRUARY, WAS TRADITIONALLY considered a day of great importance in the country year, for it was the day that marked the return of the sun. Pastorally, the name Candlemas derived from commemoration of the purification of the Blessed Virgin Mary. On their first visit to church after giving birth, mothers would carry a candle, which was blessed.

Candlemas is the day when snowdrops (Galanthus) are supposed to push their way up through the ground. Their association with this day is also due to the purity of their colour and form.

ST VALENTINE'S DAY

ST VALENTINE'S DAY IS STEEPED IN HISTORY and folklore. Many believe St Valentine to have been a Christian priest who was stoned to death on 14 February in the early days of Christianity. Claudius II had decreed marriage illegal for his soldiers, as it sapped their fighting strength, but Valentine performed marriage services clandestinely for the sake of true love. Another legend relates that on the night before he was martyred he restored the sight of the jailor's blind daughter and left her a farewell message 'From your Valentine'.

It was the Victorians who started the fashion for sending cards on this date. The Penny Post was introduced in 1840, and it was the decades following this that became the golden era of the Valentine card. Such cards were not always well-meaning, but today the custom has survived with the best possible sentiments.

Valentine's Day is one of the high points of the florists' calendar, as flowers are accepted as being a token of affection and love. Red roses were at one time considered the only flower to represent this occasion, but now a much wider selection of flowers is given. Red tulips are a popular gift, as are all other red flowers available at this time of year.

Flowers are more expensive during the run-up to Valentine's Day, as the increase in demand creates greater production costs. Take care when purchasing that flowers have not been held back too long in cold storage in order to keep them in bud. Such flowers will go over extremely quickly. Look for crisp green foliage and full flower buds.

A template of the heart-shaped wreath was made from the backing of a hard-backed envelope. This was then glued to the wreath. A thin layer of foam was glued onto the backing and 20 dried red roses positioned to repeat the heart shape. A wire or ribbon threaded through the top of the heart will enable it to be hung up.

A tied bunch of red and yellow parrot tulips, red roses, burgundy roses, anemones, Eucalyptus and fern has been wrapped in a square piece of cellophane. Before tying, water was poured into the cellophane through a small opening and then the square was tied up with raffia. Take care when adding the water that the stem ends remain in contact with the cellophane, by gripping the cellophane and stems tightly together. See Tied Bunches (page 142–3).

MOTHER'S DAY

THE IDEA OF HONOURING MOTHERHOOD is a long-established custom. Indeed, in ancient times the Greeks used to have a special three-day festival to honour Cybele, the mother of the Gods.

Traditionally in England servants were allowed one day's leave a year to visit their homes and the church of their birth. This became an established event, which took place on the fourth Sunday in Lent. On their way home the serving girls would gather flowers and leaves from the hedgerows to give to their mothers, and it is from these times that the tradition of giving flowers on Mothering Sunday has arisen.

In America, Anna Jarvis, after the death of her mother, wanted recognition for all mothers. She was able to convince the Government of the need for a special day, which was set up as the second Sunday in May. President Wilson urged all Americans to 'display the flag in their homes on this day as a public expression of our love and reverence for the mothers of our country'. To express this love Anna Jarvis chose the carnation as the flower to represent the day. White carnations are traditionally sent to the mother whose own mother is no longer living, and pink or red carnations are sent to a lady whose mother is still alive.

Flowers that are easily transported are ideal on this occasion. Baskets of flowers, tied bunches, flowers presented in cellophane, a few daffodils from the garden bunched with a few stems of *Skimmia* or conifer and tied with a yellow ribbon, are all a delightful present from a young child.

White carnations (Dianthus), America's flower for Mother's Day, arranged in a simple crescent to complement a figurine. ARRANGER: HEATHER MILLER.

A Mother's Day basket, arranged by Lucy Ryan, aged 6.

Another Mother's Day basket, arranged by Sally Ryan, aged 8.

MAY DAY

ACCORDING TO CELTIC CUSTOM, 1 May was the first day of summer and a day of great festivity. Traditionally long sprays of hawthorn (*Crataegus monogyna*) were gathered from the woods and used by the young people to decorate the church and village. Queen Anne's Lace (*Anthriscus sylvestris*), ox-eye daisies (*Leucanthemum vulgare*) and greenery were also used for decoration and for crowning the May Queen. In Elizabethan times the village youth danced round a maypole that was 'covered all over with flowers and herbs'.

At the turn of the century girls would decorate their dolls with wild flowers. They would then go 'May dolling' around the village, carrying their doll covered with a cloth. They would knock at doors and ask whether occupants would like to see the May doll, in return for which the children would receive sweets or a farthing.

*A glass bowl with lily-of-the-valley (*Convallaria majalis*). Flowering bulbs have been planted in John Innes no. 2 compost. The top of the compost has then been covered with moss. After flowering the bulbs can be returned to the garden. On the European continent there is a delightful custom of giving bunches of lily-of-the-valley on 1 May to celebrate Labour Day and to show friendship.*

EASTER

EASTER IS THE OLDEST CHRISTIAN OBSERVANCE after Sunday. Easter Sunday is a movable feast, which usually falls between the middle of March and the middle of April.

The word Easter is a derivative of Eostre – the Anglo-Saxon spring goddess – and is thus derived from pagan rituals. Some 3,500 years ago Egyptians made hot-cross buns, but then the cross represented the four phases of the moon. The Chinese started the custom of presenting eggs as a rite of spring and our tradition of giving chocolate eggs developed from this.

In the Christian faith Easter is the most important festival. On Good Friday, Christians remember the Crucifixion and, on the following Sunday, Christ's Resurrection from the dead. Flowers form an important part of Easter's celebration. In many churches flowers are reintroduced into the church after 40 days of absence during Lent. Lilies (*Lilium*) are much in evidence, for their symbolic association with this festival.

The return of spring brings hope and joy to many at this time, at the moment of nature's rebirth. Daffodils (*Narcissus*) and other spring flowers are inexpensive at this time of year and a large bunch in a glass vase needs no other embellishment. Do remember that daffodils emit a poisonous sap from their stems, so do not mix them with other flowers unless they have first been on their own for 24 hours, and remember not to re-cut the stems.

This is a quick and easy way to display narcissi. Group several bunches in the hand. Take an elastic band up to just below the flower heads and cut the stems level. Impale the stems on a pinholder and wrap an iris leaf around the stems, inserting the end of the leaf through a slit in the leaf.

*In a typically Scandinavian arrangement an assortment of hand-blown eggs, decorated by children with acrylic paint, and yellow and white feathers are hung from branches of birch (*Betula*).*

*A stunning array of Easter lilies (*Lilium longiflorum*) and Singapore orchids (*Dendrobium*) on a chimney piece, created simply and easily by filling three long trays with foam to cover the length of the mantelpiece. Church candles have been secured in place (see page 97) and assorted long-lasting evergreen used to cover the mechanics and to sweep down the sides of the fireplace. An arrangement like this is in keeping with the more reflective side of Easter.*

THE SUMMER SEASON

IN ENGLAND, JUNE AND JULY are the hat season – for Royal Ascot and the Henley regatta hats are a must.

Ascot is perhaps the most famous event in the world for the wearing of hats. In the Royal Enclosure, to which entry is permitted only to ticket-holders who have been nominated and seconded by members, the wearing of hats, skirts (as opposed to trousers) and covered shoulders are compulsory. But it is not only in the Royal Enclosure that hats abound. Ascot is the occasion where size and outrageous daring win the day. It is an occasion where anything goes!

Henley is the more informal of the two occasions. Along with the Oxford and Cambridge boat race, this represents the height of the British rowing season, when teams from all over the world congregate at Henley-on-Thames to pit their prowess against the best. Hats and dress are informally smart.

Katherine Parsons, Jane Blacklock and Sophie Sutcliff wearing straw hats embellished with a few parchment flowers.

HARVEST FESTIVAL

GIVING THANKS FOR THE SAFE GATHERING of the harvest is one of the oldest celebrations, particularly enjoyed by country people throughout the world, whatever their religion. In many parts of England this custom is often called the Harvest-Home. During the final act of gathering in the harvest, which traditionally took place sometime during September or October, depending on the weather, there was a ceremonial cutting of the last sheaf of corn. The farm workers believed that the Corn Spirit was driven back and took refuge in this last sheaf. Part of the sheaf was then taken and used to weave a corn dolly, in which it was believed the Corn Spirit would reside. In the evening there would be a harvest supper, often held in a large barn so that all the workers could attend. The barn would be decorated with corn, flowers and foliage and a splendid supper would be supplied by the farmer to show thanks for all the hard work. In many parts of England the corn dolly would be kept in a safe place until the sowing of the seed the following year, when it would also be sown, to ensure a successful harvest.

Thanksgiving celebrations take place all over America on the fourth Thursday in November. This is in appreciation of the first successful harvest gathered by the newly arrived settlers in New England. They were helped in the planting and the reaping of

*A dish containing foam is placed within a circular wreath. Hydrangeas, blackberries (*Rubus fruticosus agg.*), rosehips and the turning leaves of the Boston ivy (*Parthenocissus tricuspidata*) are massed together in autumnal abundance.*

*An unfired, rolled clay pot is filled with nasturtiums (*Tropaeolum*), tobacco plants (*Nicotiana*),
lady's mantle (*Alchemilla mollis*) and other gleanings from the garden.*
ARRANGER: MARGARET OPPÉ.

their corn by the Indians, who were invited to join in the three-day festival of thanksgiving. The tradition has endured over the centuries and in 1863 President Lincoln pro-
claimed Thanksgiving Day a great national holiday for all. In Canada harvest or
Thanksgiving takes place on the second monday of October and flowers are an important
part of the festive feast. Long-lasting vegetables such as squash, marrow, pumpkin, car-
rots and turnips are celebrated before being put away for food during the harsh winter.

This is an ideal time to combine flowers with fruit and vegetables. Although ripening
fruit does give off ethylene gas, which shortens the life of cut flowers, there is an affinity between them that is hard to beat. Cocktail, kebab sticks or special flower arranger's
plastic picks can be impaled onto the fruit, which is then inserted into the foam. Blue-
black aubergines, red, orange and green peppers and yellow bananas (*Musa*) give a
smooth texture and strong form. Crinkly-leaved cabbages (*Brassica oleracea*), prickly
pineapples (*Ananas*), ridged melons (*Cucumis mela*) can all be used to create exciting
contrasts.

This is the time of year when the turning colours of the leaves remind us of the cycle
and pattern of life. The green leaves change to brown, through a myriad of different yellows, reds and oranges. Before they turn this final colour they can be enjoyed in mixed
arrangements, where they will last up to a week, depending on their development.
Leaves of the Boston ivy (*Parthenocissus tricuspidata*) are particularly effective, as are
those of members of the maple (*Acer*) family.

Many plants have a second flowering at this time of year to give rich and varied
colours in the garden and hedgerow. They can be successfully combined with hips and
haws, seedheads, nuts, cones and foliage, in all its autumnal glory, to display the boun-
tiful abundance of Harvest-Home.

*A natural preserved maple leaf collected
in the autumn in the Canadian woods and
then handcrafted*
LOANED BY ANN MILLER

*A terracotta pot contains late garden roses,
berries, hips and leaves, showing the changing
colours of autumn*
ARRANGER: CYNTHIA WILLIS

HALLOWE'EN

HALLOWE'EN, OR THE EVE OF ALL HALLOWS (All Saints), occurs on 31 October. It is the night when supernatural forces are supposed to come forth, when spirits walk and witches fly. For many years good-natured fun and games have taken place on this night. In recent years trick-or-treating, an American custom, has also become commonplace in parts of Britain. Children dress up in spooky costumes and go from door to door, soliciting sweeties.

A fun idea at this time of year is to hollow out a pumpkin or turnip (*Brassica rapa*) and place a jam jar or vase inside, in which to place a tumbling mass of autumnal flowers. Such vegetables should last up to a week in a cool place.

Shining apples (*Malus sylvestris*), bright orange, black and red, are the symbols of Hallowe'en.

*An arrangement suitable for a buffet party or for display in a front window. The paper bats and pumpkin (*Cucurbita maxima*) give atmosphere to the design and are well incorporated to create overall unity.*
ARRANGER: ANN REID.

BONFIRE NIGHT

IN BRITAIN, 5 NOVEMBER IS THE DAY when bonfires are lit and fireworks are set off in gardens and on open land throughout the country. The tradition stems from 1605, when Guy Fawkes was captured minutes before setting light to a cache of gunpowder deep in the cellars of the Houses of Parliament, in an attempt to rid the country of James I. Guy Fawkes was tried, found guilty of treason and executed. Effigies are still placed at the top of bonfires and set on fire, to the loud accompaniment of rockets and fireworks.

For an arrangement for a party on this night you could choose plant material that simulates fire – think of red and orange dahlias and carnations. This is one of the few occasions when green foliage does not add to the impact and effect. Use autumnal tinted foliage, such as vine (*Vitis*), Boston ivy (*Parthenocissus tricuspidata*) or the last of the flowering currant (*Ribes sanguineum*). Alternatively, use glycerined or sprayed plant material. The illusion of smoke can be achieved with traveller's joy/old man's beard (*Clematis vitalba*) or pampas grass (*Cortaderia selloana*). Fireworks can be represented by dried exotics, bulrushes (*Typha*), onion (*Allium*) seedheads, gay feather (*Liatris*) and twisted cane.

An atmospheric arrangement for Bonfire Night.
ARRANGER: ANN PANNETT.

CHRISTMAS

CHRISTMAS IS PERHAPS THE ONLY TIME OF THE YEAR when the majority of homes and places of comradeship, business and worship are decorated with evergreens, cones and berries to add to the festive celebrations of this special time.

It was around AD 440 that 25 December was arbitrarily set as the day on which Christ was born. It was, however, established close to, or on, the day of the winter solstice or the shortest day – a time when the sun was at its lowest and pagan festivals were celebrated to ensure fertility in the coming year. Evergreens were used to decorate the home, for they represented the continuity of life, and their use has continued uninterrupted to the present day. The only exception came during the Civil War and Commonwealth, when evergreens were branded as pagan and even mince pies were forbidden, due to their supposed resemblance to cribs.Before the arrival of the Christmas tree in Queen Victoria's reign, evergreens were formed into circles, globes or wreaths and decorated with ribbons, apples and other fruits. Today Christmas is distinguished from the many other occasions celebrated with flowers by the use of certain colours and plant material accessories.

An arrangement to give festive cheer is positioned on a desk top. Fresh red roses and carnations are combined with silk poinsettias and foliage that includes Elaeagnus, Mahonia, ivy and looped New Zealand flax (Phormium tenax). ARRANGER: MARIE SLANN.

COLOUR

FOR TRADITIONAL CHRISTMAS DECORATION there is one colour scheme that never dates or goes out of fashion. Red and green, sometimes highlighted with a touch of gold or silver, are the colours of Christmas, whether composed of fresh, dried or artificial plant material.

Red and green are complementary colours, which show each other at their most vibrant and vital, and they are recognized as the Christmas colours in many parts of the world. They conjure up an image of berries against shiny holly (*Ilex*), the robin redbreast in the evergreen tree, the warmth of the fire – nature at its most comforting.

The combination of white and green is also widely used, the imagery being snow on the land and the purity of the Virgin birth. The colour combinations of blue and silver, orange and red, orange and silver, yellow and gold can also give pleasing colour schemes at this time of the year.

Three large cream candles have been placed in the centre of a wet-foam ring. The ring has been decorated with fresh Eucalyptus, chocolate Pittosporum (P. tenuifolium 'Tom Thumb'), creamy white roses (Rosa cv.) and finished with dried slices of orange (Citrus sinensis).

ACCESSORIES

THE SIMPLE ADDITION OF CANDLES, ribbon and a touch of glitter can alter the atmosphere of a favourite design that is on show the whole year round and give it seasonal sparkle.

Candles

Lit candles give off an aura of warmth and comfort. The gentle glow softens all it surrounds and adds to the mystery of Christmas. It goes without saying that candles should never be left burning and that care should always be taken that they do not burn too low.

Generally speaking, brightly coloured candles are more difficult to work with, as they can easily dominate the flowers. Shocking-pink, sunshine-yellow, Bristol-blue and orange candles can look startlingly effective, but if you are unsure then pastels, greens, creams and deep colours are a safer bet.

Candlelight is not kind to all colours – the softness of the light ignores blue and dark-coloured flowers, so that they disappear and their form becomes hard to distinguish. Candlelight is kinder to pastel and bright colours, so this might be a criterion when choosing your flowers for a candlelit dinner.

Festive topiary with mossed balls. ARRANGER: ILONA BARNEY.

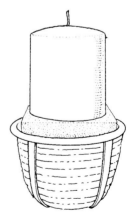

A large burgundy candle sits securely on foam and is surrounded by a mass of golden fruits and burgundy flowers.

Ribbon

Ribbon can complement and enhance many arrangements of flowers at this time of year. It is choosing the right ribbon for the right occasion that needs a little care. The addition of a wired tartan bow to an arrangement of green holly (*Ilex*) and red carnations (*Dianthus*), or of a golden ribbon to link with a gold candle, yellow roses and the bright variegated leaves of *Elaeagnus* or *Euonymus*, enhances the overall effect. Inexpensive polypropylene ribbon can be used in wreaths exposed to the elements, as it is waterproof. Single-faced, plush pile velvet in rich, deep red and green gives sumptuous bows. Gold and silver metallic ribbon created from paper or Lurex gives an exuberant lift. And paper and hessian bows are ideal when included in arrangements with a more rustic feel.

Paint and Glitter

Spray paint and glitter can be added to glycerined, fresh, dried or artificial plant material. Gold is universally popular and always looks festive. It can be purchased at Christmas time in many department stores and multiples, along with silver and glitter sprays. For other colours, car spray paints, available from any car accessory shop, are a good substitute. Place the objects to be sprayed in a deep cardboard box just big enough to contain the items in a single layer. Other objects to be sprayed can be placed on top of items already sprayed, so that any excess spray reinforces the first coat.

A 'Simply Garland' cage is the base for this hanging arrangement of fresh foliage and cock'scomb (Celosia), beautiful artificial open red roses from CI of Blackpool, ribbon and two festive bells.
ARRANGER: MARIE SLANN.

A topiary tree of preserved Eucalyptus, fruiting ivy and lotus (Nelumbo) seedheads, some of which have been sprayed gold. A square of fabric has been used to cover the plastic pot containing the tree.

Information on how to create bows is given on page 97.

FRESH PLANT MATERIAL

CHRISTMAS IS THE TIME OF YEAR WHEN EVERGREENS are of special importance. Many fresh evergreens provide not only a wonderful texture and background to berries, fruits and flowers but also an unforgettable fragrance.

All the conifers are useful. If you can, buy blue spruce (*Pinus pungens*) or noble pine (*Abies procera*). It might be relatively expensive in comparison with other conifers, but it will last right through the festive season, giving off a delicious fragrance, and it is thick and luxuriant. Deran Foliage in Wales (for their address see page 306) provides a mail-order service. Dark green conifer, Leyland cypress (*Cupressocyparis leylandii*), is inexpensive and available from most florists. Give it extra pep by adding sprigs of cream or yellow variegated conifer, such as *Thuja plicata* 'Zebrina'. These conifers are readily available from garden centres and grow reasonably quickly.

For flowers and foliage available at this time of year refer to the borders on pages 26–9.

Ivy, *Elaeagnus* and *Skimmia* with its bright berries are long-lasting and easy to grow. For other foliage available at this time of year refer to the border of evergreen plant material on page 30–1. Also refer to the borders of florist's flowers on pages 32–3.

A special flower available at this time of year is the long-lasting amaryllis (*Hippeastrum*). Just one or two creates a very special effect. Two are needed at different heights in a low dish for an instant arrangement.

Carnations, gerberas and anemones are also widely available in a multitude of colours, including a vibrant red.

*Conifer, pine (*Pinus*), variegated holly (*Ilex*), berried Skimmia and dried poppy (*Papaver*)
seedheads in an all-foliage Christmas arrangement.*

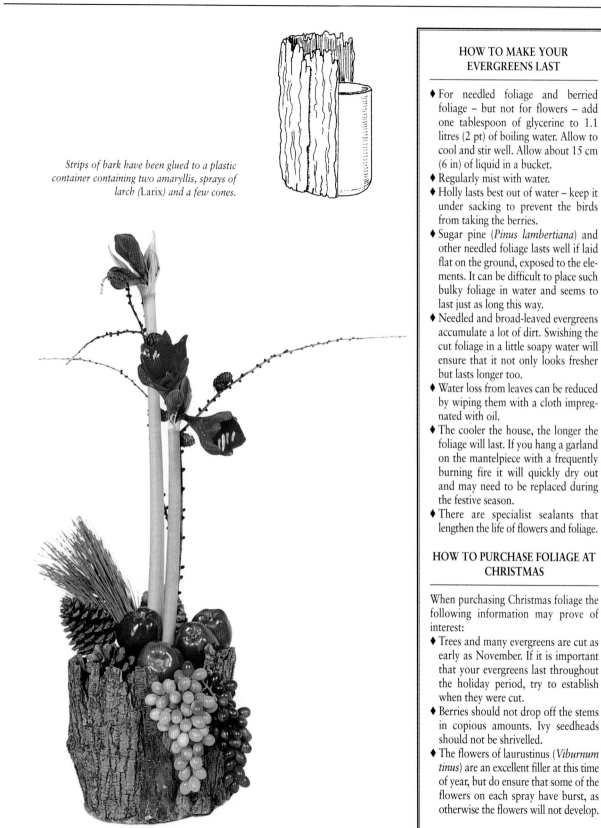

Strips of bark have been glued to a plastic container containing two amaryllis, sprays of larch (Larix) and a few cones.

HOW TO MAKE YOUR EVERGREENS LAST

- For needled foliage and berried foliage – but not for flowers – add one tablespoon of glycerine to 1.1 litres (2 pt) of boiling water. Allow to cool and stir well. Allow about 15 cm (6 in) of liquid in a bucket.
- Regularly mist with water.
- Holly lasts best out of water – keep it under sacking to prevent the birds from taking the berries.
- Sugar pine (*Pinus lambertiana*) and other needled foliage lasts well if laid flat on the ground, exposed to the elements. It can be difficult to place such bulky foliage in water and seems to last just as long this way.
- Needled and broad-leaved evergreens accumulate a lot of dirt. Swishing the cut foliage in a little soapy water will ensure that it not only looks fresher but lasts longer too.
- Water loss from leaves can be reduced by wiping them with a cloth impregnated with oil.
- The cooler the house, the longer the foliage will last. If you hang a garland on the mantelpiece with a frequently burning fire it will quickly dry out and may need to be replaced during the festive season.
- There are specialist sealants that lengthen the life of flowers and foliage.

HOW TO PURCHASE FOLIAGE AT CHRISTMAS

When purchasing Christmas foliage the following information may prove of interest:
- Trees and many evergreens are cut as early as November. If it is important that your evergreens last throughout the holiday period, try to establish when they were cut.
- Berries should not drop off the stems in copious amounts. Ivy seedheads should not be shrivelled.
- The flowers of laurustinus (*Viburnum tinus*) are an excellent filler at this time of year, but do ensure that some of the flowers on each spray have burst, as otherwise the flowers will not develop.

A Christmas cone of fresh foliage, artificial flowers and fruits gives a warm welcome in the entrance hall.
ARRANGER:
MARY FISHER.

DECORATIONS AROUND THE HOME

A MIXTURE OF FRESH, DRIED and artificial plant material is commonly used around the home at Christmas.

The Front Door

There are many ways of creating front-door hangings but perhaps the one most commonly seen is the circular ring or wreath. The basic wreath, constructed from green conifer or blue spruce (*Picea pungens*), may be purchased and decorated or it can be made at home, using a coat-hanger pulled into a circle onto which Sphagnum moss is bound. Fresh plant material is most commonly used for the front door, as it is actually refreshed by exposure to rain. See Technique 13 on page 100.

The Staircase

Garlands are ideal for the staircase. They can be twined round the banister or placed to one side, if it is a staircase that is viewed predominantly from one angle. Artificial garlands are very easy to use, and even the most basic can be made exciting by the addition of cones, artificial berries, ribbon or bunches of dried flowers (see Technique 14 on page 101).

Anemones in a range of colours have been added to this Christmas garland of noble fir and fresh foliage.
ARRANGERS: PEARL KNIGHT, MARIE SLANN AND JOAN WARD.

The Dining Room

The Christmas table can be decorated in many ways. Most of the arrangements in this chapter can be placed on the table – the cone, the circular wall hanging, a short length of garland along the length of the table, a terracotta pot containing a candle with a few Christmas roses (*Helleborus niger*), fresh or artificial. Ivy (*Hedera*) or Alexandrian laurel (*Danae racemosa*) can be trailed across the table or garlanding the corners, as for the wedding table on page 216.

A festive table centrepiece of fresh and artificial plant material.
ARRANGER: MARY FISHER.

The Kitchen

At Christmas time the kitchen is often a hive of activity, with little room for festive decoration. The decoration shown here is ideal – it is made in seconds simply by inserting a sprig of noble fir into the centre of an apple and tying a tartan ribbon around the base.

A short length of noble fir has been impaled in each of the apples and a length of tartan ribbon tied at the base.

The Hall

n the hall there is often little room for large arrangements. A hanging ring is ideal – it
can take the place of a painting during the festive season. It can be positioned at eye
evel and allows manoeuvrability where space is at a premium.

long-lasting wreath of ribbon, fruit, moss and dried plant material
ung on wooden panelling.
RRANGER: JENNIFER TOWERS.

The mantelpiece is ideal for a showy arrangement that takes only a small amount of plant material: candles, ribbon and evergreen foliage, with a few silk poinsettias for seasonal colour.
ARRANGER: MARIE SLANN

The Sitting Room

◁ *A mossed tree with a starfish.*

▽ *Sliced dried fruits threaded on gold thread and wrapped in a square of cellophane – an ideal gift for a flower-arranging friend.* ARRANGER: LOIS DENBURY.

LARGE-SCALE ARRANGING

Sometimes, as flower arrangers, we are invited to arrange the flowers for a very special occasion. This usually means working on a much larger scale than normal and perhaps entails enlisting extra help. Examples are civic occasions, charity balls, the opening of a new building, royal visits, school speech days, concerts, and of course weddings and church festivals.

With luck, one is given plenty of time in which to plan for the event, although on some occasions you may be given only a few days' notice. In either case, careful planning and organisation of time and materials are very important.

This design of polychromatic flowers arranged to evoke an atmosphere of the past would make a spectacular display in a foyer or on a stage for a grand occasion. The lower placements take the eye down to ground level and, because the lowest placement is a little to the back, this gives added depth. Notice how the different shapes of the flowers hold the attention, an outline of spiky larkspur (Consolida) and foxgloves (Digitalis) contrasting with the large roses at the centre of the design.
Arranger: Nikki Leadsom.

PREPARATION

A PRELIMINARY VISIT TO THE VENUE is a must. You need to find out what stands and containers are available to you. If these are not suitable, or unavailable, you will have to borrow or even have the mechanics specially made. The siting of displays is also of great importance. Arrangements need to be visible above people's heads, even when standing, if at all possible. This is where pedestals and columns come into play. A local wrought-iron worker may be able to make a larger-sized pedestal than normal. Alternatively, a handyman can make a stand to your specifications out of rigid cardboard tubes or piping from a builder's merchants, finished off with an attractive paint finish.

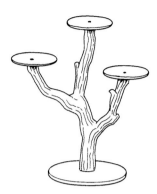

a

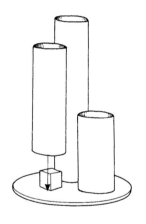

b

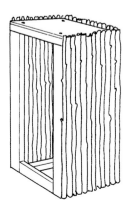

c

Wherever you decide to place an arrangement, it must never impede the proceedings of the event in question. Displays may start at ground level or from a few feet up. If working from the ground, consider carefully how much will be seen or hidden by a mass of people. If hidden, then such a design may be better placed in an entrance, where people attending the event will pass it and be able to appreciate it fully.

Sometimes organizers ask you to place flowers in a certain position to mask an unsightly object. This is rarely successful, and a far better option is to place the display in such a position that it draws the eye away from the eyesore and towards the flowers.

On an initial visit you need to find out where the water supply is and where the broom cupboard is located. This will give you a chance to get on the right side of the caretaker, which is no bad thing. He or she is likely to welcome a few leftover flowers!

Once you have decided where the arrangements are to be placed, that they are of a size in scale with both the building and the occasion, and in harmony with the design and decoration of the venue, you need to work out careful costings. Sometimes, albeit rarely, you will be given unlimited resources. On the other hand, many organizations work to very tight budgets and in these cases one has to be ingenious to create maximum effect at minimum cost.

This type of parallel design can be as long, or as short, as you wish. The length of this one is about 125 cm (4 ft 1 in). Containers sold for window-boxes may be suitable, or plastic troughs placed end to end. The tall, upright placements of flowers are balanced by the visually heavy grouping of flowers and foliage in the base, which is sometimes called groundwork or tapestry. When choosing flowers for this type of design, take care to choose a good variety of different forms: simple rounded forms, linear and trumpet forms – some double and some single.
ARRANGER: MICHAEL BOWYER.

CHOICE OF FLOWERS

IT IS WORTH BEARING IN MIND that at certain times of the year flower costs increase greatly – for example, at Easter, Mother's Day and Valentine's Day. As the flower world is international, events in other countries, such as Women's Day, May Day, can also affect their availability in your own country.

When budgets are tight, look around you to see what is plentiful. Devise displays in spring using masses of *Forsythia* which, when blooming, seems to be growing in every garden in every street. In summer dahlias are plentiful and large enough to put on a good show. Later in the year abundant supplies of golden rod (*Solidago*) could be employed mixed with Chinese lanterns (*Physalis alkekengi* var. *franchetii*). In late autumn Michaelmas daisies (*Aster novi-belgii*) and chrysanthemums (*Dendranthema*) are plentiful and inexpensive.

Colour will also play an important part in your choice of flowers and foliage. Companies, local councils and schools may have particular colours associated with them, which they may specifically ask you to include. Remember that receding colours, such as blue and violet, do not show up well from a distance and can look like 'black holes' in an arrangement. If you are expressly asked to use colours such as royal blue or deep purple, these should be arranged where they can be viewed at close quarters and where the lighting is good. Again, the entrance may well be a good position. If the location is particularly dim, then only flowers with high luminosity will show up well. These are the tones that have a lot of white in them, such as creams, pale yellows and pinks. A walk around the garden at twilight will enable you to pick these out.

Larger displays usually necessitate larger flowers. Suitable garden types would be peonies (*Paeonia*), hollyhocks (*Althaea*), delphiniums, foxgloves (*Digitalis*), larger roses (*Rosa* cv.), hydrangeas, rhododendrons and Bear's breeches (*Acanthus*). Even if garden supplies are plentiful, some flowers will probably have to be purchased. Larger flowers available all year round are lilies (*Lilium*) (which are always effective), painter's palettes (*Anthurium*), gerbera and sunflowers (*Helianthus*), whilst seasonal varieties include *Allium*, amaryllis (*Hippeastrum*), African lily (*Agapanthus*), sword lily (*Gladiolus*) and proteas. Flowers such as carnations and roses, which would assume the role of focal flowers in a smaller display, become filler flowers when used in large arrangements.

Once you have decided which flowers to use, the next step is to find out where they are available. Someone with a large garden may be more than willing for you to pick quantities of flowering trees, such as lilac (*Syringa*), mock orange (*Philadelphus*) and *Viburnum*, if you prune carefully and do not ruin the overall shape of the bush. Most people feel honoured that their material will be used at an important occasion.

If you are buying flowers in large quantities there are several options open to you – you can buy from your local florist or wholesaler, if you have access to one; flowers can be ordered over the telephone from suppliers at flower markets (like New Covent Garden) and dispatched to your nearest mainline railway station, or you may have a grower or market gardener nearby (this can be useful if buying a large quantity of one type of flower). You will also need to calculate when to pick up your order. Roses need to be collected one to three days beforehand, depending on the time of year. Easter lilies (*Lilium longiflorum*) may need up to a week or ten days before they are at their prime. And amaryllis can take nearly two weeks to open fully in the coldest months of the year. It is always best to let your blooms open up gradually, rather than trying to force them by the warmth of a fire.

Having obtained flowers and foliage, the next step is to condition everything very well indeed. Methods of conditioning various types of plant material are considered elsewhere in this book (see page 94). However, it is the scale of the operation that will differ slightly now. Where do you store – or even lay your hands on – upwards of 20 or 30 buckets? Supermarkets may not be able to cope with a specific large flower order, but most of their flower supplies arrive at the store packed into buckets, which are quite often simply thrown away – it is worth asking if they have any spare.

If you do not have the space in your home to store all the materials prior to the event, then the garage may be pressed into use. But beware: after a really cold night you could find that the water has frozen in the buckets, and on a very hot day the temperature inside a garage can become extremely intense. If space is a problem, you may be able to store materials at the venue itself.

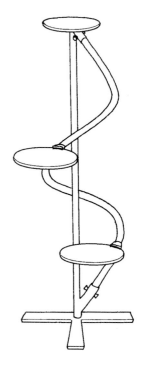

This design consists of three placements on a spiralled wrought-iron stand. The flowers are lilies (Lilium, 'Joy'), green bells of Ireland (Molucella laevis), pale pink Peruvian lily (alstroemeria), with yellow gerbera picking up the yellow in the dark blue Iris. Trails of ivy have been bound around the spiral to give it bulk and make it more prominent than the upright, central column. If well conditioned, the ivy will last well out of water for several days.
ARRANGER: MICHAEL BOWYER.

SETTING UP

TRANSPORTING EVERYTHING YOU REQUIRE is the next consideration. As well as mechanics and plant material, do not forget to pack some dustsheets, dustpan and brush, as well as your workbox and water sprayer. For a long stint of arranging, body and soul must be kept together and refreshments therefore need to be packed.

Check how easily all the containers, stands and flowers will fit into your vehicle. Will you need help, or perhaps need to make more than one journey?

If you are transporting flowers on a long journey in hot weather it is probably best if the plant material can travel in water. Standing buckets in boxes or plastic crates can prevent them toppling over. Some arrangers with access to a good handyman have special wooden frames made to fit their vehicles, into which buckets can then be placed. Some flowers, such as open lilies, are best transported upright at all times of the year, as their petals break easily when packed into boxes. When packing boxes, the best support for flowers is other flowers. Full boxes prevent them from rolling around. Line the boxes with thin polythene and mist gently before putting the lid on.

Foliage can be packed in dustbin liners, which can then be used at the end of the exercise for all the rubbish.

Even if you have decided to tackle all the arranging on your own, some assistance will probably be needed with fetching, carrying and removing the debris, if you are not allowed to leave it on the premises. Some thought should be given as to what will happen to all the arrangements once the function is over, and whose responsibility it will be to remove everything. Perhaps a local hospital or retirement home would enjoy having the displays to decorate their premises.

MARQUEES

STABILITY IS THE KEY TO ANY LARGE-SCALE ARRANGEMENT, but this is doubly true if you are ever asked to decorate a marquee, as the ground underfoot may well be turf or uneven paving slabs. You may even find that the site is sloping – gently or otherwise – which makes floor-standing designs out of the question. In addition to the usual table decorations, you might like to consider garlands or swags around the edges of the marquee, which prevents the designs from being jostled by the guests and puts them at, or above, eye level.

Hanging arrangements are also popular. Besides the hanging basket described on page 00, you could consider huge circlets of flowers arranged in garland cages, attached to a hoop either cut from plywood or made from iron and suspended by four ropes. The finished effect is like a floral chandelier.

Marquee poles lend themselves to other types of decoration. Do make enquiries beforehand, though, as some modern marquees are self-supporting and have no poles. Garlanding poles can be most effective. Work out how many stems of flowers and foliage you need for 30 cm (1 ft) and then multiply that figure by the total length of the garlands. Spray carnations really come into their own for this, because they can be cut down to individual heads, which will go a long way. For the technique of making garlands, refer to page 101. Do remember that the weight of a finished garland is considerable.

An alternative way of decorating poles is to use foam-filled cages (florettes), which are commercially available in three sizes. Three to four cages can be fixed around each pole well above head height. They can either be arranged in situ from a stepladder or made previously and then fixed in place. If you do arrange them prior to the event, remember that they will be looked at from below and should be arranged accordingly. Long trails of foliage and ribbon look good hanging down from the cages, with ribbon loops fixed into the tops.

When planning, find out if the marquee will be lined, and if so, with what. Unlined marquees, although not beautiful, are neutral in colour. Lined marquees can be really sumptuous and will set off your arrangements magnificently but do investigate the colour of the lining material. You may even be offered a choice. Ask whether the poles will be covered in the same material. If you can, ask to see a sample of the material to be used, as the contractor's idea of a suitable lining may not fit in with your floral ideas! Some modern rigid-frame marquees are constructed of a thick plasticized material, which is usually left unlined. Once again, beware. They sometimes come in a very bold white and deep blue stripe, against which only white and the strongest of yellows will stand out, and which requires a good backing of plain foliage.

Sometimes, when decorating a marquee, you are working against the clock, because the marquee may come into existence only hours before the event, which means that your planning will have to be all the more careful. This can be eased by befriending the contractors erecting the marquee, if you intend to hoist hanging decorations and attach items to the poles.

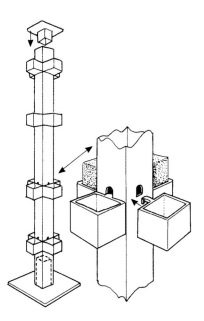

This four-placement arrangement on a specially made iron stand is composed of peach amaryllis and roses, white lilac and tuberose (Polianthes tuberosa) outlined with branches of yellow mimosa (Acacia) and the opening buds of Forsythia. The iron stand has been draped with pale green cotton, which gives a fuller, richer effect. This idea could also be adopted in a marquee, using the same fabric as the lining to create overall harmony. The iron stand is very versatile. The containers may be positioned for an all-round or front-facing design. If extra height is required, another section can be inserted into the top of the stand, and a flat top could also be inserted. Containers can also be placed at ground level, as in the photograph.

ARRANGER: MICHAEL BOWYER.

WEDDING AND ANNIVERSARY FLOWERS

FLOWERS ARE AN IMPORTANT PART of any wedding and the anniversaries that follow. Flowers and foliage can be selected to give added joy and happiness on these special days. They can also be themed, to celebrate china, gold, silver or ruby anniversaries.

Flowers decorating a lych-gate.
ARRANGERS: JOAN WARD AND EILEEN MILLIGAN.

WEDDING FLOWERS

FIRST OF ALL, THE WEDDING. Flowers for a wedding can be daunting for the flower arranger. It is wise to leave the intricate, specialized work of wired corsages, head-dresses and wedding bouquets to the professional florist and to concentrate on decorating the place of marriage and the reception room or marquee. If you are the bride's mother and not experienced in flower arranging, it may be best to leave the flowers in the hands of friends and fellow flower arrangers, as there are so many other things to concentrate on at this special time.

The smallest, quietest wedding or a morning-dress affair with a guest list of 1,000 will both be enhanced by flowers, but where do you start? One of the first things to consider is the date of the wedding. Only a few years ago flowers out of season could not readily be obtained. Now, with new technology and sophisticated glasshouses, virtually any flower can be acquired at any time of the year. In the floral world, daffodils can jostle for show in the flower market as early as November; chrysanthemums (*Dendranthema*) have been given a new name of AYR (all year round); and freesias and iris seem to 'go short' only occasionally. With notice, virtually any flower may be obtained, but this does not make it a good idea to have out-of-season flowers. Flowers in their natural season will be less expensive and probably stronger.

A bridesmaid's head-dress and posy. Wired head-dresses and bouquets are best left to a florist who is professionally trained in the intricate skill of wiring. If you do decide to attempt the bridal flowers yourself, use a 0.20 mm reel-wire for corsages and head-dresses and a 0.56 or 0.71 mm wire for the head-dress frames and wiring of rose buttonholes.
ARRANGER: VICTORIA HOOTON.

You need to meet and speak to the bride herself. You need to know if she is a 'I have just picked these flowers out of a field' person or a more traditional bride, who would appreciate a formal, hand-wired bouquet. The flowers should be designed to complement her dress, the venue and the bridesmaids' dresses.

Flowers are usually required for the place of marriage and for the reception. It is a good idea to visit both venues beforehand when they have been decorated for another wedding. Take account of the effectiveness of the placements and the colour scheme that has been used. It is perhaps where the marriage ceremony is taking place that flowers are most important. Guests always arrive early to a wedding and flowers are often studied in great depth. At the reception the guests will be talking and meeting people and will have less time to devote to the flowers.

*A traditional hand-wired bouquet for the bride of white Singapore orchids (*Dendrobium)*, roses (*Rosa 'Iceberg' and R. 'Tara'*), Eucalyptus *and Alexandrian laurel (*Danae racemosa*).*
ARRANGER: VICTORIA HOOTON.

Flowers decorating a font.
ARRANGER: MARY FISHER.

Flowers in a Place of Worship

If the wedding is to be held in a church it is important to make enquiries beforehand regarding the following (many of these points also apply to other places of worship):

1. Find out who is in charge of the flower rota, and whether there are any special procedures that must be followed.
2. Ask if it is possible to use outside flower arrangers. Some churches are delighted for this to happen while others depend on the income derived from providing this service to fund church flowers throughout the year. Find out if there is a flower-arranging room and what equipment is available. Ideally, you should be able to arrange the flowers in situ the day before the wedding. Do check that this will be possible.
3. During Lent and Advent many churches do not allow flowers to decorate the church. You may, however, be allowed to arrange flowers just before the ceremony, on the understanding that they are removed after the service.
4. Many churches understandably object to flowers being removed immediately after the ceremony and taken to the reception, leaving the church bare of flowers for the weekend. If the bride's budget will not run to decorating both place of worship and reception, it is perhaps better to use less expensive flowers or to have fewer arrangements.

Flowers decorating wooden panels at the inner entrance to the church.
ARRANGER: PHOEBE TOWERS.

5. Consider the colour of the altar cloth at the time of the wedding. An orange altar cloth would not be sympathetic with pink flowers. See if an alternative is available and permitted.

6. If possible, decorate the windowsills, as these bring colour from the front to the back of the building. Pew-ends present similar opportunities.

7. If the bride wants a wealth of flowers, ask the vicar, priest, verger, pandit or church flower arrangers if pillars and archways may be decorated. If so, ask whether small nails can be inserted into the fabric of the building if these are not already in position.

Perhaps the best place for flowers in a church would be:

• on a pedestal close to where the wedding service will take place (or on two pedestals, if budget allows)

• on two further pedestals each side of the aisle at the entrance to the building

• as pew-end hanging arrangements on alternate pews

• on the window ledges

• on an arch over the porch. Many churches have the mechanics for this and nails in position. This is a lovely place to have photographs taken.

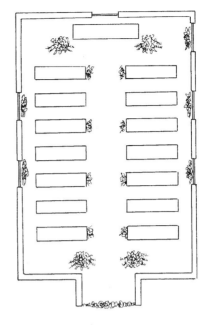

Decoration of the interior of a church for a country wedding.
ARRANGERS: JOAN WARD, MARY FISHER, PHOEBE TOWERS, EILEEN MILLIGAN, BARBIE THOMPSON, BETTY CORMACK.

Reception

Once the marriage ceremony is over, the bridal party and their guests make their way to the reception, which may take place in a hotel, hired hall, marquee or even on a boat. If there is to be a stand-up buffet, then pedestals need to be firmly secured. If the room will be crowded, they may best be avoided as an over-enthusiastic guest may well send one flying. Flowers are better positioned high up in the room, on a mantelpiece, for example.

It is a good idea to visit the venue first and see where flowers would be most effective. The following places are where flowers can best be appreciated:

• Long, low arrangements on a mantelpiece, such as the one on page 181, look attractive. The same shape of design can be used to decorate the front of a drinks table. It can be created from trails of ivy, mixed foliage and a few bold flowers.

• If there is a sideboard, then a display using fruits, vegetables and bunches of herbs makes a wonderful scented focal point.

• A pedestal or large arrangement in the reception area, or perhaps close to the receiving line, can be very eye-catching.

• Decorate the wedding cake or buffet table with garlands.

ARRANGER: VICTORIA HOOTON.

Flowers are often arranged to enhance the wedding cake. They may be displayed in a small vase on the cake itself, but loose flowers can also be threaded through the cake and on the table. Use flowers that will stand without water for several hours.

To decorate the table long sprays of *Danae* can be intertwined, perhaps lightly wired together for extra security and the ends stapled to the corners of the table. Orchids or other long-lasting flowers can be threaded through the *Danae*. Alternatively, mini-decos by 'Oasis' can be placed on the four corners of the table and decorated with a few flowers, perhaps with some toning ribbon.

• Table centrepieces are attractive – the tables are usually round, seating six, eight or ten. You must beware of not making a table arrangement so tall that one cannot talk over it. A maximum of about 30 cm (12 in) is ideal. An alternative is to make it so tall that guests can talk under it!

Round arrangements such as those on pages 108-9 would be ideal. For a country wedding you could line terracotta pots, fill them with foam, insert a thick, cream church candle and add cow parsley (*Anthriscus sylvestris*), lady's mantle (*Alchemilla mollis*), seedheads, wild grasses or anemones. Alternatively, prepare baskets of flowers with handles, which the guests can take home with them afterwards.

ARRANGER: VICTORIA HOOTON.

WHITE AND CREAM FLOWERS

SPRING

Tulip (*Tulipa* sp.)
Daffodil (*Narcissus* sp.)
Anemone coronaria
Freesia sp.
Iris sp.
Arum lily (*Zantedeschia* sp.)
Hyacinth (*Hyacinthus* sp.)
Easter lily (*Lilium longiflorum*)*
Lily-of-the-valley (*Convallaria majalis*)

SUMMER

Achillea ptarmica '*The Pearl*'
White roses such as 'Vanilla',
'Eskimo' and 'Tinneka', and spray
roses such as 'White Princess'
Larkspur (*Consolida* sp.)
Sword lily (*Gladiolus* cv.)
Snapdragon (*Antirrhinum majus*)
Phlox sp.
Delphinium sp.
Sweet pea (*Lathyrus odoratus*)
Dahlia cv.

AUTUMN

Casablanca lily (*Lilium CasaBlanca*)*
Chrysanthemum (*Dendranthema*)
Peruvian lily (*Alstroemeria* sp.)
Carnations (*Dianthus* sp.)*
Euphorbia characias
Hydrangea sp.
Madagascar lily (*Stephanotis floribunda*)

WINTER

Euphorbia sp.
Christmas rose (*Helleborus niger*)
Amaryllis (*Hippeastrum* sp.)
Singapore orchid (*Dendrobium* sp.)*
White spray carnations*

* Flowers available all, or virtually all, year round.

Tips for Wedding Flowers

- Lilies are majestic and look lovely in wedding arrangements. Purists dislike removing the stamens, but I thoroughly recommend that all stamens are removed as the flowers open. If the stamens remain in place they can cause untold damage by staining, which is extremely difficult, if not impossible, to remove completely. Plucking, rather than cutting, gives them a more natural look. When purchasing lilies choose those on which one flower is beginning to open on each stem. Buy them approximately five days before the event and monitor their development.
- Where economy and lack of time are the order of the day, consider creating arrangements of masses of well-conditioned Queen Anne's lace (*Anthriscus sylvestris*) in the late spring, perhaps with the addition of marguerites (*Argyranthemum frutescens*). In the summer, lady's mantle (*Alchemilla mollis*), alone or with a few focal flowers, can create a wonderful effect. Great bunches of baby's breath (*Gypsophila*) can be used on its own or with Easter lilies (*Lilium longiflorum*). In the autumn think of Michaelmas daisies, dahlias, hydrangeas and berries. During the winter months use lots of evergreens with a few gerberas, lilies or some focal silk flowers.
- The most effective way to pack bridal flowers is to lay them on masses of scrunched-up tissue paper, which has been lightly misted. The flowers should then be carefully lain on the paper and covered by a few more sheets of tissue, which can again be lightly misted. The box should be stored in a dark, cold room or cellar. The flowers will last like this for several hours.
- As the seasons vary, so do the flowers that are available at the most competitive prices. White and cream are by far the most popular colours for wedding flowers. On this page there is a list of some of the more widely used white and cream flowers in their season.

Flowers Suitable for Corsages and Head-dresses

These flowers can be used whole or broken down:
Hyacinth
Stephanotis
Narcissus
Hydrangea
Rose – spray and small-headed varieties
Freesias
Lily-of-the-valley
Singapore orchid

Preserving the Wedding Bouquet

The wedding bouquet can be preserved by pressing or by using a desiccant, the procedures for which are explained on pages 102-3. There are a few extra tips that relate to the preservation of wedding and other special-occasion flowers.

• When you have preserved the flowers, either by pressing or by using a desiccant, you must be aware that the colour of the flowers will fade if exposed to strong sunlight. If the flowers have been preserved with a desiccant they will reabsorb moisture and discolour, unless they are sprayed with a sealant and placed behind glass. So display of the flowers in the form of a picture or a cone of flowers, placed under a Victorian or reproduction cloche or bell, is ideal.

• It is a good idea to ask the florist to let you have a few extra of those flowers that will be part of the bouquet, especially if you wish to use a microwave, as you need to remove all the wire from the stems. This can, of course, cause irreparable damage.

• Take a photograph of the wedding bouquet before it is dismantled. Although it is unlikely that you will use all the flowers from the bouquet, as this would create a very large picture, it is rather nice to re-create the form or shape of the bouquet.

• The backing to the picture could be of the same material as the wedding dress. Stretch the fabric and glue it to the back of the backing, not the front. You could incorporate sprigs of lace or tiny lengths of ribbon into the design.

• If you wish to place desiccated plant material behind glass, ensure that the photograph frame you use has a deep recess. The recess needs to be at least 5 cm (2 in) deep, and more if you have large flowers. A local carpenter will make this up for you and specialist shops also supply them.

• Use tweezers to position your plant material and a glue that dries clear, such as Copydex or UHU. Do not use a glue gun. When satisfied with your design use a sealant spray. Clean the glass and seal. Ensure that the glass does not press against flowers preserved with desiccant.

An unwired bridesmaid's posy for a winter wedding.
ARRANGER: ANN KENDRICK.

An unwired wedding bouquet for a winter wedding.
ARRANGER: ANN KENDRICK.

Jewish Weddings

In the Jewish religion the wedding ceremony takes place under a canopy supported by four poles. This canopy is called a huppah. This tradition originated in the Middle Ages, when marriages took place outdoors as an omen that the marriage would be blessed by as many children as 'the stars in heaven'. The canopy distanced the ceremony from the market place. Today, the huppah poles are often elaborately decorated with flowers.

Buddhist Weddings

Buddhists love bright, strong colours as a symbol of happiness and celebration. Each Buddhist country has its own wedding customs, but flowers are always offered to Buddha, for they symbolize worldly possessions and pleasures. Their transient life symbolizes human life and represents the correct attitude towards material and sensual things.

In a Korean Buddhist wedding ceremony the appointed young girl gives the bridegroom five red roses, which he offers to Buddha. The girl then gives the bride two yellow roses, and she will likewise offer these to Buddha.

Among Chinese Buddhists white and black are traditionally regarded as the colour of mourning. The wedding ceremony is conducted by one of the Venerable Masters, and the bride often carries a bouquet and the groom a buttonhole.

A typical display of flowers in a Buddhist temple.

Muslim Weddings

A Muslim wedding is a relatively long process. Depending on the region and the prosperity of the people, there will be various stages comprising proposal, engagement, *manyun, mehndi, barat, nikah, rukhsati, saij, valima and chauthi. Manyun* entails applying a paste of turmeric, flour, rose petals and oil to the whole bodies of the bride and bridegroom. *Mehndi* is the occasion when mehndi leaves are mixed with chemicals and applied to the hands and feet of the bride and to the hands only of the bridegroom. There is no fixed time for this ceremony, the main consideration being that the colour should not fade away before the *nikah* or *rukhsati. Barat* is the marriage procession, which is led by the bridegroom on a horse, camel, in a car or on foot to the bride's house. *Nikah* is the registration of the wedding and is usually conducted at the bride's house. Both bride and groom will wear *sehra* (lots of garlands of flowers), which cover their faces completely until the *nikah* ceremony is completed. *Rukhsati* is the giving away of the bride. Flower petals are thrown at the couple as they make their way to the bridegroom's house. *Saij* (or *saje*) is the bridal bed, which will be decorated with flowers. Lots of red rose petals will be scattered on it. *Valima* is the feast given by the bridegroom the day after the *rukhsati*, and *chauthi* is the occasion when the bride goes to her parents' house for a few days.

At all the above occasions flowers are used in the form of garlands, bouquets and bracelets. They are also thrown over the heads of the bride and groom and their families and friends. Horses and carriages are decorated with flowers.

In some areas Muslim weddings take place in the home, or in a tent or marquee, rather than in the mosque. The bridegroom's family bring the wedding dress to the bride's family the day before the wedding and this is exchanged for other gifts from the bride's family.

Hindu Weddings

The wedding ceremony often takes place in the home or a hall, rather than in the temple, and is considered both a religious and social occasion. There are certain days that are considered auspicious for weddings, and the family will consult the priest as to which day would be best. Many flowers are used at the wedding ceremony to decorate the place of marriage, and fragrance is of the utmost importance. The bride's family, often the children, are involved, welcome the guests and distribute flowers to them as they enter. The pandit (priest) has red and white flowers in a dish, and as he blesses the bride and groom he puts flowers in the palms of their hands. The bride and groom exchange sumptuous garlands, mainly of red and white flowers decorated with very fine silver strands, strung on cotton, which they wear around their necks as they are married. Jasmine is widely used for its intense, heady perfume, but roses and other sweet-scented flowers can be included. *Hibiscus* is also commonly used. In some communities there is a curtain of flowers around the bridal bed.

The female guests at the wedding all wear flowers – just as they do at any special occasion. Garlands are entwined around buns in the hair, along plaits or behind the ears. There is joy and celebration in this use of sweet-scented flowers.

ANNIVERSARY FLOWERS

ALL ANNIVERSARIES ARE SPECIAL, but perhaps the most important landmarks are silver and golden wedding anniversaries.

Silver Weddings

A suitable container for such an event could be a silver bowl, a silver sprayed tin or plastic container, a silver candlestick with a candlecup, an aluminim foil container or a low dish that will not be seen. A base could be a silver tray, a cake board or a silver doily. This could then be placed on a white lace cloth over silver foil.

White and silver flowers would portray your theme but be careful of using only white flowers as this can look rather bridal. This could be avoided by adding simple bows of silver ribbon. Alternatively fronds of artificial ferns can be sprayed with white paint and then glitter or silver sequins applied. Poppy seedheads, chinese lanterns and many other dried flowers and seedheads can also be sprayed silver.

Sterling Silver roses that are ideal for mixing in silver wedding anniversary arrangements are available most of the year. Silver and grey foliage include:

Wormwood (*Artemisia* sp.)
Elaeagnus x *ebbingei*
Gum tree (*Eucalyptus* sp.)
'Silver dust' (*Senecio cineraria*)
Jerusalem sage (*Phlomis fruticosa*)
Curry plant (*Helichrysum italicum*)
Ballota pseudodictamnus
Hosta sieboldiana
Rue (*Ruta graveolens*)
Sea holly (*Eryngium alpinum*)
Common rosemary (*Rosmarinus officinalis*)
Brachyglottis syn. *Senecio* 'Sunshine'
Stachys byzantina
Cotton lavender (*Santolina chamaecyparisus*)

*For a silver wedding celebration, lisianthus (*Eustoma*), veronica (*Hebe*) and 'Sterling Silver' roses have been arranged between two silver candlesticks.*

Golden Wedding

Fifty years of marriage certainly merits celebration. The warmth and mellowness of gold is found in much plant material such as roses, daffodils and golden rod (*Solidago*), 'Californian Glory' (*Fremontedendron*). Candles can be gold, green or golden-yellow. Gold ribbon can easily be incorporated into a design. Dried plant material may be sprayed gold. When using an aerosol spray remember that a smooth texture will shine whereas a rough texture such as that of a teasel will look less effective. Gold paper or material can cover a base or a container.

Golden and cream foliage include:
Golden privet (*Ligustrum ovalifolium* 'Aureum')
Elaeagnus pungens 'Maculata'
Choisya ternata 'Sundance'
Euonymus japonicus 'Aureopictus'
Hedera helix 'Gold heart'
Lonicera nitida 'Baggesen's Gold'
Aucuba japonica 'Crotonifolia'
Spiraea japonica 'Goldflame'
Hosta fortunei 'Aureomaculata'

A mass of golden-yellow roses has been arranged in a wet-foam ring for a golden wedding celebration. A glass bowl has been placed within the ring, in which candles and petals gently float.

SHOW WORK

COMPETITIVE EXHIBITING IS A UNIQUE PART of the art of flower arranging. Flower arranging started as a purely decorative art, but soon shows and competitions were organized. In competitive exhibiting, importance is placed on communicating a theme. This type of arranging has a particular logic, and it often takes the arranger time to enter into the frame of mind necessary for 'showing'. This chapter is designed to assist this process, by breaking it down into easy stages, which, like a game of charades, need to communicate clearly an idea or theme.

There are a couple of misconceptions that should be abandoned at the outset. The first is that there is an overriding competitive streak and a great deal of aggressive behaviour among competitors. This is generally untrue, for there is considerable camaraderie in show work. Many creative people who work on their own greatly enjoy meeting the like-minded. For many competitors, the staging period is the most important part of the competition, not the prize-winning. Until you have experienced this, it is perhaps hard to believe it.

The second great misconception is that to win prizes you have to spend large amounts of money. It is the creative use of plant material, in any form, that is rewarded by a prize, not the abundance or exoticism of the material itself.

You may ask why people want to enter shows. The answer varies enormously, from person to person. It could be motivation, self-satisfaction, winning praise from others, being accepted by the 'establishment', getting to know other arrangers and making new friends, wanting to learn from others, or the sheer enjoyment of creating and interpreting with plant material, which is so different from arranging for decorative purposes.

Contemporary seascape
Plant list: Driftwood, Euphorbia griffithii 'Fireglow', Rosa 'Lambada', Fagus sylvatica atropurpurea, Cimicifuga 'Purpurea'. At first sight there only seems to be one accessory in this exhibit – the sea animal encrusted squid pot. However, in addition there are some pieces of terracotta sponge and two pieces of sea fan coral. Both these items, which have been in my possession for many years, are considered 'animal'. Such items are now endangered, fuelled by the fact that nowadays we find them more attractive. Increasingly we seek to preserve and conserve such animal life, so that future generations can see their beauty, preferably in their natural habitat under the sea. The exhibit has a somewhat contemporary feel. It tries to convey an air of mystery and the unknown, associated with the sea.
DESIGNER: CRAIG BULLOCK.

GETTING STARTED

BEFORE ENTERING YOUR FIRST SHOW, visit as many shows of varying standards as possible – this will give you a head start. Plan as you view the exhibits. Are there types or styles of exhibit that particularly appeal to you? What was the outcome of the judging? Did the judge give comment cards and, if so, was there a common thread (a competitor's base, for example, might be judged too large for the space allowed for the exhibit)? It is a good idea to note the exhibits with bases that are in good proportion to the arrangement or to the space provided. Making good use of viewing shows, before entering your own first show, can give you a great deal of experience without being sidetracked by an exhibit of your own.

Choice of show is important. Start with a local show in order to gain experience. Experience is one of the keys to being a good competitor. Choosing a local show where the judge(s) are qualified by NAFAS is also a good idea. The show will then be judged in accordance with the latest schedule definitions produced by NAFAS, which has spent many years devising and creating standardization for competitions. Being judged by an unqualified person often means that more of the judge's taste is applied, rather than an objective approach. By reading the schedule definitions it becomes clearer what is meant by the particular terms used.

How to Choose a Suitable Class Title

This is the interesting part. All competitors get excited when the schedule drops through the letter box, although the problem they often find is that either all the titles appeal or none do.

When you first enter a show, look for a class that has wide appeal and allows an open interpretation. Try to create a design that you are comfortable with, or choose one for which you already have a collection of accessories to incorporate into the design. For example, such a class might in the past have been worded as 'my favourite book' or 'a song title' – such classes are still going strong at many shows. A more up-to-date approach to this kind of class would be to describe it as 'inspired by ...', leaving the inspiration to the arranger.

Another approach is to choose a title where interpretation is linked to one of the principles or elements of design. 'Captivating Colour' or 'Nature's Harmonies', for instance, means that the exhibit will rely mainly on design skills and less on interpretation.

An Approach to Interpretation

Having made your choice, how do you interpret the title? You might consult a thesaurus for words and associations, or a dictionary for the exact definition of the words in the title. You might ask someone who is not connected with flower arranging, for they will have a mind which does not immediately translate the title into flowers. Remember it is the title (not the source) that is of prime importance, unless the schedule actually states where the quotation comes from. Some people get so carried away with the source, or with some deep meaning associated with it, that they

forget that, however intellectual, well-read or well researched the judge is, he/she can never be an expert in all fields.

One underlying rule for competitors is that 'the judge is a fool'. At first this sounds disrespectful, but in this communication game, simplicity is often the key to interpreting the theme. When judges look at an excellent piece of show work, they feel that the competitor has 'hit the nail on the head'. The interpretation is obvious and it makes one think, 'Why didn't I think of that?'

Some titles are very open, giving the individual competitor maximum creative space. Sometimes, as in charades, you can 'do the whole thing', but on other occasions you have to (as it were) 'break it down into syllables'. In such cases you may give a title card to the judge to establish which part you are interpreting. Take, for example, a class called 'The World's Wild Places'. If you decide that you are going to create all the wild places, or as many as you can fit into the space allowed, then you may well be heading for a design that is divided into sub-sections and an exhibit that does not have unity. A more arresting approach is to concentrate on one wild place and to give it a title card so that the onlooker and judge do not have to rack their brains to understand what on earth the exhibit is trying to convey.

Check that the title you have chosen does not have a specific inclusion or exclusion in the class description that does not suit you. For instance, a class entitled 'Cargoes' might state 'featuring dried plant material', when you have a greenhouse full of exotic plants and foliage that you want to use.

Remember to look in your schedule definitions if you are unsure of the meaning of a term used in the schedule. If it is not covered in the schedule definitions, check the dictionary definition and with the secretary of the show, to cover yourself. Remember that plant material must always predominate.

Inspiration

Where does inspiration come from? This is a question that is often difficult to answer, and for each of us there will perhaps be a different answer. You soon realize that the possibilities are boundless. Inspiration could come from sculptors, painters, land artists, poets, writers, dancers, other flower arrangers, the theatre, nature, architecture, and so on. Often you are not inspired at the time of choosing an exhibit. It may be weeks, months or years before you see a schedule when inspiration first fuels a floral idea for an exciting class title. Different titles will appeal to different minds.

Sometimes no inspiration comes ('can't think of a thing') and the more you seek it, the more it seems to evade you. But then it hits you – all of a sudden, out of the blue, at a time when you least expected it. The most important thing is always to be receptive, keeping your eyes open.

Much inspiration comes from other arrangers and not always from people of the present day. The past also plays its part, just as it does in fashion or music. The two photographs here show work by Winifred Simpson and Lilian Martin, artists who will long be remembered for their flawless, evocative and atmospheric exhibits, which chilled the spine of the onlooker.

The advent of new-style clubs, like the Club in the Park, has brought futuristic exhibits to major competitions – not always with success, but arresting the attention of the onlooker. One arranger who has pushed out the boundaries is Carol Firmstone. Her foundation of teaching art studies adds a new lease of life to the floral creator, bringing the arranger into line with many other present-day artists.

The main part of this story is told by the plant material. The shadows on the background seem to highlight the interpretation of 'ghosts'. The use of evocative plant materials, for example, silk tassel bush (Garrya elliptica), Helleborus orientalis, Fritillaria persica and the rare Kalanchoe beharensis attracts both viewer and the judge's eye.
ARRANGER: *LILIAN MARTIN.*

Backgrounds, Bases and Accessories

Backgrounds have several uses. They enhance the appearance of the plant material, assist in the interpretation and creation of atmosphere and can also be used to hide mechanics. A background should not be used, however, if it does not contribute to the overall exhibit, and it must not predominate over the creating with plant material.

Bases can bring together and unify a collection of separate arrangements and accessories. In the past it was generally thought that they were always needed, but this seems to be changing as we move from the 1990s. If a base is to be used it must contribute to the overall exhibit.

Accessories often present the greatest problem for the competitor, as so often these are relied upon to give the greater part of the interpretation. The problem arises when these are made from non-plant materials. It is much better if accessories are made from plant material, as greater reward is given by the judges for this extension of creativity with plant materials.

If you have to rely on accessories made from non-plant material, one way of blending these so that they do not overtake the importance of the plant material is to age or distress them. Accessories should look genuine, even if they are not.

Title Cards

Many an exhibit has been spoiled by a poor title card. You will see some competitors create a most attractive exhibit and then place upon it a title written badly and on white card, almost as an afterthought. That is exactly what a title card should not be – it should be in keeping with the whole exhibit, in both atmosphere and context. The style of script should also follow these criteria. Consider how the same title can be made to look quite different, using different scripts and cards.

Word processors mean that the production of such title cards can be done without taking a course in calligraphy. If you do not have access to a word processor, the dry, rub-on lettering has its uses. This also comes in handy when wanting to inscribe letters directly onto a stone or a leaf, which might be rather difficult to pass through the printer!

What Does the Judge Look For?

Before considering what the judge looks for, ask yourself what first-prize winners have in common.

They often fall into one of two camps: either they have excellent design skills or they show strong and clear interpretation. Over the years, judges have differed as to whether design or interpretation is more important, so it would seem that if you concentrate on both these issues and create an exhibit with clear interpretation and excellent design, you are in the running for a high award.

To help you understand what it is that the judge is looking for, look at your copy of the NAFAS schedule definitions. The judge's manual issued by NAFAS is another key source of information to every competitor.

Here are some of the questions that the judges ask when looking at the exhibits before them:

- Is the exhibit according to schedule? (Consult your schedule definitions booklet to establish what the present NAFAS xrules are – there are not many – the rest deals with definitions.)
- Does the exhibit interpret the title of the class?
- Does the exhibit use well the elements and principles of design?
- Is the exhibit well staged, groomed and presented?
- Are all the materials used in good condition?
- Has the exhibit got distinction?

You may ask what distinction is – a difficult question to answer. Some dictionaries define it as a distinguishing mark or mark of special honour, so this seems to be the place to say that there is room in show work for a more subjective outlook from the judge and, judges being human, that is the way it is.

▷ *Foliage Pedestal*
Plant list: Polygonatum biflorum, *selection of ferns, lady's mantle* (Alchemilla mollis), Hosta *'Sum and Substance'*, H. *'sieboldiana'*, H. *'Frances Williams'*, H. *'Krossa Regal', golden oats (*Stipa gigantea*), pendulous sedge (*Carex pendula*), Ligularia dentata *and plain bearded Iris. Often when we start flower arranging we cannot see that there might be much beauty with no flowers in the design: our views can change, however, as we acquire the taste and learn to love foliage (particularly if we grow it ourselves). This exhibit, which could be entitled 'Poolside Majesty', is classified as a pedestal exhibit. The pedestal is a metal stand with dried giant hogweed (*Heracleum mantegazzianum*) stem over the top. The only accessory is a mossy stone, and the title card is another flat stone with dry, rub-on lettering. DESIGNER: CRAIG BULLOCK.*

△ 'Earth's Core'. This exhibit relies almost totally on plant material. The only accessory used is the piece of old rusty sheet which extends the wood. The skilfull blending of colours could be likened to that of an artist blending paint.
DESIGNER: CAROL FIRMSTONE.

Practical Points

The 'mock-up' is a most important stage of the exhibit. This is where all your ideas come together and possibly where paring down has to take place. This stage will raise many more questions about the mechanics, for example: how do I hold that up there? Make sure at this 'practice' stage that the size of your exhibit is carefully marked out in all three dimensions. Do not feel that you have to use the exact plant materials that you intend to use in the completed exhibit. When you do the real thing it is often difficult to repeat the exact materials, and you may be tempted to feel that it was better in the mock-up than it is on the show bench.

You must give careful thought to the type of plant material you need and can obtain. Order any florist's materials well in advance to be as sure as possible to obtain them. Make a list of all the suitable plant material from the garden that should be available at the time of the show. Do not get upset if some materials are not available; rather, be excited by the things you know you have. A positive approach is a much firmer foundation on which to build.

Condition all your plant material well so that there is no chance of it wilting. If in doubt, do not use it.

Prepare a check-list of all your exhibit and competitor's requirements so that nothing is forgotten. Place all your materials carefully, so as not to damage anything on the way to the show. Do not forget your tool box and, if you are using it, your floral foam. It can be a help to label with your name on all your boxes, etc. This can save any confusion.

The way in which you work when you get to the show is totally personal, but do allow yourself time for a break, especially as you may return with what seems to be a fresh pair of eyes.

Just before you leave, take time to look around your exhibit and check such things as water, whether your exhibitor's card is on the exhibit and within the size allowed, and give yourself a last opportunity to assess the whole exhibit. If permitted, you might at this stage wish to photograph it, not only to remind you of the completed exhibit but also to enable you later, in the cool light of day, to judge the exhibit yourself.

With sufficient preparation you will, hopefully, have thoroughly enjoyed the experience and be well pleased with the result – ever the judges may think!

INTERNATIONAL COMPETITIONS

COMPETING ON THE INTERNATIONAL SHOW BENCH is somewhat different. Interpretation is a more difficult area to convey, with the hurdles of different languages and differing cultures to be overcome. The judge may well come from another part of the world. It seems therefore that in this type of competition, design and innovative arranging are particularly high on the agenda.

The World Association of Flower Arrangers (WAFA) came into existence in 1981 and held its first competition in Bath in 1984. WAFA has just a few rules but no schedule definitions. This seems to leave the creative platform wide open, although it could also be perceived that the judge may be influenced more by his/her own country's definition of what constitutes, for example, 'an abstract'. This can produce a less consistent approach to judging or, on the other hand, a more worldly approach. Because of this wide-open platform and possibly less consistent judging, there seems to be less pressure on both the competitor and the viewer to take note just of the prize-winners. The inventiveness and creativity of all competitors can be fully appreciated. At this type of competition there is much outstanding work, which will excite and inspire even the most experienced of exhibitors.

THE WAY FORWARD

'WHAT IS GOING TO BE NEXT?' is the common cry. There has been great concern recently when exhibits containing no flowers at all have won prizes and, indeed, major prizes. There is so much emotion on this subject, but it should always be remembered that the first aim of NAFAS is 'To encourage the artistic and creative use of natural plant material in all its forms'.

And what of a possible way forward? Should there be room at competitions for some categories to be non-competitive, providing space for more creative experimentation and allowing the viewer to be the judge? Food for thought.

Whatever you consider to be the way forward for you, I hope that there is one thing we all share in our competing and exhibiting – a fair and friendly process of creating designs of great beauty with natural plant materials.

A traditional arrangement of purples, mauves, grey and chocolates. Plant list: Nectaroscordum siculum, Rosa 'Little Silver', red masterwort (Astrantia rubra), Phormium tenax 'Sea Jade', Armeria formosa, Euphorbia dulcis 'Chameleon', pink Iris silica, Parahebe sp. purple beech (Fagus sylvatica atropurpurea), Rosa glauca, Cimicifuga simplex atropurpurea, Huchera var. diversifolia 'Palace Purple', Eucalyptus sp., purple Centaurea, purple sea lavender (Limonium) and purple larkspur(Consolida sp.). This exhibit is very traditional in design, relying on other objects to help convey the interpretation. It could be entitled 'Junk Shop Finds' or 'From Antiquity'. It concentrates on having a 'pretty' type of attraction, which of course not all competitive exhibits have. The accessories have been incorporated at the base, and the addition of a second placement helps to lessen any dominance they might have. The whole is tied together on a faded damask-covered base, which is sprayed with a little black paint to deaden the new appearance it originally had. DESIGNER: CRAIG BULLOCK.

EUROPE

BELGIUM

BELGIUM IS ONE of the Low Countries, historically one of the most prosperous parts of Europe, but often its battleground. Flemish is the language spoken in the northern part of the country and French in the southern.

Flower arranging perhaps had its real origin in the paintings of the Flemish and Dutch artists of the sixteenth and seventeenth centuries. Painters such as Jan Brueghel, the 'Velvet', Daniel Seghers, Jan Davids, de Heem and Soreau were masters in painting flowers, bouquets and still lifes. Their influence has been considerable regarding colour, opulence and the love of combining vegetables, herbs and country flowers. They have also influenced the making of garlands – Brueghel had a fondness for painting garlands of flowers mixed with fruits and vegetables.

△ *A modern, abstract arrangement with wood.*
ARRANGER: *BELGIAN FLOWER ARRANGEMENT SOCIETY.*

◁ *An urn of fruits and foliage.*
ARRANGER: *BELGIAN FLOWER ARRANGEMENT SOCIETY.*

In Belgian flower arranging today there is a love of opulence, exuberance of garden plant material and a delicate use of colour. In the north of Belgium there are many glasshouses famous for their range of fresh plant material.

Many Belgian florists have taken the tied bunch to an art form: a few perfect flowers are mixed with an eclectic assortment of foliage, wrapped in a circle of paper and tied with raffia. The giving of flowers is very prevalent in Belgium and no one would consider going out to dinner without taking a box of chocolates or a bunch of flowers to show their appreciation. Flowers are usually given to the hostess the first time you visit a house and should be given or sent afterwards, if attending a dinner party.

If you receive an official announcement of a wedding it is customary to send flowers to the '*adresse du jour*'on the day of the wedding. White flowers are sent on the occasion of first communion and on the confirmation of a child. These are often seen on windowsills during the week following the occasion, as it is customary to 'display' them. Flowers are also sent to someone moving to a new house.

Chrysanthemums (*Dendranthema*) are placed on graves on 1 November (All Saints' Day) and cemeteries are a mass of flowers. As chrysanthemums are associated with this custom, they are not usually sent as gifts.

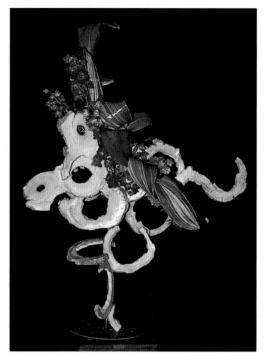

△ *Driftwood, delphiniums and twisted variegated cast iron plant* (Aspidistra elafior) *leaves.*
ARRANGER: BELGIAN FLOWER ARRANGEMENT SOCIETY.

◁ *A blue container holding all-green flowers and foliage.*
ARRANGER: BELGIAN FLOWER ARRANGEMENT SOCIETY.

CZECH REPUBLIC

THE CZECH REPUBLIC is the most westward of the former Soviet bloc countries and lies at the very core of Europe. Economically one of the strongest of the former East European countries, it has a grand architectural and cultural heritage, especially in Prague, and its heart is now beating strongly again.

People of the Czech lands (Bohemia and Moravia) have always purchased flowers for birthdays, namedays, weddings and funerals. The people of the Czech lands give flowers as other people give cards, and the namedays celebrating Jan, Josef, Frantisek, Vaclav, Anna and Marie have become almost national occasions, due to their popularity. Flower arrangements for Easter and Christmas are hugely popular in the numerous churches throughout the country.

During the Communist regime all flower shops were called *kvetiny*, which means 'flowers' in Czech, because they were all owned by the State. Only a small variety of flowers was available. Flowers were picked from gardens or purchased outside cemeteries for putting on graves. Pot plants were, however, commonly seen.

Mineralized roses were much in evidence: paper roses were hung in a shower of mineral water in the many spas that exist throughout the Czech Republic. The minerals crystallized on the surface of the rose, giving the appearance of a rose made of stone.

In the cities, and particularly in Prague, dramatic changes have taken place over the past few years, since the Velvet Revolution, which followed the collapse of the Iron Curtain. The changes are particularly evident in the availability of consumer goods and flowers are no exception. New florists' shops are opening daily alongside the designer clothes boutiques. They are staffed by young assistants with natural, creative skills, who are readily able to adapt and create their own new styles and designs. Every type of flower is now available, and arrangements range from modest posies to structured arrangements, influenced by many countries and in particular Germany.

Dried flowers are extremely popular, probably due to the very cold winters and hot interiors of homes and offices. Artificial flowers and fruits were traditionally manufactured in the Czech Republic, but with new technology producing very realistic plants, flowers and fruits, imports are generally winning.

Flower arranging and floristry are flourishing commercially in the new Czech Republic, though as yet it has not taken off as a hobby.

Each year Flora Olomouc organizes a horticultural exhibition round the city centre of Olomouc. There are exhibits by schools, research institutes, flower producers and importers in four pavilions in an area of approximately 5,000 sq. m (6,000 sq. yards). It is organized in conjunction with a State-run gardening school in Melnik.

An arrangement typical of the country regions, where the long-lasting carnation is much appreciated. The choice of red and white flowers is popular.
ARRANGER: *ALENA BRODSKA.*

A jug holding country flowers.
ARRANGER: ALENA BRODSKA.

A sophisticated fleur-de-lys design typical of those found in many of the sophisticated flower shops and hotels in the cosmopolitan capital of Prague.
ARRANGER: JEAN GEESON.

FRANCE

FRANCE HAS A MOST FAVOURABLE GEOGRAPHICAL POSITION in Europe, bounded on three sides by sea. In the Pyrenees, the Auvergne and the Alps there are alpines and other plants that thrive in a cooler climate. In the south there are mimosa (*Acacia*), African lily (*Agapanthus*), palms, *Agave*, New Zealand flax, bamboo and *Yucca* and forests of *Eucalyptus* and maritime pine (*Pinus pinaster*). Many of these plants are also found in the west of France, due to the warm Gulf Stream. Further north and west, where the climate is cooler, are found all the flowers of the European continent.

Everywhere in France, whatever the climate, you will find roses (*Rosa*), delphiniums, hydrangeas, rhododendrons, statice (*Limonium*) and *Achillea* in gardens. In the countryside, flower arrangers have become excellent gardeners, growing and exchanging all the species that one might want to see in an arrangement.

On 14 July (Bastille Day) tricolour bouquets (blue, white and red) of poppies, cornflowers and marguerites are sold in the streets. May, October and December are the months when most flowers are bought, due to the dual occurrence in May of May Day – when sprigs of lily-of-the-valley (*Convallaria majalis*) are given to friends and family to bring good luck – and Mothering Sunday. On All Saints' Day (*Toussaint*), on 1 November, large, single-headed chrysanthemums are placed on the graves of loved ones. Carnations that provide so much variety of form and colour are

A basket of roses, lilies, chrysanthemums and green tomatoes, inspired by the traditional Flemish arrangements seen frequently in French paintings of the eighteenth century.
ARRANGER: OLGA MENEUR.

The delicate colours within the alabaster container are perfectly enhanced by the fruit and flowers.
The classic feel of the arrangement is uplifted and modernized by the ribbon of Typha that encircles it.
ARRANGER: JACQUELINE BOGRAND.

not popular with restauranteurs and actors who believe they may bring bad luck.

There has been a continuous evolution in the art of flower arranging in France over the centuries, as in painting, sculpture, dance, jewellery and architecture. Flower arranging today seeks to be modern and unfussy, using contrasts in texture, blocks of colour, shape and volume. The focal point is no longer centred but placed at attractive points of the design. Currently there is a tendency to look for continuity between the container and the flowers, so that the whole arrangement appears organic. Great importance is given to leaves, which are manipulated to create forms that are different from those of nature. They are grouped, trimmed, cut and positioned in a manner attractive to the eye.

Nature is subjected to the will of the artist. But, like traditional flower arranging, the end result is beauty. That said, it is not beyond the bounds of credibility that traditional arrangements will make a come-back.

Jacqueline Bogrand, President of the flower arranging section of the Société Nationale d'Horticulture de France, writes the following on the modern flower arrangement, 'Predominance is given to graphism, to the impact of unusual and strong elements. As in sculpture, the abstraction of all figurative ideas. Sculpture, sobriety and strength dominate the modern arrangement just as classical arrangements always seduce by their luxuriance, charm and poetry, their subtle harmony.'

Monique Gautier, Director of the French School of Flower Arranging, adds, 'Nothing is more contrary to the dynamism of an arrangement than the static. Everything must contribute to the rhythm. Dare to be different and remember that the best arrangements will become the classics of tomorrow.'

An arrangement made from leftovers. The material comprises a block of foam, a small dish, wires, arum lilies, arum lily stalks, Dianthus barbatus *(sweet william), spray carnations,* Nigella damascena *and one stem of* Alchemilla mollis. ARRANGER: MONIQUE GAUTIER.

The green Pandanus *form a frame for the massed yellow tulips, which are surrounded by* Chamaerops livingstonia. *No vase is used. The entire arrangement is vegetative.*
ARRANGER: OLGA MENEUR.

GERMANY

GERMANY IS THE LARGEST AND MOST CENTRAL of the European countries. Famous for sausages, beer and good white wine, it stretches from the Baltic in the north to Switzerland and Austria in the south. After 30 years of being two separated countries, it is now one – the Iron Curtain having fallen.

Flowers have always been used and enjoyed throughout German history: in the Middle Ages they were used to create small wedding bouquets composed of spicy, fragant herbs.

Christmas and Easter are the two main occasions when floral arrangements decorate the home. On the first Sunday in Advent the first candle on the *Advent Kranz* (wreath) is lit. The whole family sits round the table and sings carols. On each of the following three Sundays a further candle is lit, the final one being lit on the last Sunday before Christmas. This is a long-standing tradition in every German home.

On Christmas Eve the Christmas tree is erected, but never before this date. Real candles are often lit on the tree itself, which will rarely be decorated with tinsel or bright lights. Instead, glass balls, delicate silver strands, artificial fruits and wooden toys are hung from the tree. It is taken down after 6 January – the day of the visit by the Three Wise Men. Presents are also given and received on Christmas Eve, when there is an intimate family gathering. Carols are sung and the main Christmas meal is enjoyed. On Christmas Day itself the extended family is invited. The tree and the wreath are the two main Chrismas decorations.

At Easter time hard-boiled eggs are painted on Good Friday, which are then eaten on Easter Sunday before going to church.

Branches are brought in from the garden, placed in a big vase and Easter eggs hung from the branches. After church the Easter bunny will have left eggs in the garden and the children will have to find them – an Easter egg hunt.

But flowers are given on many occasions. They are used to decorate concerts, openings, sport festivals, hotels, restaurants, castles and churches. Even if visiting someone for *Zum kaffee trinken* (afternoon coffee and cake), or going to see a friend or relative in hospital, you would first visit the florist to buy a small bunch of seasonal flowers arranged with a spray of foliage. You would tell the florist the occasion and the amount you wish to spend and a suitable bunch would immediately be made up.

During the last 10 to 20 years floristry in Germany has developed remarkably and a large number of new designs have appeared. Flowers and floristry are strongly influenced by interior design, forms, styles, architecture and colours. At present the mega-trend is 'Nature and the Environment'. The ecological consciousness of customers has increased: plastics, mica, glitter and artificial flowers are no longer in demand. Flowers may be purchased not just from florists but from supermarkets, stalls, petrol stations and railway stations. But nearly always the flowers are ready-mixed in tied bunches and often wrapped in brown paper, coloured tissue paper or cellophane.

The trend is towards natural, uncontrived flowers, reflected in the popularity of large roses, hydrangeas, peonies, *Hibiscus*, lisianthus (*Eustoma*), *Helleborus*, dahlias, *Celosia*, sunflowers (*Helianthus*), lavender (*Lavendula*), ivy (*Hedera*), *Hebe* and other flowers typical of a cottage garden. Foliage is an important component and a typical hand-tied bouquet includes many varieties.

A floral ring for a summer party.
DESIGNER: WALLY KLETT

Ribbons, gold wire and other materials are sometimes incorporated.

Many designs include a construction. This is perhaps best described as a framework of strong regular stems, secured at the joints with raffia. Suitable stems are dogwood (*Cornus*) and willow (*Salix*). Constructions are often incorporated into hand ties (tied bunches). For a simple hand-tie two short, smooth stems are bound together with raffia or twine to form a cross, with a third to form the stem. Only a few bold flowers and one or two strong, waxy leaves need to be added, placed at differing heights. The stems are bound with raffia, twine or hessian ribbon.

An innovative and exciting design.
DESIGNER: *WALLY KLETT*

To make this garland all the plant material has been wired and taped and linked with gold reel-wire.
DESIGNER: *WALLY KLETT.*

HOLLAND

HOLLAND, OR THE NETHERLANDS as it is properly called, is bounded by Germany to the east and Belgium to the south. Historically it is a trading and agricultural nation, famous for its flat countryside, its canals, its windmills, and of course for its national flower, the tulip. The canals serve both as drainage and a means of transport. The famous windmills were built principally to drain water from the land into the canals.

The botanist 'Carolus Clusus' (Charles de L'Écluse) introduced tulips into the Netherlands from the Black Sea region of Central Asia, and the first tulips bloomed there in 1594. The name derives from the Arabic word *tulipam*, meaning turban, which the bulb is said to resemble.

Tulip bulbs came to be viewed as prized possessions. Early in 1637 tulip-mania reached its peak and a 'Semper Augustus' bulb fetched as much as 13,000 guilders. As a comparison, two years later the same amount was spent by Rembrandt van Rijn on his house in Amsterdam. In those days fresh tulips were exclusive to the rich; the poor had to content themselves with articles bearing a representation of the flower, and this led to the development of the tulip motif on tiles, pottery and many other household artefacts.

Efforts were long made to grow a tulip that bloomed at Christmas time. This led to the production of the short-stemmed, small red tulip, 'Duc van Tol'. During World War II numerous families cherished a pot with three of these small tulips as their only Christmas decoration at home. When people were starving during the winter of 1944 many ate tulip bulbs, because there was nothing else to eat. Today, when Queen Beatrix goes on a State visit she often takes a present of tulip bulbs to her host country.

A hand-tie of irises bound with rope or ribbon. By splaying the stems wide, the tied bunch stands up easily. It has been placed in the centre of a large shallow bowl. The iris leaves have been turned inside-out and looped, then placed around the arrangement.
DESIGNER: LEO KOOLEN.

Despite the fact that Holland is a small country, it is well known worldwide for trading, especially in flowers. Its capital, Amsterdam, lies about ten miles west of the city of Aalsmeer, where the biggest flower trade centre in the world is located, with a surface of 715,000 sq. m (approximately the size of 120 football pitches laid side by side). Every day 14 million flowers and one and a half million plants are sold, more than 80 per cent of which are destined for the overseas market. Nearly one and a half billion stems of roses in 200 varieties are sold each year. Tulips (*Tulipa*), carnations (*Dianthus*), chrysanthemums (*Dendranthema*), freesia and gerbera are also sold in vast numbers.

A Dutch household without flowers and plants is unimaginable. Compared to other countries, the Dutch spend a relatively large sum of money on cut flowers. House plants are also popular and are arranged along the windowsills of many homes as an attractive alternative to net curtains.

Flower shops and stalls abound throughout Holland. Fragrance is important, and when flowers are purchased they are wrapped but rarely enclosed, so that the perfume is able to escape. Ribbons are seldom used. Florists are frequently asked to create informal tied bunches, and flower arrangements in containers are given on more formal occasions.

Every year on the first Saturday in September one of the greatest flower parades in Holland takes place in Aalsmeer. Many of the floats are 12 m (40 ft) long and 4 m (13 ft) high and covered with thousands of flowers.

▽ *A swirling mass of tulips in a low bowl complements the form and texture of a ceramic tulip bulb.*
DESIGNER: LEO KOOLEN.

◁ *A festive arrangement for Sylvester's Night (31 December). Bells of Ireland (*Molucella laevis*), scarlet plume (*Euphobia fulgens*), Gloriosa, Narcissus, Aspidistra leaves, starfish (*Astropecten*) and pussy willow (*Salix caprea*) have been used to create an appropriate firework effect.*
DESIGNER: LEO KOOLEN

IRELAND

IRELAND IS USUALLY ASSOCIATED with the colour 'green', and indeed the 'forty shades' can be seen throughout the land. The soft, rainy climate has a great deal to do with this, but Ireland also has sunny days when the countryside can be seen in all its splendour.

Despite the relatively small size of Ireland, different areas can grow different plants. In the south, which is touched by the warm Gulf Stream from Mexico, the climate is almost Mediterranean and the lush growth everywhere is beautiful. However, the west of Ireland, from Kerry to Donegal, is lashed by Atlantic gales and storms in winter and here the beauty lies in the gnarled trees covered with the most beautiful lichens. The native heathers and furze (*Ulex*) give great splashes of colour against the lichen-covered rocks. Driftwood abounds here and is much used in conjunction with flowers.

In the woodlands, and throughout the countryside generally, numerous wild flowers abound.

There is a wide diversity of plant material, from the native trees to the now interesting shrubs available in the many garden centres around the country. Many plants now being imported from Australia and New Zealand are settling well into their new sur-

roundings. *Pittosporum* of many hues, *Griselinia* and of course the numerous *Phormium* sp. can now be seen as part of every garden. In lime-free areas rhododendrons and azaleas provide riotous colour in the spring and early summer. The soft rain is kind to plantain lilies (*Hosta*), which are so useful in the summer months, as are the elephant's ears (*Bergenia*) that are available in many different sizes.

Ireland's national emblem is the shamrock (*Trifolium* sp.). Many long years ago St Patrick used this plant to illustrate the doctrine of the Trinity, when teaching the people of Ireland. It is of course worn by everybody on 17 March, St Patrick's Day, and is sent round the world to emigrants to remind them of their homeland.

Foliage and driftwood feature greatly in Irish flower arranging. Landscape exhibits are popular and new trends coming from other countries are inspiring arrangers to use their plant material in different ways. The vertical horizontal style is spectacular in tints, tones and shades of green, combined with the varying textures of the foliage available.

As a Celtic race, the Irish are regarded as being creative and dreamers. So one of Ireland's strongest areas in flower arranging is interpretative work. Many examples can be seen in the exhibitions and flower festivals held throughout the country.

◁ *Three terracotta pots have been placed with stones on a brown earthy-coloured base. Three pieces of driftwood provide weight. A branch of* Corylus avellana *'Contorta' adds height. Moss softens the line of the base and the driftwood. The blue polyanthus adds weight and depth.*
*The composition is completed by the addition of daffodils (*Narcissus *'February Gold') on the left, and the yellow colouring is repeated on the right with the tulips. Ferns and winter flowering heather complete the picture.*
ARRANGER: NUALA HEGARTY.

▷ *An arrangement of foliage of contrasting forms and textures. The foliage includes* Aspidistra elatior, Mahonia x media *'Charity',* Thuja plicata *'Zebrina',* Griselinia littoralis *'Bantry Bay', variegated* Cordyline, Phormium *'Sea Jade' and bells of Ireland. Dominance is provided at the focal area by* Bergenia *'Sunningdale' and by succulents. The fruits of the* Mahonia *are trailed down over the front of the pot.*
ARRANGER: NUALA HEGARTY.

ISRAEL

ISRAEL FINDS ITSELF AT THE EASTERN END of the Mediterranean. Its climate and soil are ideal for the cultivation of many varieties of flowers and a wide range, such as Orchids, gerbera, Michaelmas daisies (*Aster novi-belgii*), turban flowers (*Ranunculus asiaticus*), kangaroo paw (*Anigozanthos*) and baby's breath (*Gypsophila*) is grown and exported. A programme introduced for the Protection of Nature ensures that there are masses of wild flowers all year round, but a visit in spring is a must, as the desert in bloom is a breathtaking sight.

Israelis love flowers and they play an important role in their lives. Flowers decorate the home, are an integral part of functions and an essential part of the Jewish religion and tradition, as many of the Jewish holy days and festivals are agriculturally based.

Fridays in Israel conjure up visions of people carrying home their bunches of flowers bought from florist shops or vendors. From the manual worker to the head of industry, the Sabbath would be incomplete without flowers in the home. Candles that are lit for the Sabbath and religious holidays may not be extinguished, so take care when combining them with flowers.

All weddings are religious ceremonies and are performed by the rabbi under a *chupah*, the wedding canopy. Ceremonies range from the simple to the ultra-religious, from the plain to the extravagant. None would be complete without some form of floral decoration.

The blossoming of the wild almond (*Prunus dulcis*) heralds the coming of spring and the time to sow grain and plant trees. On the 15th day of the month of Shvat (Tu b'Shvat) the New Year of the Trees is celebrated. Old and young join in tree-planting ceremonies and this has become the traditional time for floral demonstrations and competitions.

△ *An all-white table arrangement for Rosh Hashanah, the New Year, with the white denoting purity. Red apple candlesticks hold beeswax candles and stand alongside the traditional plate of sliced apples and honey, which will ensure a sweet New Year. Plant material includes gerbera, Eustoma, Michaelmas daisies, Nephrolepis, Arachniodes adiantiformis.*
ARRANGER: GINA ETING.

Hebrew counting uses alphabetical characters: 18 is written as *chai*, which means Life, and a gift of 18 flowers wishes 'long life'. Chanukah is the Festival of Lights, which lasts for eight days and celebrates the victory of the Maccabees over the Greeks in 165 BC. Every evening another candle is added to the nine-branched candelabrum called the Chanukiah, which is frequently decorated with flowers. Shavouth is the time to celebrate Moses receiving the 10 commandments. And the figure seven is important, for it represents the 'Seven Species', which are date (*Phoenix dactylifera*), grape (*Vitis vinifera*), olive (*Olea europaea*), fig (*Ficus carica*), pomegranate (*Punica granatum*), wheat (*Triticum aestivum*) and barley (*Hordeum vulgare*). Synagogues are deco-

rated with foliage, and children, wearing garlands of flowers on their heads, offer up baskets of fruit and vegetables. Succouth is the Festival of Booths or Tabernacles. It is an eight-day festival commemorating the 40 years in the desert, and celebrates the late summer harvest. Most families and institutions construct temporary booths outside in the garden or on their balconies where they are 'under the stars': all meals are taken in the 'Succouth'. The symbolic 'Four Species' are the embryonic palm frond (*Pheonix dactylifera*), the citron (*Citrus medica*), the myrtle (*Myrtus communis*) and the willow (*Salix*). These, together with flowers, foliage, fruit and vegetables are made into swags and garlands to decorate the booths.

◁ *For the festival of Purim flowers have been arranged in a special foam collar that fits onto a bottle of 'Rothschild wine'. Wine is given for the man, flowers for the lady. The contents include* Sandersonia aurantiaca, *tulip (*Tulipa*), narcissus, Euonymus, mimosa or wattle (*Acacia dealbata*), leather fern (*Arachniodes adiantiformis*).* ARRANGER: GINA ETING.

ITALY

ITALY IS A LONG PENINSULA stretching out into the Mediterranean, separated from the rest of Europe by the snow-capped Alps. Its climate differs considerably from place to place and its flora is consequently varied. The coasts, especially on the Riviera and in the south, have mild temperatures and a Mediterranean vegetation. In the north there are areas with a continental climate and cold winters. Around Lakes Maggiore, Como and Garda, the milder climate has allowed the creation of wonderful gardens with rare specimens of trees and flowers.

Flowers are greatly loved by the Italians but they are also a source of income, having been exported abroad since the end of the nineteenth century. Cut flowers are grown mostly on the Riviera, near the French border and in Tuscany. All kinds of flowers can be found in Italian markets, but the most commonly grown are roses, carnations (*Dianthus*), gerbera hybrids and chrysanthemums (*Dendranthema*). The latter are arranged almost exclusively to decorate tombs, as they are considered the flowers of the dead.

The largest displays of flowers are for weddings. These used to consist primarily of carnations and *Asparagus setaceus* fern, but nowadays a wider variety of flowers could well be used. At Christmas most houses are decorated with branches of holly (*Ilex*), mistletoe (*Viscum album*) and pots of poinsettia (*Euphorbia pulcherrima*). On 8 March, Woman's Day in Italy, a sprig of mimosa (*Acacia*) is offered to all women. But roses are still the favourite flower and men give red roses on many occasions. On Palm Sunday the priest blesses olive (*Olea*) branches and palms that have been artistically woven. The biggest and most beautiful arrangements are made in the town of Bordighera, which sends one to the Pope every year. On Maundy Thursday altars are decorated with a profusion of flowers and pots of wheat (*Triticum*) that have been germinated in a dark room. On Corpus Christi village streets are strewn with carpets of petals, over which the procession has to pass.

The use of flowers has been observed throughout Italian history since the time of the Romans. At Pompeii and Rome archaeologists have found frescos, vases and mosaics showing baskets, thyrsi and garlands of flowers and fruits. During the Middle Ages those flowers painted close to the Virgin, by artists

Mass and space arrangement. The shiny red painter's palettes (Anthurium andreanum) against the rough dull fungus give depth. The succession of enclosed spaces builds up the rhythm in the design, along with the close harmony in form and colour that links the container – an eternit pipe with a lead band – to the plant material. ARRANGER: ANNA BARBAGLIA.

• Plant material is restricted to give bold design and maximum impact.

• In all arrangements painted and non-vegetative material may be used.

• The container is a major feature of the arrangement. It is usually sculptural, with bold, clean lines and of neutral colour, to enhance the design.

Free-form Arrangements
The modern free-form design is generally asymmetrical and is characterized by repetition of the lines and the alternation of space and mass.

Line Arrangements
In the modern line arrangement, the line – generally asymmetrical – is the dominant feature. The container must not dominate.

Mass Arrangements
For the mass arrangement, the typical design of the Italian Institute of Flower Arranging Decoration for Amateurs (IIDFA), mass is the main feature and its apparent stillness strengthens the design. Flowers are arranged in groups, so that depth is maximized by the juxtaposition of advancing hot and shiny colours with those that are cool and dull and consequently recede. Containers must be massive to support the visual weight of the arrangement. Articles of clay, metal, plexiglass or rusty iron are sought out and used to create exciting new designs.

Layer Arrangements
To create layer arrangements different surfaces are placed together vertically, horizontally or obliquely. Flowers often give only a touch of colour. Layer arrangements can be created in both modern and antique containers.

*Free-form arrangement. The sprays of Canary Islands date palm (*Phoenix canariensis) *are bent to create space. Rhythm is created by repetition of the round forms. The two gourds (*Cucurbita) *stabilize the design and are united on one side by the* Ligularia *leaves and on the other by the lilies.*
ARRANGER: CARLA BARBAGLIA

such as Giotto di Bondone and Simone Martini, had a symbolic meaning (Madonna lily (*Lilium candidum*) for instance stood for her purity). With the Renaissance, decorations became richer and flowers were used not only in churches but also in the home. They were painted with naturalistic accuracy, as can be seen in the work of Sandro Botticelli. Growing interest in the classical world brought garlands back into vogue. Gardens were created around palaces and villas, and the search for order and rationality resulted in the creation of regular, symmetrical patterns based on geometric formulae. This style of Italian garden had an important influence on garden design over the following centuries.

With the beginning of the Baroque period, flower arrangements in paintings show traces of the gloomy and restless spirit of the Counter-Reformation. Michelangelo Marisi da Caravaggio started the Italian still life tradition, with his famous painted baskets, now at the Pinacoteca Ambrosiana.

The eighteenth century replaced the Baroque spirit with a quest for simplicity and the frivolity of the Rococo period. Flowers, and in particular roses, decorated tapestries, wallpapers, dresses and pieces of furniture. They were usually in soft pastel shades and were arranged in garlands or baskets, from which they flowed gracefully.

The nineteenth century saw the rule of the middle classes and gardens and flower arrangements became simple and calm. People liked oval or round, almost massed, arrangements of roses, camellias, carnations, lilac (*Syringa*), peonies (*Paeonia*), ferns and kentia palm (*Howeia fosteriana*) leaves. Art nouveau was called 'Liberty' in Italy. There was a wide use of wisteria, iris, sunflowers, poppies (*Papaver*) and hydrangeas, which were used to create asymmetric designs, usually with open and sinuous lines.

In Italy the vogue for flower arranging began early in the 1960s. Modern Italian flower arranging can be classified as:
• free-form
• line
• mass and space
• mass using different forms
• layer – the latest creation of Rosnella Cajello Fazio.

In all designs strong contrast of texture and form is evident. Colours are well defined and also show strong contrast. In Italian flower arranging only fresh or dried plant material is used but arrangements often incorporate objects such as stones, metal and plexiglass.

*Line arrangement. Rhythm is created by the movement within the form of the wood and is reinforced by the placement of the two parallel bird-of-paradise flowers (*Strelitzia reginae*).*
ARRANGER: ANNA BARBAGLIA.

◁ Mass arrangement using different forms. In this design,
reminiscent of the warm Mediterranean, the shiny smooth
Aeonium contrasts with the rough matt textures of the container,
the Melianthus and the dates. The tips of the kentia palm were
doubled over to form a neat mass effect.
ARRANGER: CARLA BARBAGLIA.

▽ Layered arrangement. A combination of smooth and uneven
parallel layers is created with gum (Eucalyptus) bark and the
dried red leaves of water lilies, supported on sticks and painted
with transparent varnish. The Calathea leaves and painter's
palettes (Anthurium) give touches of colour.
ARRANGER: CARLA BARBAGLIA.

MALTA

VIEWED FROM THE AIR, the island of Malta looks like a honey-coloured speck in the centre of the blue Mediterranean. On a surface area of only about 260 sq. km (100 sq. miles) it sustains a population of 360,000 and over a million visitors a year. The landscape is craggy and very rocky. It could be described as a land of stone and prickly pear (*Opuntia ficus-indica*), yet it is by no means a desert. Ochre-coloured cliffs, covered in wild thyme (*Thymus*), cascade into the azure sea.

Summer is long, hot and dry, lasting from April right through October. During these months the land is parched and stark. Many a flower arranger's garden, however, is ablaze with flowering climbers and shrubs such as hibiscus, bougainvillaea, plumbago, tecomas, jasmine and antigonon. These are resistant to heat and drought, and give a striking splash of colour well into autumn. Their flowers are often used to decorate tables for *al fresco* meals. October to May is the rainy season, with cool yet gloriously sunny days. There is a sudden transformation in the landscape, and the country comes alive with carpets of wild flowers.

Most gardens are situated at the back of the house and are surrounded by high walls to give protection from prevalent strong winds. Flower arrangers with gardens tend to cultivate foliage plants.

A wonderful selection of flowers is available from the florist all year round, as these are grown commercially under glass. A variety of palms, *Pittosporum*, *Ruscus*, *Cycas*, *Sansevieria*, *Ligularia*, *Aspidistra*, *Aloë* and *Yucca* are indigenous to the Mediterranean and are easily grown. The Maltese national flower is the *Centaurea spatula zerafa*.

Flower arrangers often undertake to decorate churches, cathedrals and palaces – the former *auberges* of the Knights of Malta – with large and lavish displays of flowers on formal and State occasions. Thousands of blooms are used for these events, which are always the highlight of the flower arranging year.

The King of Spain gave Malta to the Knights of St John in 1530 and they ruled the island for 300 years. Known as the Knights Hospitallers of St John of Jerusalem, they were members of Europe's noble families and were sworn to celibacy. Many high-ranking Maltese are still members of the Order, although their present-day role is mostly ceremonial and philanthropic. Their ceremonial dress is a black robe with the white eight-pointed cross – now known as the Maltese Cross.

Weddings provide another happy occasion for flower arrangers to get together to decorate the Baroque churches on the island and the old houses where the wedding receptions take place. Masses of flowers are used on these festive occasions for a large-scale decorations.

△ *Maltese landscape – a collage by Mary Mangion.*

'World's foliage' by Mariuccia Michallef Grimaud.

'Medina Cathedral Flower Festival.'
ARRANGERS: MEMBERS OF THE MALTA FLORAL CLUB.

A spring arrangement with anemones, contorted hazel and moss, with one long
Cymbidium *leaf to give contrast. The round balls are made*
of moss fixed to foam spheres.
ARRANGER: ROLF TORHAUG.

NORWAY

NORWAY IS A LAND OF SUNSHINE, rain and snow, located in the far north of Europe. In this place of climatic contrasts, the south of Norway experiences hot, dry weather during the summer months. The west coast benefits from the warm Gulf Stream and enjoys mild and pleasant days. In contrast, the far north has many cold and rainy days. During the winter the entire country is dressed with a layer of snow, but from April to September the land is green, covered with a multitude of colourful wild flowers, which appear even more colourful the further north one goes.

The Atlantic Ocean surrounds nearly two-thirds of the country. Fjords cut deeply into the land, but high up in the mountains there are wide expanses of wild country covered with the most beautiful and exciting material for flower arranging. Here there are cones, moss, pine and other fresh foliage. Reindeer moss (*Cladonia rangiferina*) grows abundantly, and as yet there are no restrictions on it being gathered for export or for the home.

Flowers are given on many different occasions in Norway, such as when visiting friends and for anniversaries and birthdays. Although flowers are used to decorate churches for weddings and funerals, it is not the custom to arrange flowers there on a weekly basis. Flowers are often purchased for decorating the home, especially at Christmas, Easter, National Day on 17 May and Mothers' Day, which always occurs on the second Sunday in February, when the Norwegian-grown tulips are at their best.

△ *A mossed ball sits in the opening of the vase. The single* Ligularia *leaf is placed through the ball into the water beneath. Other plant material includes* Hydrangea, Bromelia, Aspidistra, Magnolia, *and contorted hazel (*Corylus avellana Contorta*).*
ARRANGER: NILS NORMAN IVERSEN.

Because the cost of energy in Norway is low, certain flowers can be grown in hothouses throughout the year and their quality is excellent. Daffodils are widely used in arrangements at Easter time. But with the exception of the rose, which is by far the most commonly purchased flower and available all year round, Norwegians tend to buy and arrange flowers that are in season. In spring there are forget-me-nots (*Myosotis*), daisies (*Bellis*), tulips (*Tulipa*), cowslips (*Primula veris*), mimosa (*Acacia*), anemones (*Anemone*) and poppies (*Papaver*). In summer sweet pea (*Lathyrus odorata*), marguerites (*Argyranthemum frutescens*), cornflowers (*Centaurea cyanus*), roses, lady's mantle (*Alchemilla mollis*), pot marigolds (*Calendula officinalis*) and delphiniums are widely used, and in autumn chrysanthemums, lilies (*Lilium*), berried branches, Michaelmas daisies and dahlias. Towards the end of the year exotics, such as *Anthurium*, *Protea* and orchids, are incorporated into designs. Red tulips (*Tulipa*) and amaryllis (*Hippeastrum*) are particularly popular.

Flower arranging societies have not yet been established in Norway. Clubs are primarily interested in growing plants such as roses, fuchsia and bonsai. Floristry, however, is a respected profession, needing four years of training in specialist schools.

▷ *A typical Scandinavian arrangement using only a few stems of plant material but with every stem placed for maximum effect. Rolf Torhaug has used Bells of Ireland (*Molucella laevis*), Star of Bethlehem (*Ornithogalum umbellatum*), Allium, moss and a* Phalaenopsis *leaf.*
ARRANGER: ROLF TORHAUG.

▷ *Thick wires were inserted into the snake grass (*Equisetum hyemale*) to give them strength and were then bound with more snake grass. Flowers with their ends in glass tubes are tied to the snake grass and embellished with red wire.*
ARRANGER: NILS NORMAN IVERSEN.

POLAND

THE POLISH PEOPLE ARE JUSTLY PROUD of their fine country situated in the heart of northern Europe. In the north lie the flat plains adjoining the Baltic Sea. In the south lies a more mountainous region that bears the breathtakingly beautiful Tatra Mountains. Despite Poland's troubled history, the resilience and fortitude of its entrepreneurial people has led to the Poland of today being an exciting, fast-developing country.

One of the distinctive features of Polish life is the importance of flowers in everyday life. Poles give flowers to express their feelings – in gratitude, sympathy or appreciation, as a symbol of friendship and reconciliation.

Different flowers suit different occasions. Carnations are very popular, but roses are regarded as more sophisticated for joyous occasions. White flowers, such as chrysanthemums, usually accompany condolences. Exotic flowers are expensive and, as such, are valued as a generous gesture. Most occasions require cut flowers rather than potted ones, which are most popular when visiting graves on All Saints' Day. Cut flowers are generally presented upright and without a wrapper.

Availability of flowers used to depend on the season, but today glasshouses supply all kinds of flowers all year round. Purchasing flowers is therefore more a question of price than availability.

When paying a visit you are expected to take flowers for the lady of the house. Welcome, farewell and school ceremonies, weddings, theatrical performances and official celebrations cannot do without flowers. On the day of elections, the first person who casts his or her vote in a polling station receives flowers.

Colours of flowers symbolize different attitudes. Red is associated with love, yellow with jealousy, and white with innocence. White and red flowers are frequently used on patriotic occasions.

Flower growing and selling is big business in Poland. Good florists are well known for their bouquet-making, and people will travel miles to buy a bouquet from a well-known florist. On certain days (for example, Valentine's Day, Graduation Day and namedays) supplies of flowers are sold out almost immediately.

Red and white roses and a cloud of Gypsophila *reflect the colours of the Polish flag.*
ARRANGER: BARBARA BIELECKA.

*A small bouquet of
flowers typical of
those prepared
by kiosk sellers.
Glory lilies (Gloriosa
superba) and
asparagus fern
(A. setaceus) have
been pushed through
the actual structure
of a fleshy leaf.
Arranger: Rosemary
Wetherell.*

*Palms of dried flowers are taken to the church
on Palm Sunday.
Arranger: Rosemary Wetherell.*

RUSSIA

RUSSIA IS THE LARGEST PART of the former Soviet Union, stretching from Leningrad (or St Petersburg as it is now known) on the Baltic Sea to Vladivostok on the Pacific, and spanning 11 time zones. The climate is distinctly continental, with hot, dusty summers, and is famous for its extremely cold winters.

The countryside is mostly flat and noted for the absence of stone, which is why it is famous for its red-brick architecture. The winters are long and hard, and one quarter of the rainfall falls during July and August. Hence the need to import flowers into Russia from flower-growing countries such as Holland.

Flower arranging in Russia developed in conjunction with gardening. In 1630 Tzar Alexei Mikhailovich ordered the first formal gardens to be laid and over 800 lilies, pansies and other flowers (100 varieties in total) were delivered from abroad. In 1667 the Russian artist Nikolai Pavlovets painted a famous painting of the Blessed Virgin Mary in a garden, with bunches of flowers in the foreground. Other famous paintings of flowers that followed were by Tolstoy, Fyodorov, Khrutscy, Potatuyev and Kramskoy. Flowers are, and always have been, used in the decorative arts – in tapestries, woodcarvings, wood paintings and on vases. Flower patterns decorate traditional clothing, particularly shawls, which are now sold mainly as souvenirs.

Although flowers are expensive and are considered a luxury item, they have always been an important part of Russian life. They are given on every special occasion, such as birthdays, namedays, weddings, anniversaries, house-warming parties and as a sign of gratitude. It is considered very bad luck to give an even number of flowers and most, but not all, Russians are superstitious about this. The number four is particularly avoided, as this is associated with death. On an occasion where several bouquets are presented, perhaps at a birthday party, the host will periodically check that no room contains an even number of flowers. When visiting a concert many of the audience will take bunches of flowers, which they will present to the artists of their choice after the performance.

Flower arranging is supported by the Russian Ministry of Culture. In Moscow and the big cities virtually everyone lives in apartment blocks and so gardens are not available. Plant material for arranging is grown on windowsills or taken from pot plants. Plastic and artificial plant material is used extensively.

Flowers are sold both in kiosks and specialist shops. There is a fine row of kiosks located by the Park of Economic Achievements in Moscow. Perhaps the most popular flowers are roses and carnations, but lilies, chrysanthemums, irises, gerbera hybrids and statice are also sold.

Bouquets are very simply assembled – three or five roses with a sprig of foliage, or perhaps three or five carnations or tulips. Different types of flowers are not combined in bouquets. Carnations are popular because they last a long time and are available all year round. In spring tulips and mimosa are commonly seen, in summer roses and chamomile flowers (*Anthemis*), and in autumn chrysanthemums.

Roses have a special significance for Russians. They are sold in ones, threes and larger bunches. Due to their known high cost, they are widely given. The Russian people are generous hosts, the giving of presents is widespread and, even though money is short, they will not hesitate to show their appreciation of visitors.

A number of city-dwelling Russians have *dachas* – modest wooden cottages in the countryside, to which they generally retire in the warmer months of spring and summer. Generally people concentrate on the cultivation of fruit, potatoes and other vegetables in their *dacha* gardens. Much of what is produced here is pickled for consumption during the long, hard winter months. Flowers tend to be grown in areas of land that are not suitable for food cultivation, along pathways or next to fences.

Red is an important colour and in eighteenth-century literature the words beauty and red were often used interchangeably. Red Square is so called because of its great beauty. Red implies goodness and beauty – hence the large number of red roses and other red flowers in the market place.

Japanese ikebana has had a very strong influence on Russian flower arranging. Now, due to visits from European flower arrangers, new influences are taking hold and Russian styles are becoming more diverse.

An exhibit at a flower-arranging show at Sochi.

An Easter arrangement at an exhibition in Sochi.

An odd number of red carnations
with asparagus fern.
ARRANGER: LYLIA KADER.

SPAIN

SPAIN LIES TO THE SOUTH-WEST OF EUROPE, occupying most of the Iberian peninsula. Its coast forms the western boundary of the Mediterranean, but Spain also has an Atlantic coastline in the north-west and south-west. The country is predominantly high, hot and arid.

Carnations are the traditional symbol of Spain and are represented in paintings, festivals and dress. Mantillas – ladies' headdresses – carry a red, white or other coloured carnation, according to the festival.

During Holy Week there are processions all over Spain, when effigies of saints are carried through the streets. The saints are festooned with roses, sword lilies (*Gladiolus*), lilies and carnations. For the Corpus Christi procession in June the petals of roses and other flowers are tossed onto the procession as living confetti.

In the Costa Blanca a wide variety is grown of both foliage and flowers, wild and cultivated. In the countryside in spring there is a wonderful choice of wild flowers that closely resemble the larger cultivated plants, such as crocus, gladiolus, *Muscari*, bee orchid, *Allium* and *Narcissus*.

Roses, lilies, anemones (*A. coronaria*), freesias, sweet pea (*Lathyrus odoratus*), geranium (*Pelargonium*) and marguerites (*Argyranthemum frutescens*) are commonly grown and are available in the florists' shops. There are also many flowering shrubs such as jasmine, honeysuckle (*Lonicera*), *Bougainvillaea*, *Weigela*, oleander (*Nerium oleander*), *Hibiscus* and *Lantana*. Foliage plants include the various pines, palms, rubber plants (*Ficus*), various ivies (Hedera), flax (*Phormium*) and many lovely grasses. There is an amazing array of two-colour spray carnations. These look lovely mixed with baby's breath (*Gypsophila*) for delicate pretty arrangements.

One of the most delightful foliages is that of the hibiscus. Its dark, shiny leaves give a smooth, glossy background to the vibrant colours of the lily and gladiolus.

Ceramic pots of various designs, and pots made of shaped dried leaves, are often used as containers. The latter look lovely when used with larger foliage and with flowers in brilliant orange, scarlet, deep red and purple colours. Also used frequently with these containers is a wide selection of citrus fruits and vegetables. When large ceramic pots are used, a green plastic container is fixed into the neck of the pot and either a pinholder or foam placed in position.

▷ *Gerberas of mixed colours with palm leaves.*
ARRANGER: DORI TILEY.

▷ *Red carnations and red gladioli.*
ARRANGER: MANANA CRESPI FONTES.

THE UNITED KINGDOM

THE UNITED KINGDOM COMPRISES England, Scotland, Wales and Northern Ireland. Although sharing a long history, each country maintains its own culture and traditions. The climate is generally similar throughout – temperate and maritime. It is seldom excessively hot in summer or cold in winter. It is, however, wet and windy much of the time. This mild, wet climate creates the lush green nature of its predominantly deciduous vegetation.

England

Throughout history, flowers have been used in England for medicinal and culinary purposes. Their fragrance has been employed not only to bring delight to the senses, but to combat the rather unpleasant odours of less sanitary times. From Stone Age times, when flowers were carved on the walls of caves, flowers have also been used in a representational form. They appear in the illuminated manuscripts of the Middle Ages, on china and pottery, on tapestries, wallpaper and fabrics. The red and white roses were even the badges of the competing sides in the Wars of the Roses in the late Middle Ages. The herbalist John Parkinson wrote in the early seventeenth century that a house was decorated with 'fresh bowls in every corner and flowers tied upon them and sweet briar, stock, gilly flowers, pinks, wallflowers and any other sweet flowers in glasses and pots in every window and chimney – for sight and scent'.

Styles of arranging have changed through the ages. They have adapted to the ever-changing styles of art, interior design and new inventions in technology. With the British love of gardens and gardening, the use of an abundant amount of garden plant material has often featured in British flower design. Georgian and Victorian periods gloried in this abundance. The Edwardian period saw a more restrained use of plant material. In the 1930s Constance Spry brought abundance back into the home. Although many styles are practised today, it is for the traditional garden style that the English are so well known.

A pedestal arrangement using garden plant material.
ARRANGER: MARY FISHER.

Scotland

Mary Law writes: 'Experienced Scottish cooks often remark that Scotland has one of the best larders in the world, just as the flower arranger is never lost for choice in plant material. Many famous plantsmen have hailed from here, and an interest in foliage is always high on the artist's list. With an abundance of natural wood and plants, it is no wonder that the floral artist turns to his own wealth in the garden.

'Our National Heritage is very important to the Scottish people. A design for a Hogmanay celebration would possibly include arching sprays of Scots pine (*Pinus sylvestris*), ivy (*Hedera helix*), golden *Cupressus*, Chinese witch hazel (*Hamamelis mollis*), silk tassel bush (*Garrya elliptica*) and touches of heather (*Calluna*). This would form a suitable background for the inclusion of rich red carnations and amber-coloured chrysanthemums.

'In January, the birthday of the poet Robert Burns calls to be remembered in flowers, and here the options are endless. His love of nature makes a landscape design of driftwood, wooden ferns, *Hedera helix* and white single-spray chrysanthemums to represent the modest daisy. The sweeping foliage of broom (*Cytisus*) could depict a windswept design for "O Wert Thou in the Cauld Blast". No one can resist using lovely red roses and these, teamed with the grey foliage of western hemlock (*Tsuga heterophylla*), would suitably signify "My Love is Like a Red Red Rose".'

A wreath with a tartan bow.

Wales

Sylvia Lewis recounts: 'From the rugged north to the gentle south of the Principality of Wales, the dainty wild daffodil, *Cennin pedr*, appears in early spring. *Cennin* is actually Welsh for 'leek', but the association arises because the daffodil leaves are so similar to those of the leek (*Allium porruco*).

'On St David's Day, on 1 March, the bright yellow flower of our national emblem is much in evidence, worn with pride. Dressed in national costume, children celebrate at school with *eisteddfod* – a competition in verse and song. A prize-winning psalm for Wales was written by Christopher Thomas, aged 10, and included the following verse:

> Behold the daffodil and leek – the proud emblems.
> We give thanks to you O Lord
> for the music and the harp of Wales.'

Northern Ireland

The Reverend William McMillan writes: 'For over 25 years I have used floral art to celebrate some of the major festivals in the Christian calendar. My church – a unique Georgian meeting house in Dunmurry on the outskirts of Belfast – attracts thousands of visitors to our yearly festival, staged at either Christmas or Easter.

'Flowers express the deepest emotions of the human heart and, when used symbolically, they speak louder than many sermons. It has been my privilege to stage many similar festivals in cathedrals and churches throughout Northern Ireland. These, ignoring the political and religious divide, have expressed the faith, hope and dreams of many, and as such have witnessed the reconciliation and peace in a unique and challenging way.'

The Welsh wedding of Rhian Davies and Gareth Parry. The floral arches were decorated with roses, honeysuckle, carnations, myrtle and rosemary. The Brymawr folk dancers are dressed in authentic traditional Welsh costume.

Dried swags by Betty Birney for the annual flower festival in Dunmurry.

AUSTRALASIA, ASIA AND AFRICA

AUSTRALIA

AUSTRALIA IS AN UNBELIEVABLY vast country. It is the largest island and the smallest continent in the world – 8 million sq. km (over 3 million sq. miles) in total. The land area is almost equal to that of the United States but it has a population of only around 17 million. Australia lies in the Southern Hemisphere, with a vast coastline of some 20,000 km (12,500 miles) washed by the waters of three oceans and four seas. Roughly one-third of the country is situated above the Tropic of Capricorn, having a tropical climate, the remaining two-thirds having winter rainfall.

It is a land of many changes, from lush tropical rain forest, through fertile and wet plains, mountainous regions and forest areas to a wonderful coastline and the largest mass of arid desert. Each state has natural species of flora to suit the climate of that region. No matter how arid the area is, after the rain it becomes a wonderland of colour.

Flowers are an important part of life in Australia. Most homes have a garden. There is a trend towards low-maintenance gardens, as during the hot, dry summer months water is not always plentiful. Most flower arrangers grow plants for foliage, the most popular being small palms, New Zealand flax (*Phormium*), privet (*Ligustrum*), myrtle (*Myrtus*), *Aralia*, *Philodendron*, conifers and a variety of ferns.

Flowers are given on all occasions, from the beginning of life to the end, and on all celebrations in between. Roses, carnations, orchids, painter's palettes (*Anthurium*) and chrysanthemums (*Dendranthema*) are extremely popular, as are *Banksia* and *Protea* in season. People tend to buy longer-lasting flowers. At flower markets a wide variety of flowers and foliage is available from all the different parts of Australia and from overseas. Spring flowers from the Northern Hemisphere, for instance, are available in the Australian autumn.

Flower arranging is very popular throughout Australia, but in such a vast land, clubs are small and often isolated by distances of many hundreds of miles from the next.

The most popular style uses a restrained amount of plant material. Interpretative work is popular, as the designer can use much or little plant material, according to what is available. Sculptural work is becoming more popular, as the wonderful nuts, seedheads, wood, vine and palm spathes that are widely available are so long-lasting. Foliage arrangements are another popular choice, using a wonderful array of succulents. These can be designed as pedestal or modern arrangements, or as leaf sculpture.

Pincushion flowers (Leucospermum), *mimosa* (Acacia) *and bear grass* (Xerophyllum).
ARRANGERS: KATHERINE DEWE MATTHEWS AND BETTY MACMAHON.

*Lemons, limes (*Citrus*) and avocados (*Persea*) with* Hibiscus *flowers.*
ARRANGERS: KATHERINE DEWE MATTHEWS AND BETTY MACMAHON.

CHINA

CHINA IS ONE OF THE WORLD'S LARGEST, most populous and geographically diverse countries. With climates ranging from cold, high desert to coastal tropical wetlands, its flora and fauna are similarly diverse. So too are its peoples, who span a vast linguistic and ethnic spectrum. Culturally, however, China has enjoyed several thousand years of relatively harmonious and continuous evolution. Despite periodic internal upheavals, self-imposed economic and political isolation has led to the development of a unique approach to life.

The Chinese have always considered that flowers should be placed in their proper setting and treated with due deference and respect. Writing during the Ming dynasty, Yuan Lhung-lao said, 'Talk of all that is ugly, plain and common is held in deep disgust by flower spirits. It is better to sit in dull silence than be disliked by flowers.'

Auspicious juxtapositions of ideas, shapes, colours, textures – even lines of the day, month and year – as well as orientations of objects, from bowls to buildings, assume an importance in Chinese life that is incomprehensible to the untutored Westerner.

Flowers have traditionally been one of the most dominating and recurring motifs in Chinese art. Even the imperial robes were decorated with symbolic flowers. And throughout their history the Chinese have selected and graded flowers into ranks of importance and endowed them with deep symbolic meanings. For example, pine (*Pinus*) is associated with longevity, bamboo with scholarly attributes, while the lotus (*Nelumbo*) – grown exclusively in lakes and ponds – symbolizes purity and perfection and is also the flower of Buddha. The peony (*Paeonia*) is the flower held in the highest esteem of all, symbolizing wealth and honour. Its importance in imperial gardens was always emphasized by its setting in raised marble flower beds. The chrysanthemum (*Dendrathema*) was first grown as a herb and has been cultivated since AD 600. Even today the chrysanthemum is celebrated with its own important autumn festival and with huge displays in public parks.

The principal colour of happiness is red, both for decorations and flowers. Red also expresses the stronger male characteristics. At weddings, red was traditionally worn by both bride and groom, while pomegranates (*Punica granatum*) with their many seeds were often given to promote the birth of many children – especially sons.

The proper use of red and white colours reflects the combination of yang and yin, leading to maximum good fortune at festivals and joyous occasions.

Flowers are important as offerings to Buddha in temples or on family altars, where the ancestral tablets are placed and flowers and fruits offered. During the 4 or 5 April Festival of 'Pure Brightness' – the date varies according to the lunar calendar – the ancestral graves are visited, washed and decorated with flowers.

But the most important family gathering and gift-giving event is the New Year Festival at the end of January. In the flower markets pots of small, golden orange trees are bought for nearly every home. The golden fruit symbolizes the wish for wealth and prosperity for the new year. Branches of plum (*Prunus*) blossom are arranged, and bowls of a special white *Narcissus* – symbol of the season – are brought into homes.

A bronze antique vase on a flower table. The pine is a symbol of long life, the chrysanthemums are an autumnal flower and there is a bowl of apples, an auspicious fruit. Included is a carved god of longevity. This would be a traditional grouping for a scholar's room.
ARRANGER: PAMELA SOUTH.

The classic Chinese style of flower arrangement was developed by the educated mandarin scholar class. Senior mandarins relaxed by making flower arrangements, drinking wine and burning fragrant incense as they composed erudite poems with their friends. The style they favoured was linear, rhythmic and asymmetrical, with limitation of material and space within the design. Vases had their own bases and were placed on small stands or flower tables, often grouped at different heights and with accessories such as incense burners, scholars' writing materials and scrolls, plus bowls of auspicious fruits. As early as 1595 an influential and historically important book on flower arrangement was published for the instruction of would-be scholar arrangers.

A classical composition or grouping often incorporated hidden symbolic meanings. For example, the names of the flowers (as expressed in written Chinese characters) might be re-combined to form auspicious homophonic phrases particularly appropriate to the occasion or season being celebrated.

Porcelain was, of course, invented by the Chinese, so there have traditionally been beautiful vases in which to place flowers. The rim of the vase was never obscured by the arrangement, in order that the beauty of the vase and the flowers might complement one another. China is also said to have made the first baskets specifically for the display of flowers. Peasant-style arrangements – often in baskets – were exuberant, colourful and crowded, symbolizing abundant good wishes for the happiness of the recipient or for the occasion. China also invented silk, so naturally it became the first country to make silk flowers.

In the early years of the twentieth century interest in flower arranging waned. The Cultural Revolution of the 1960s proved to be an even greater setback.

During the last few years, however, with the general 'relaxation' of a once rigidly centralized society, a spontaneous revival of public interest in many older forms of cultural and artistic expression has occurred within China. The first All-China Flower Arrangement Exhibition since the founding of the People's Republic in 1949 was held in Shanghai in September 1990. The 10-day exhibition was attended by an estimated 100,000 people. Class titles included 'The Flowers in a Bride's Hands', 'The Basket of Flowers for Birthday Celebrations' and 'The Flower Arrangement on a Table for the Honoured Guest'.

It is difficult for any observer to determine the extent of the revival of flower arranging skills in a country so vast. What is

An antique basket filled with mixed flowers and hydrangeas. An abundance of flowers means 'full of good wishes'. This arrangement would be suitable for an auspicious occasion, such as a birthday.
ARRANGER:
PAMELA SOUTH.

clear is that there is official encouragement. Much of the excellent floral work seen in local exhibitions was initially sponsored by official bodies, such as horticultural institutes and offshoots of the national Ministry of Agriculture.

Within the educated and managerial classes, flower arranging is slowly re-establishing itself as a legitimate means of personal artistic expression.

Among the wider peasant classes, in what is still a predominantly agricultural society, controlled and formalized flower arranging has never existed, but informal groupings of flowers have always been used to beautify homes and to celebrate special occasions.

Across the nation, florist's shops are springing up in many major cities, and in the evenings flowers grown by the peasants can often be purchased in impromptu back-street markets. The giving and receiving of flowers, as a mark of personal esteem, has undergone a considerable revival.

A brass antique container and incense-burner using scented flowers.
ARRANGER: PAMELA SOUTH.

JAPAN

JAPAN CONSISTS OF FOUR MAIN ISLANDS surrounded by more than 1,000 smaller islands. The length of the country from north to south creates a climate with extreme variations. There are hard winters in the northern island of Hokkaido, but in the southern part of Kyushu and on small islands like Okinawa the climate is tropical. Hokkaido became well known for the Sapporo Winter Olympics, and at its annual Ice Festival beautiful sculptures are carved out of the snow and ice. The islands of Japan are very mountainous, mostly volcanic, the most famous mountain being Mount Fuji. This leaves very little flat land for agricultural purposes, which is mainly used for the cultivation of rice.

The mountains of Japan are covered with pines, with wild azaleas (*Rhododendron*) and maples (*Acer*) giving beautiful colours in the autumn. The cherry blossom (*Prunus serrulata*) – the Japanese national flower – is another lovely sight in the spring. Parties called *Hanami* (flower viewing) are held to admire these beautiful blossoms and to toast them with *sake* (rice wine) and song.

There are many festivals in Japan, some national and some applicable only to certain regions. The Doll's Festival (called Hina Matsuri) is celebrated all over Japan on 3 March. Beautiful dolls depicting the Emperor and Empress, the ladies-in-waiting, retainers and musicians are displayed on a red tiered stand. Offerings of peach (*Prunus persica*) blossom and rape (*Brassica napus*) are also placed with a small doll in a basket and floated on the river, to take away evil spirits from a child.

Another well-known festival is the Tango no Sekku (Boys' Festival) on 5 May when the sobu iris (*I. ensata syn. I. kaempferi*) is used, since its leaf resembles the blade of a sword. The iris leaves are put in the boys' bathing water to make them brave. At the same time you see lots of carp, mostly made of silk, flying from the rooftops of houses.

In the summer the Bon-o-Dori Festival is intended to entertain the dead, who after seven years are permitted to return briefly. They are guided by lanterns placed on the water or around the shrine where the dances are being held.

The gardens in Japan are well known for their simplicity, their blossom in springtime and their colours in the autumn. They are usually small, with pine, bamboo and flowering shrubs, such as camellias and azaleas, but rarely many annuals or perennials. They seek to preserve nature in miniature, and thus a stream will represent a river, and a rock a hill or mountain.

In Japan red is the colour for celebration. When a new business opens it is customary for friends and business associates to send large red and white wreaths, which stand outside the business premises on tripods.

Ikebana

One could not talk about Japan without mentioning ikebana. Over the last 600 years ikebana has become one of Japan's traditional art forms, practised by men and women alike, and a vital element in the contemporary world of art.

This specialist art started many centuries ago, with the offering of the lotus plant to Buddha. The three stages of the flowers and leaves symbolized the future (the bud or curled leaf), the present (the open flower or wide-open leaf) and the past (the seedpod

The tea ceremony room. On the left are tea utensils consisting of an iron kettle and a water container.
ARRANGER:
KAZUYO KIDO.

and the withered leaf). The styles of arranging the flowers began to differ. At first they were rather stiff and upright in tall bronze vases, but Chinese paintings of landscapes influenced the later style, which became known as the Rikka. These huge, man-high arrangements, whose principal placements were mountains, waterfall, rocks, source of the river, the river and the town, were placed in the courtyards of palaces and temples. With these arrangements the first ikebana school was born, called the Ikenobo School of Ikebana. Its temple was in Kyoto and the school still has its headquarters there.

Other changes came – the arrangements became smaller and could be placed in the home in a special shallow alcove in the main room, known as a *tokonoma*. With the changes came different schools with their own headmasters (and nowadays also headmistresses) with their own styles, but all related to the basic asymmetrical triangle arrangements, with the three principal branches symbolizing Heaven, Man and Earth. There are now more than 3,000 different schools of ikebana in Japan, handed down through the generations from father to son, daughter or adopted son. Time has also played an important part. Like any art, ikebana is alive and changes over the centuries due to outside influences. The Ohara School, for instance, developed the pinholder (Kenzan) and placed arrangements in low containers, in order that they could be viewed from different angles and placed on Western-style tables and sideboards. One of the better known schools in Japan, and in the world, is the oldest one, Ikenobo; one very modern and still fairly young school is the Sogetsu School. The Enshu School-Isshin Kai is one of the very few that is still highly classical. Its style is always a Seika and the asymmetrical triangle is easy to recognize.

Another well-known Japanese art is the tea ceremony. In the small room where the tea ceremony takes place a small arrangement is placed in the *tokonoma*. The arrangement is delicate and made of local materials – there are many rules about which kinds may, or may not, be used. The style of arrangement is called *cha-bana* (*cha* meaning 'tea' and *bana* or *hana* 'flower').

A classical Enchu arrangement.
ARRANGER: TINEKE ROBERTSON.

NEW ZEALAND

NEW ZEALAND HAS VERY VARIED climatic conditions: the south experiences strong winds that rush over the open plains, while in the north there are virtually tropical temperatures.

New Zealanders live close to nature and tend to take the profusion of plants around them for granted. Parks, forests, native bush, coastlines, farms and mountains are generally within easy reach of most people. In addition, New Zealand is a nation of gardeners. Little wonder, therefore, that many people wish to bring plants indoors and design with them to enhance their homes, workplaces, social functions and special occasions. An interest in floral art is a natural progression for many who want to learn more about the art of designing with plant material.

Floral Art Society of New Zealand members prefer to be called floral artists or floral designers. 'Floral' is taken in its widest botanical meaning, and encompasses any part of a plant – flowers, foliage, fruits, vegetables, bark, seaweed, mosses, lichens, spathes, vines and roots.

New Zealand's climate encourages the growing of a huge range of plant material. The horticulture and floriculture industries are highly developed, so the variety and quality of plant material are extensive and inexpensive. Plant material arrives almost daily from markets around the world to add an exotic flavour to the range available.

Flowers and foliage for the home often come from the garden, but with flowers available from florists, supermarkets, petrol stations and greengrocers, these are often bought to supplement the garden supply and to enjoy something different. Wonderful artificial fruits and flowers are now available and these are being used more and more. Home entertaining usually includes flowers for buffet and dining tables. In the North Island, where hibiscus grow, their blooms are popular table flowers, since they do not need to be put in water.

Christmas in New Zealand falls in midsummer. The traditional colours of red, white and green still feature, with roses (*Rosa* cv.), lilies (*Lilium*), conifers, ivy (*Hedera*) and holly (*Ilex*) firm favourites. Living Christmas trees of pine and Douglas fir (*Pseudotsuga menziesii*) are popular, but because of their lush, soft new growth at this time of the year there are problems of wilting in the summer heat.

Native plants in New Zealand are not noted for their brightly coloured flowers. The predominance of white or small flowers is usually attributed to the fact that most are wind-pollinated, rather than insect-pollinated. Some natives do, however, have showy flowers, such as Sophora tetraptera with its bright yellow tubular flowers, and the red pohutukawa (*Metrosideros*), which makes such a splash in the landscapes of the north around Christmas time. The lush variety of greens of the wonderful native foliages more than make up for the lack of bright colour. Cascading *Dacrydium*, bold, shiny *Meryta sinclairii* and *Myosotidium* leaves, the rough, fine textures of *Hebe* and *Podocarpus totara* (Totara), together with *Pseudopanax*, *Griselinia* and New Zealand flax provide a rich tapestry from which the floral artist can choose. The grey-leaved astelia and senecio are favourites. Other popular native materials include ferns, skeletonized ponga (*Cyathea dealbata*) bark, weathered puriri (*Vilex*) wood, black beech (*Nothofagus*), supplejack vine (*Rhipogonum scandens*), shelf fungi and mosses. Exotic favourites for floral design include Asiatic lilies, roses, *Strelitzia*, proteas, leucadendrons, Chinese gooseberry or kiwifruit vine (*Actinidia chinensis* syn. *A. deliciosa*) and statice (*Limonium*).

Pseudopanax lessonii *('Gold Splash'),*
pohutukawaa *(*Metrosideros kermadecensis)
blooms and black fungus covering Coprosma
branches in a tall pottery container.
DESIGNER: LORRAINE MCMILLAN.

Sophora microphylla, Metrosideros, *Regal lily (*Lilium regale*),
chrysanthemum, carnations (*Dianthus) *and Love-lies-bleeding*
(Amaranthus) *arranged on a stand constructed from*
Eucalyptus *stems.*
DESIGNER: MARGARET MORRISS.

*Wall hanging with New Zealand flax (*Phormium hybrid),
Coprosma *berries,* Pittosporum eugenioides, *black beech*
(Nothofagus solandri) *and* Meryta sinclairii.
DESIGNER: HELEN POTTER.

The New Zealand Way

New Zealanders have earned a reputation as a DIY and innovative nation, and these traits are certainly part of the floral art world. Designers often make their own containers or create designs without obvious containers. Mechanics and stands are continually being created and copied, and give a versatility and freedom to designs that are not bound by the constraints of a container. The typical floral artist's workbox contains a hammer, nails, drill, strong wire, straps and glue gun, as well as the more traditional tools. The use of accessories is limited and special backgrounds are seldom seen.

Designers employ a wide range of styles and design. Their work encompasses traditional and modern styles, and they have a great interest in new trends and ideas. New Zealanders love to travel, both within their own country and overseas, so they are constantly soaking up new ideas and influences, which they explore and adapt. They use colour in a bold, clear-cut way, reflecting the strong, clear light of the Pacific skies. The swirls and curves of Maori art and craft, the vines and strong forms of the New Zealand native forests, contribute to a preference for strong lines and bold plant material. Floral artists revel in the profusion of nature's bounty in which they live. The natural beauty of the land constantly challenges and inspires creativity.

*Supplejack vine (*Rhipogonum scandens*) and gum (*Eucalyptus*) stems forming the stand, with* Magnolia *leaves glued at the base.* Aspidistra *leaves,* Hydrangea *and sunflowers (*Helianthus*) complete the design.*
ARRANGER: MARGARET MORRISS.

SOUTH AFRICA

SOUTH AFRICA, WITH ITS GREAT VARIETY AND WEALTH of natural beauty, is recognized as one of the countries richest in indigenous flora. Its magnificent scenery, wilderness areas, botanical gardens, parks and nurseries as well as beautiful private gardens, have contributed to the healthy growth of flower arranging as a hobby and art form. The wide range of climatic, geographic and cultural variations makes for a fascinating diversity of flower arranging styles. It is difficult to identify one particular style of design that is common to all of South Africa.

The western part of the Cape Province (Namaqualand) is very beautiful. From August to September the flowers are magnificent and unequalled in the world. In a relatively small area there is an amazingly large variety of indigenous species, especially of the huge Proteceae family, which is tolerant of the winter rainfall and strangely poor soils of the area. Flower arrangers from the Cape delight in showing off their magnificent flora, often skilfully offset by dried kelp, vines and spathes. Bold, free-form line designs and naturalistic massed arrangements are popular and may include the attractive foliage, cones and berries of the leucadendron or the leathery sword-shaped leaves of the bird-of-paradise flower (*Strelitzia reginae*). Table designs include locally grown grapes, melons (*Cucumis*), apples (*Malus*), wheat (*Triticum*) and barley (*Hordeum*), driftwood and sea shells.

Moving north through the arid areas of the Karoo to the Free State, the geography becomes one of vast, open farming spaces. The climatic extremes of very cold winters, blistering hot summers and low rainfall produce many interesting succulent species. Once the rains come, spring is greeted by many flowering trees and shrubs, which come into profuse blossom, along with a colourful array of flowering bulbs. The vleis are covered with thousands of white arum lilies (*Zantedeschia*), and fascinating grasses abound. Arrangers enjoy using colourful groupings of flowers, with driftwood and dried plant material as a framework. In winter, when there are few flowers, modern and abstract designs are popular.

The provinces of the greater Transvaal encompass a high plateau, rugged mountains and the subtropical Lowveld. The extremes of temperature have also influenced styles. Many arrangers favour designs using a minimum of plant material. Interesting lines and unusual forms are combined in pleasing free-form, modern, abstract and sculptural arrangements. The gardens of the Lowveld have an abundance of luxurious foliage, and here colourful traditional and modern grouped mass arrangements are popular.

KwaZulu-Natal stretches from the grandeur of the Drakensberg Mountains through the rolling grasslands, down to the subtropical region adjacent to the warm Indian Ocean. English-style gardens predominate in the cooler midlands, where flowering trees such as peach, cherry, plum, and shrubs such as azalea, rhododendrons, and garden perennials abound. Beautiful traditional arrangements reminiscent of Constance Spry are favoured. Every three years, in September, Kirstenbosch has a very large show in Cape Town in the Goodhope Centre, where vast displays of indigenous flora are used.

In the coastal subtropical areas informal, flowing and line mass designs generally include a variety of luxuriant and colourful foliage combined with bougainvillaea, heliconia, ixora and anthuriums. Arrangers also enjoy grouping and layering of flowers and foliage.

The Eastern Cape falls between the Cape and KwaZulu-Natal, so arrangers have the best of both worlds and enjoy making traditional and modern, massed and line designs, with strelitzias playing a special role.

During October most towns and cities have Rose Festivals. The Addo Rose Show, with over 25,000 roses on display, has been likened to the Chelsea Flower Show.

To conclude, all styles and types of design can be seen in South Africa and it is fortunate in having a tremendous wealth of attractive plant material from which to choose and a ready availability of beautiful hand-woven baskets, fabrics and clay pots in all shapes and sizes, inspiring designers to experiment with unusual combinations of exciting textures and vibrant colour mixes.

Modern mass arrangements of indigenous plant material in an Ali Baba container.
ARRANGER: EMMIE PABST.

◁ *An informal mass-type arrangement for the patio. Dramatic heliconias are used for the outline, with muted bromeliad spikes seen at a lower level. Stems of vibrant red croton (*Codiaeum*) give colour and rhythm. Two heads of* Dracaena *foliage are placed on the left. The fan-shaped leaves of the dwarf fan palm (*Chamaerops humilis*) form an area of radiating and diagonal lines on the right. A grouping of rounded flower heads of* Ixora *gives weight to the central area. Textural interest is provided by the inclusion of sprays of shiny green seeds from the areca palm (*Chrysalidocarpus lutescens*). The looped, hand-made beaded Zulu belt gives a typically local flavour to this design.*
ARRANGER: ROSEMARY LADLAU.

▽ *The upturned hand-carved bowl was the inspiration for this continentally influenced design. Strong vertical thrusts of* Strelitzia reginae, *spiral ginger and yellow ginger (*Hedychium sp.*) balance the visual weight of the dark container. The round, ball fruit of the screw-pine (*Pandanus utilis*) echoes the carved pattern on the wood. Textural interest is supplied by the smooth, shiny anthuriums and the aubergines (*Solanum melongena*). The horizontal lines are extended with the cat's-tail fern (*Asparagus densiflorus 'Myers'*) and yellow mottled* Anthurium *leaves, while the hybrid gerbera, an upmarket cousin of the indigenous* Barberton *daisy, adds further form interest.*
ARRANGER: ALTHEA HIGHAM.

THAILAND

THAILAND IS SITUATED IN THE HEART of south-east Asia and is the gateway to Indochina. It is a land rich in resources, with soaring mountain ranges in the north, sprawling plateaux in the north-east, and white sandy beaches on turquoise seas in the south. The climate is tropical, with long hours of sunshine and high humidity. There are three seasons: hot from March to June, rainy from July to October and cool from November to February. The geographic and climatic conditions make the country ideal for the cultivation of many varieties of flowers.

Flower arranging has been enjoyed in Thailand since ancient times. Thao Srichulalak and Nang Nophamal refer to flower arranging as a popular pastime for women. Flower arranging skills were learnt at Court and were practised by women of wealth and noble birth.

Since then Thai flower arranging has been recognized as a fine art, requiring the qualities that are admired and respected in good housewives.

'Phum'
This arrangement is used at royal ceremonies and other rites. It is placed on altars, presented to Buddha, to senior monks, the Sangha and members of the royal family as floral tributes. The art originated at the royal Court, where the gracious art of flower arranging was considered an essential accomplishment. The arrangement is made from globe amaranths (Gomphrena celosiodes), which have been dyed in different colours. Each flower is pierced by a sharp bamboo stick, which holds it fast to a clay centrepiece. A predesigned pattern is made by the use of different colours.

It was Nang Nophamal who invented the floating lantern in the shape of a lotus (*Nelumbo*) made from colourful flowers and adorned with candles and incense sticks. This floating lantern was placed on the river at the royal ceremony of Chong Prieng on the night of the full moon of the twelfth lunar month. The King was so delighted by this that he declared the night of the floating lanterns to be an annual event – a tradition that has been continued to the present day. The floating candle is usually made of banana (*Musa*) leaves and decorated with flowers.

Thai flower arranging necessitates intricate artistry, evidence of which can be seen in floral bouquets, garlands, floral lace and chains. Flowers are contrived or rearranged in different forms – rose (*Rosa*) or lotus petals, for example, are pleated to create garlands or to make imaginary flowers, such as Wok Kha. Phut-jeep or crepe jasmine flowers (*Ervatamia coronaria*) are made into bracelets for the Buddhist Lent candle.

The traditional skills are taught in girls' schools and may be further studied at colleges throughout the land. The Thai people love flowers, seeing them as a reflection of the peacefulness and calm inherent in the Buddhist faith and in their own gentle nature. Lotus flowers are used to remember the Lord Buddha, since the lotus is the flower to which he compared humans.

Hangings 'Khrueng Khwaen'
Decorative hangings are hung by windows where the flowers' fragrance can best be appreciated.

'The wrist garland'
*This type of garland represents the art of garland-making at its best. A good wrist garland must exhibit a high degree of neatness and delicacy as it is usually an offering to Buddha, members of the royal family, guests on state visits, respected public figures and personalities. It can also be used as a decoration. The material used here includes Gardenia buds, rose petals, orange jasmine (*Murraya paniculata*) leaves, red sage buds (*Salvia fulgens*), water chrysanthemums, rak or Black varnish tree (*Melanorrhoea usitata*), Hibiscus and Ban-buree (*Allamanda*).*

THE AMERICAS

BARBADOS

THE TINY ISLAND OF BARBADOS, only 35 km (22 miles) long and 19 km (12 miles) at its widest point, is the most easterly of all the Caribbean islands, isolated in the Atlantic Ocean. A bedrock of fossilized coral stone differentiates Barbados from other islands in the Lesser Antilles chain. Large boulders of ancient coral litter the landscape.

Barbados enjoys a tropical climate: June to November marks the rainy season, when an average of 150 cm (60 in) of rain falls. Sometimes torrents fall within a few hours, to create rushing rivulets throughout the island. Vegetation quickly becomes lush and green. During the high tourist season, from December to the end of March, breezes blow and evenings are delightfully cool. Flowers return to perfume many gardens.

The British colonized Barbados in 1627 and governed the island until independence in 1966. Some still call it 'Little England'. They left behind them their Parliament (the third oldest in the world), their Anglican Church and their love of flowers.

For most Barbadians, flowers are a part of life. The Barbados Horticultural Society was founded in 1927 to promote horticulture in all its branches, and for over 25 years it has staged an annual flower show, at which anyone is eligible to win a prize for their best bloom.

When the English first came to these shores they brought with them many of the approximately 700 species of plants that now grow wild in Barbados and blend into the landscape. Barbados is home for ornamental plants from Africa, Asia, South America and the South Pacific, and Bajan floral designers are just as quick to cut African dracaenas or Asian angelica from their gardens as they are to cut the native bay rum (*Pimenta racemosa*) from their woodlands. This handsome small tree is known for its dark green glossy leaves, which are both aromatic and flavourful.

Temperatures never go below freezing in Barbados so there is always a plethora of garden foliage available. Fronds of Boston fern (*Nephrolepis exaltata* 'Bostoniensis'), golden feather palm or areca palm (*Chrysalidocarpus lutescens*), and lady palm (*Rhapsis excelsa*) are staples. The green heads of Egyptian papyrus (*Cyperus papyrus*) often replace more colourful flowers. The

This triangular arrangement is typical of those made for Bajan parties. The foliar skeleton consists of three cultivars of Dracaena, Dracaena reflexa *'Song of India,* Dracaena angustifolia *'Honoriae', corn plant (*Dracaena fragrans angustifolia *'Massangeana'), and a red-veined croton cultivar. Hybrid green* Anthurium *'Midori' and red* Anthurium *'Tropica',* Alpinia purpurata *'Eileen McDonald', the pink ginger,* Dendrobium *'Sonia' and 'KB White',* Oncidium *'Gower Ramsay', and pink and gold parrot's flower or parrot's plantain (*Heliconia psittacorum*) hybrids fill the centre of the arrangement. The exotic, dangling* Heliconia chartacea *'Sexy Pink' is the jewel in the crown.*
ARRANGER: *DAVID YEARWOOD.*

branches of variegated Dracena reflexa 'Song of India', crotons (*Codiaeum*) or yellow screw pine (*Pandanus baptistii* 'Aureus') are as bright as a blossom and the large leaves of Swiss cheese plant (*Monstera deliciosa*) and tree philodendron (*P. bipinnatifidium*) bestow a jungle ambience to the simplest creation.

Exotic gingers (*Alpinia purpurata*), lobster claws (*Heliconia*) and waxy-red painter's palettes (*Anthurium*), all commercially farmed on the island, ensure a unique Bajan touch.

Flowers are in great demand for holidays like Valentine's Day and Mother's Day. Valentine's Day colour schemes are red and white. Shops import roses from Colombia and the United States, and local red anthurium mimic Valentine hearts. The larger parish churches are decorated with flowers for fund-raising festivals and major feast days, such as Easter, Whitsuntide and Christmas. Easter and Christmas displays highlight the liturgical colours of yellow and white. Tuberoses (*Polianthes tuberosa*), white *Anthurium*, yellow marigolds (*Calendula*) and, for Christmas, the tall golden spikes of Christmas candle (*Senna alata*) are in great demand. Like snow-on-the-mountain (*Euphorbia leucocephala*) and poinsettia (*Euphorbia pulcherrima*), Christmas candle is a large shrub that only flowers when the days are at their shortest – December and January.

BERMUDA

LAPPED BY THE WARM WATERS of the Gulf Stream, Bermuda is the most northerly of the world's coral islands, and is considered to be semi-tropical. Situated 650 miles off the Eastern Seaboard of the United States and 1,000 miles north of the West Indies, the approximately 180 islands and islets are coral reefs built on the tops of long-extinct volcanoes and comprise a total of 22 square miles. The topography is hilly and due to the porosity of the rock there are no rivers or lakes and only a few tidal ponds.

Imported plants have all but supplanted the original inhabitants, two of the most notable being *Hibiscus* and *Oleander nerium*, whose vibrant colours splash the landscape. Perhaps the most prized of the endemics is Bermuda cedar (*Juniperus bermudiana*). It is a most beautiful wood with a deep red colour and wonderful aroma and was used for building ships, houses and furniture. Bermuda palmetto palm (*Sabal bermudiana*) is another 'original'. Once hats made from the Bermuda palmetto were all the rage in London.

Another plant, Bermudiana (*Sisyrinchium graminoides*), is the national flower. A small, purple wildflower with yellow centre

*This two-tiered centrepiece is for a dinner party at the Prime Minister's residence. Rum-barrel arrangements often decorate Barbadian flower festivals. Here plumes of the pampas grass (*Cortaderia selloana*) are mimicking the sugar-cane (*Saccharum officinarum*) arrows that shoot out from the cane fields at the end of the year. Anthurium 'Linda DeMol' and Heliconia chartacea 'Sexy Pink' confirm its tropical origin.* ARRANGER: DAVID YEARWOOD.

which blooms in the spring, its likeness can be found adorning everything from bone china to T-shirts. An introduced flower with which Bermuda has become synonymous is the Easter lily (*Lilium longiflorum*). These flowers used to be an important export crop and now each year Her Majesty the Queen receives an Easter bouquet.

In the seventeenth and eighteenth centuries, rosemary (*Rosemarinus*) was used decoratively for funerals and weddings. The first mention of a rose (*Rosa*) was by a shipwrecked Spanish sailor in 1639, and by the late nineteenth century it was recorded that 'white roses are in great profusion, as many as 2,000 blooms have been used in the Easter decoration of Trinity Church alone'. With the island being an important stop-over for vessels trading between Europe, the Americas and the West Indies, we can assume that, as with the styles in housing, furniture and clothing,

the floral decorations in the home would follow those of England and Europe.

As tourism is Bermuda's main industry, many flower-related items have been made to satisfy the demand for souvenirs. The late John Lennon was inspired by the freesia 'Double Fantasy' while visiting Bermuda, and named his album after this fragrant flower.

Arrangers in Bermuda keep up with latest trends, bringing home new ideas from their travels and using them as catalysts for their own creativity. It is a very cosmopolitan community, and this is reflected in the flower arranging, with no particular style dominating. If Bermuda is to be recognized for its flower arranging it would probably be in the way that all-foliage designs are so excellently handled, due to the natural abundance of such wonderful plant material.

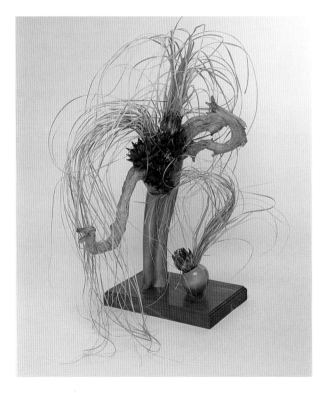

A contemporary design.
ARRANGER: JEAN MOTYER.

A foliage design.
ARRANGER: JUDI DAVIDSON

CANADA

CANADA IS FORTUNATE TO POSSESS some of the world's most spectacular natural scenery. It is a vast, varied but largely uninhabited land, with most of its population located in the historic heartland of Ontario and Quebec. Canada spans the continent from the Pacific Coast, through the Rocky Mountains and the Great Plains to the Great Lakes, Quebec and the Maritime Provinces bordering the Atlantic, but also stretching through the Great Wild North to the Arctic Sea.

Floral art in Canada, like painting, sculpture and music, has been influenced by many cultures. While there is little record of the native people using fresh flowers in art, plant forms were traditionally used in decorating crafts and clothing.

This design incorporates arum lily (Zantedeschia aethiopica), Royal palm (Roystonea) and Epipremnum sp. ARRANGER: PEG SPENCE.

It was land that brought many people to Canada, and it is still bringing them, land that could be their own. It is the land, its mountains, rocks, forests and inland lakes, that is reflected in paintings, in sculpture and in music. To some degree the land can be seen in Canadian floral design too, in naturalistic placements, in the use of native plants and in the images created, sometimes stark, sometimes vibrantly colourful and frequently evocative.

Flower arranging emerged as a recognized art form shortly after World War II, when garden clubs and horticultural societies incorporated decorative sections in their flower shows. At first these were judged by American judges, but within only a few years schools were established to accredit Canadian judges and teachers.

Canadian flower arrangers have become familiar with all aspects of flower show work, and in particular with the many variations in design, from the history of floral design to the present. The fine points of traditional work, modern and abstract, have been studied and incorporated. The long tradition of Japanese flower arranging (ikebana) has also made an impact.

After the long winter, spring finally bursts forth, crowning last year's fungus with new colour. Materials include: Phellinus ignarius, Ganoderma adspersum, Spongipellis 'Pachydom', Chinese wisteria (Wisteria sinensis) and Tulipa 'Garden Party'.
ARRANGER: MARISA BERGANINI.

Variations in decorative design are not the sole criterion for flower arrangers. They must also have considerable horticultural knowledge, perhaps not so much of the culture of plants, but of plant names, both common and botanical. This is essential information for competitors, as is the care of house plants and cut specimens. Because Canada's winters are long, except on the west coast, arrangers take special interest in drying and preserving plant material. The forcing of spring branches is also part of an arranger's repertoire. So Canadian flower shows are not restricted to the growing season. Early spring designs may incorporate forced branches, while late autumn and winter shows frequently have decorative classes that specify dried arrangements.

*This design comprises baby's breath (*Gypsophila paniculata*), winged statice (*Limonium sinuatum*), pampas grass (*Cortaderia selloana*) and driftwood. ARRANGER: JOYCE DIETRICH.*

Canadian flower shows demonstrate wide variety in their competitions. Garden clubs and horticultural societies encourage designers to be growers, and growers to be designers. Flower shows feature both horticultural specimens and flower arranging. In the design section, in addition to traditional and interpretative exhibits, special classes feature miniature designs, corsages, decorative tables, collages, plaques, wreaths, garlands, vignettes and still lifes.

It is difficult to 'label' the flower arrangements of Canada because they reflect such a wide range of elements and cultures. However, a distinction may be seen in their clear outlines, fresh colours and use of indigenous materials.

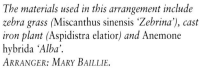

*The materials used in this arrangement include zebra grass (*Miscanthus sinensis *'Zebrina'), cast iron plant (*Aspidistra elatior) *and* Anemone hybrida *'Alba'.*
ARRANGER: MARY BAILLIE.

COLOMBIA

COLOMBIA IS THE NORTHERNMOST of the Andean countries and has access to both the Atlantic and the Pacific Oceans. It is a tropical country where around half the population derives its livelihood from agriculture. Its landscape is dominated by the grandiose range of the Andes that runs through the west of the country from south to north. The climate varies according to altitude, the lowlands being hot, humid or dry. The temperate areas are higher in altitude, and it is here that the world-famous Colombian coffee is grown. There are also cool mountain regions, and above 3,000 m (9,850 ft) the climate becomes very cold – typical of that of high altitudes in the Tropics.

Given Colombia's diversity in altitude and climate, an enormous variety of flowers and foliage is to be found. The most noteworthy flowers are orchids, of which around 3,000 species have so far been classified, most of them epiphytes. Roses (*Rosa*), Easter lilies (*Lilium longiflorum*), African lilies (*Agapanthus*), all varieties of chrysanthemums, irises, tritonias, heliconias, bird of paradise flowers (*Strelitzia*), carnations, hydrangeas, daffodils (*Narcissus*), delphiniums, gladioli, arum lilies (*Zantedeschia*) and many more are grown commercially for the domestic, as well as

A typical Colombian flower display arranged by a member of the Club de Jardinena de Medellin.

the export, market. Foliage is equally varied – silver *Eucalyptus*, quince (*Chaenomeles japonica*), myrtle (*Myrtus*), countless varieties of ferns and philodendrons being just a few of the plants used in flower arrangements. The national flower is the *Cattleya*, the most common of the native orchids.

Throughout its history Colombia has been influenced by foreign fashions in flower arranging. There is, however, a typically Colombian type of flower arrangement – the *arreglo Santaferenó* – whose name derives from the capital, Santafé de Bogotá. This makes use of whatever grows in the garden, and combines herbs, wild flowers and leaves with geranium (*Pelargonium*), begonias, violets (*Viola odorata*), pansies (*Viola wittrockiana*), carnations, poppies (*Papaver*) and marguerites (*Argyranthemum frutescens*) in an informal yet fairly elaborate way.

In the days when florists did not exist, peasants would come daily to the towns to sell the flowers they grew in their small plots. They would tie the flowers in bunches and carry them in wooden boxes called *silletas*, so that they came to be known as *silleteros*. As towns grew, the *silleteros* gradually disappeared, but in Medellin, where they had been one of the city's most characteristic sights, their lost trade is revived each year on 7 August in a spectacularly colourful parade, the Desfile de Silleteros.

A stunning display of Strelitzia.
ARRANGER: CAROLINA ARROWSMITH.

MEXICO

THE REPUBLIC OF MEXICO INCLUDES Lower California and the peninsula of Yucatan. To the west lies the Pacific Ocean and to the east the Gulf of Mexico and the Atlantic. On the lowest land, where there is a tropical climate, there are hundreds of species of cacti, *Yucca* and many types of *Agave* and mesquita (*Prosopis*) bushes. A little rain changes the whole scenery, for the land becomes covered with flowers of brilliant colours. On higher land, which experiences a more temperate climate, the pine (*Pinus*) and oak (*Quercus*) are found, together with magnolias, acacias, myrtle, mimosas and bamboo. In the forest region there are hundreds of species of trees half-buried among ferns and plants of all kinds. Many valuable trees grow here including mahogany (*Swietenia mahogani*), rosewood (*Dalbergia* sp.), Spanish cedar (*Toona* syn. *Cedrela adorata*), and plants from which ginger (*Zingiber officinale*), licorice (*Glycyrrhiza glabra*) and gums are obtained.

It was one of Hernando Cortés's men who said, 'When I beheld the scenes around me, I thought within myself that this was the garden of the world' when they landed near Vera Cruz in 1519. They discovered Tenochtitlán, a city with temples, pyramids, palaces, houses, and open markets. What surprised them most, however, was the advanced horticultural technology. There were floating gardens, connecting lakes, one with salt and one with fresh water, and an intricate system of canals. A system of hydroponics existed called *tzinanpayotl* which had been used by the Aztecs since AD 200. Cortés's men also saw a huge botanical garden with many Mexican flowers unknown to them – the first botanical garden known to the world.

*The marigold (*Tagetes *sp.) is the flower of the dead, and the yellow-orange of its petals has been used since primitive times for funerals and memorial services. Today wreaths and crosses are fashioned from the marigold.*
ARRANGER: ISABEL IBARGUEN.

Another interesting historical note concerns an Aztec figure dating from the sixteenth century and representing Xochipilli – the prince of flowers. The symbols on its body represent the various hallucinatory plants found in Mexico! Mexicans have always had a great love for flowers, and arrangements are found in most homes today, no matter how humble. In Acapulco and other cities in the Tropics you can see many tropical flowers and foliage, such as heliconias, bird-of-paradise flowers (*Strelitzia*) and painter's palettes (*Anthurium*). Other popular flowers include sword lily (*Gladiolus*), dahlias – the Mexican national flower – all types of lily, particularly the calla lily (*Zantedeschia*), camellia, azalea, fuchsia, geranium (*Pelargonium*) and poinsettia (*Euphorbia pulcherrima*) which is a native flower of Mexico. Cock's comb (*Celosia argentea* var. *cristata*) is sold only in November on All Souls' Day and the Day of the Dead.

The native Mexicans use flowers, and garlands of fruit and flowers, at Christmas and for saints' days, when they are draped around the image of a saint or carried to the cemetery to be placed on a grave. Ninety per cent of Mexicans are Catholic, so churches are always elaborately decorated. On Palm Sunday palm branches are woven into lovely ornaments and sold outside the churches.

Mexican architecture has a great love of symmetry and this is often reflected in the way they arrange their flowers.

*Three terracotta dishes in different sizes have been filled with marigolds, potatoes (*Solanum tuberosum*), mangoes (*Mangifera indica*), chillis and, in the bottom left, colorin – the coral tree (*Erythrina*), which is very popular in Mexico. This is typical of an arrangement to be seen in a church.*

Creative three-dimensional sculptural form with gourds
(Cucurbita), Boston ivy (Parthenocissus tricuspidata)
and Trumpet vine (Campsis radicans).
ARRANGER: JUNE WOOD (NCSGC).

UNITED STATES OF AMERICA

THE UNITED STATES OF AMERICA SPANS the width of the North American continent and includes the Hawaiian islands in the Pacific Ocean and Alaska to the far north-west of Canada. It was mainly wilderness 300 years ago. It was developed by people from many different European countries, who possessed an iron determination and the different skills needed to challenge the mountains, rivers, deserts and severe climatic changes from hot to icy-cold. They tamed the land for their own use and gained the freedom to govern themselves. Except for the American Indians, the Eskimos and native Hawaiians, every American is an immigrant or a descendant of an immigrant, which explains the wide diversity of talent among its people.

'Say it with flowers' is a slogan that originated in America and is recognized in every land. Virtually every supermarket has a section selling cut flowers, where the impulse purchase is made. But the florist is not losing its importance, for this is where Americans go to buy flowers for special occasions. Flowers are given on anniversaries and birthdays, for graduation ceremonies, hospital visits, on Mother's Day and on Valentine's Day.

Homes are elaborately decorated for holidays such as Thanksgiving, Christmas, Easter, Valentine's Day and the American holiday – the Fourth of July, Independence Day. Roses, gardenias (*Gardenia*), carnations, orchids and other exotic flowers are popular on these occasions. Churches are decorated by their altar guilds according to the church architecture, the degree of formality, the practices and beliefs.

A ball or large dance, often called 'the Prom', takes place annually in every high school and college. For this formal occasion a girl will wear a corsage of flowers to match her gown – orchids being perhaps the most popular choice. There are many ways to wear a corsage: it may of course be pinned on a dress, worn as a 'wristlet' or bracelet of flowers, attached to an evening bag or worn in the hair.

American traditional all-green mass design. Lines of fern, Eucalyptus and Leucothoë were placed to create the outline for this mass design. Variegated privet, Ligustrum, and Aspidistra leaves were added for colour contrast. Sedum was used to give contrast in form, and Nandina berries to give variation in size relationships.
ARRANGER: BARBARA MAY (NCSGC).

Corsages are also given on Mother's Day to mothers who live nearby. A woman will receive pink or red flowers if her own mother is still alive, and white if her mother is not. Baskets of flowers are often sent through their florist by telephone to those living further away. At Easter, mothers are also presented with spring flowers, orchids, gardenias or roses to wear to church. For weddings, the mothers of both the bride and groom wear a corsage to match their outfit. Fathers wear a *boutonnière* – a small bouquet of freesia, a rose or a carnation – in the buttonhole of the lapel.

College football is an integral part of the American life, due in part to the television coverage that it is given throughout the season, which starts at the end of September and ends with the final 'Bowl' games played over the New Year break. At high schools and colleges the mothers and girlfriends of football players wear large 'yellow mums' embellished with oak leaves to the big Thanksgiving Holiday game.

A delightful custom in America is for lengths of highways to be sponsored by groups or individuals who keep them clear of litter, and also in many cases create wild plant gardens alongside the banks. Narcissi, unusual grasses and an abundance of other self-seeding or self-spreading flowers create a beautiful sight that needs little maintenance.

Since colonial times Americans have cultivated flower gardens on their own property. Ruth Crocker of the Garden Club of America says, 'Our attitudes towards plant material are initially conditioned by what we see growing around us, what we can go out and pick. Thus there are vast differences between where a Hawaiian begins her flower arranging and where a New Englander does, and regional styles reflect these local anomalies. However, modern transportation and importing methods have blurred geographic divisions, allowing virtually everyone access to an almost staggering array of plant material.' Local plant material is therefore frequently used in designing, combined with other exotic plant materials purchased from the florist, supermarket or from specialized garden centres.

The American South has long been renowned for its hospitality. Its version of the mass arrangement, containing an abundance of plant material, is an example of welcoming splendour. Plant material is carefully but liberally selected from cutting gardens grown for this purpose, for colour harmony and textural interest, as well as gradation and variation in size and form. What makes these arrangements so special is that, despite their sheer abundance, grouping of plant materials and unabashed lushness, the spaces between the flowers are maintained, creating a loose, almost ethereal effect.

Bracelet and corsage.
ARRANGER: JANICE MURPHY.

Hawaiian arrangers choose bold, dramatic forms from the Tropics to create large, exciting abstract designs. Plant material and other components interplay so artfully that it becomes unimportant to determine which is which. It is the total image that matters. Colours are often brilliant and contrasts strong.

Flower Arranging Styles

Ann Milstead of National Council of State Garden Clubs, writes: 'There are two categories of American design involved in the development of floral design. The traditional design period includes Colonial American (1607-1720), Colonial Williamsburg (1720-80), Federal (1780-1830), Victorian (1830-1900) and the second category covers the early twentieth-century.

'Colonial American designs were very informal, simple bunches of wild flowers in cups, bowls and other available utensils of wood, clay or basketry. During the period of Colonial Williamsburg, the flower arrangements reflected the financial prosperity of the settlers in this part of the United States of America. Containers were English in style and made of bronze, alabaster, marble, pewter, porcelain or silver. The designs were generally fan-shaped with garden flowers, barley (*Hordeum*) and wheat (*Triticum*), lightly arranged at the top and more solidly clustered at the rim of the container. Sometimes the

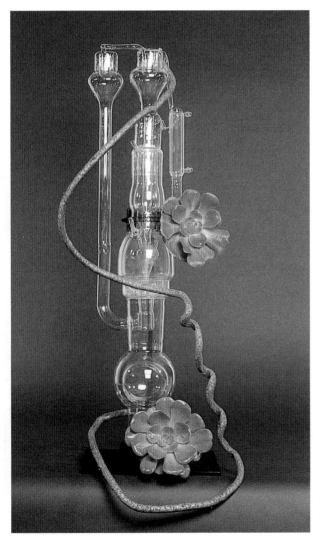

◁ *The Bionic Garden. Technology and plant material have been juxtaposed to create an arresting effect.*
ARRANGER: NANCY D'OENCH
(GARDEN CLUBS OF AMERICA).

container was completely hidden by the plant materials, and often fruit and flowers were placed on the table as accessories to create the overall effect of opulent elegance.

'In the Federal Period mass designs were popular, with formal symmetrical balance and usually greater height than width. Often fruits were used in combination with both foliage and flowers in epergnes (branched ornamental centrepieces). Containers were of Sandwich pressed glass, Paul Revere or Sheffield silver, Wedgwood and lustre-ware.

'Victorian designs were influenced by the characteristics of the European Victorian designs, as those of the early twentieth century reflected the simplification of Edwardian designs.'

American floral design is also influenced by both our European and Oriental design heritage. Oriental designs, can be traced back to 207 BC and are based on religious beliefs and nature. The Japanese developed flower arrangements as the total art form which is prevalent today. Three American designs, traditional line, traditional line-mass and traditional mass, are the result of using the lines and geometric forms of Oriental floral arrangements, and the form and style of European floral designs.

Abstract design is very popular in America, perhaps due in Ruth Crocker's words to: 'America's fascination with technology, so that all manner of materials not traditionally found in flower arranging is used in abstract work. The intent is to combine plant material with other components, in such a way as to distil the elements of design to their essence, creating a work of art – an arrangement about colour, or line, or light or space.'

'In the mid-1960s abstract designs became popular,' continues Ann Milstead. 'These designs were a break from naturalism, expressing the designer's creativity and imagination. Emphasis is placed on the use of space, depth and area of tension, which equates interest throughout the design.' These designs are a break from naturalism, expressing the designer's creativity and imagination. Emphasis is placed on the use of space and depth and areas of tension, which brings interest to the design.

Newer designs developed and created by artistic floral designers of the National Council of State Garden Clubs are presented in its Handbook for Flower Shows which it shares with its many affiliates throughout the world and is also a guide to accredit flower show judges and instructors.

Assemblage. A group of disparate objects was juxtaposed with plant materials to create depth in this abstract design.
ARRANGER: CATHERINE ARRENDALE (NCSGC).

Assemblage. An example of an Op Art abstract design using aggressive forms of equal strength to provide visual movement through the design.
ARRANGER: DEAN DAY SMITH (NCSGC).

Show Classes

Classes in a show can come under the heading of aerial, assemblage, botanical, collage, construction, illuminary, kinetic, miniature, small, Op Art, parallel, plaques, reflective, sculptural form, still life, synergistic, transparency, underwater, vibratile, vignettes and table designs.

The museum show or 'Art in Bloom' is very popular with members of the Garden Club of America. Arrangers are assigned a work of art to interpret. Staging is usually on pedestals placed next to the work of art. Curators are very careful about what is allowed in their galleries, but they are also delighted by the new museum audience drawn in by the flower arrangers. Arrangers relish the opportunity to research a work of art and the freedom to create a design in the style that they feel best interprets their assignment.

△ *The Cutting Edge, at the Philadelphia Flower Show.*
ARRANGER: GRETCHEN RILEY
(GARDEN CLUBS OF AMERICA).

FLOWER ARRANGING WORLDWIDE

This section contains information on the World Association of Flower Arrangers (WAFA), other organizations and individuals who have helped with this encyclopedia. WAFA was founded in June 1981. Irene Hawkins, Jill Findlay, Mary Napper and Dorothy Simcock were the instigators of the association. The original members were:

1. Association of Irish Flower Arrangers
2. Scuoladi Decorazione Floreale Italiana
3. The Association of Cape Flower Clubs
4. The Floral Club, Malta
5. Natal Panel of Floral Art Judges
6. NIGFAS – Northern Ireland Group of Flower Arrangement Societies
7. NIPPON Flower Designers Association
8. The Belgian Flower Arrangement Society
9. The Jamaica Panel of Floral Art Judges, and the St Andrews Flower Arrangement Club
10. Federation Mexicana de Jardineria y Arregio Floral AC.
11. Kenya Floral Arrangement Club.
12. The Garden Clubs of Ontario
13. National Association of Flower Arrangement Societies of Great Britain
14. Floral Art Society of New Zealand
15. Australian Association of Floral Art Judges[sc] Schools
16. Garden Club of Bermuda and Judges Council
17. Société Nationale D'Horticulture de France
18. Cape Floral Art Adjudicators Union
19. South African Flower Adjudicators Union (SAFU)

Other countries have since joined and up-to-date information may be obtained from NAFAS, at 21 Denbigh Street, London SW1V 2HF. You will also find contact addresses for many of the countries later in this section.

WAFA is non-partisan and promotes its objectives without prejudice as to race, language, religion or philosophical opinion. The first two objectives in the Association's constitution are to reinforce the bonds between the various members and to promote the exchange of information concerning floral art allied interests.

Also included in this section is information on other flower organizations and individuals who have helped us with this encyclopedia.

Australia

For details of flower arranging societies in Australia contact:
• Australian Floral Art Association
  Secretary: Mrs Jean Tondut
  42 Kathleen Street
  Cottesloe 6011

Barbados

Barbados has three flower arranging clubs. The Barbados Flower Circle stages a large annual show, with profits donated to the Challenor School for the Mentally Retarded. Contact:
• David Yearwood, President,
  Barbados Flower Circle,
  PO Box 655, GPO Bridgetown.
• Jennifer Weetch, President,
  Barbados Flower Arranging Society, PO Box 8W,
  Worthing, Christ Church.
• Gregory Moss, President,
  The Northern Flower Club,
  Gibbs, St Peter.

Bermuda

These are nine horticulturally related clubs in Bermuda. All clubs assist with the annual Agricultural Exhibition held each April. The Garden Club of Bermuda organises demonstrations, workshops and courses. Three international flower shows have been held there in recent years. Contact:
• The Garden Club of Bermuda,
  PO Box HM 1141,
  Hamilton HM Ex Bermuda.

Belgium

The Belgian Flower Arrangement Society, founded in 1967, now has over 2,400 members grouped in 28 local clubs called delegations, which are spread throughout the country. The aim of the association is to promote flower arranging in all its aspects. Its activities include gardening courses, visits to gardens, floral art courses, demonstrations, competitions and seminars. BFAS is affiliated to many associations and garden clubs abroad. Contact:
• BFAS,
  Kortrijksesteenweg 834, 9000 Ghent.
  Tel: 32-9-222.77.07.
  Fax: 32-9-220.15.44.

Canada

Club members of each Province are listed in The Registry of Garden Clubs of Canada. Contact:
• Marisa Berganini,
  The Registry of Garden Clubs of Canada,
  c/o Royal Botanical Gardens,
  PO Box 399,
  Hamilton,
  Ontario L8N 3H8.

Colombia

In Colombia there are 30 Clubes de Jardineria, co-ordinated by the Asociacion Nacional de Corporaciones de Clubes de Jardineria, and all of them affiliated to the National Council of State Garden Clubs. For further information contact:
• The National Council of State Garden Clubs,
  St Louis, Missouri, or:
• Club de Jardineria de Medellin,
  Carrera 52,
  No. 73-298
  Medellin.

Czech Republic

As yet there are no flower clubs but there is, however, a large residential horticultural school in Melnik which runs courses in floristry and flower arranging, collaborating with horticultural schools in Holland, Germany and Switzerland. It has been included in an international project involving the co-operation of the Czech Republic and Belgium. Each year they hold a large exhibition run by organizers Vystaviste Flora Olomouc. The styles which are taught there are wide-ranging and innovative, showing influences from around the world. Contact:
• Jan Macura (Headmaster),
  Stredni Zahradnicka Skola Melnik,
  Poabi 471, CZ-276 87 Melnik;
  Fax: 0206 623 009,
or the exhibition organizers:
• Vystavista Flora Olomouc,
  Wolkerova 17,

771 11 Olomouc;
Fax: 068 541 3370
There is also a floristry/flower arranging school at Lennicka University. Contact:
• Mendeleveltva, Lennicka a Yemedulska Universita,
  Beyrucova 345,
  Lednice na Morave, 691 44.
  Tel: 0042 627-982 11.
  Contact Ing. Neugebaueroua or Ing. Tatna Kuckova.

France

It was in 1827 in Paris that the Société Nationale d'Horticulture de France was formed. In 1962 the section L'Art Floral was formed and in 1976 it created a Diplôme d'Aptitude Florale et Artistique. In 1981 France joined WAFA. Every three years there is a 3-day exhibition in December of Christmas decorations throughout France. It is called Noël Enchanté and is run in support of various charities. Every four years there is an International Competition and every year 8 – 10 demonstrations are held at the headquarters of the society, some by demonstrators, others by florists. Contact:
• Société Nationale d'Horticulture de France, Section Art Floral,
  84 rue de Grenelle,
  75007 Paris.
  Tel: 0033 1 44 39 78 78
  Fax: 0033 1 45 44 96 57

Germany

Wally Klett has been working with the German Florist Association as a teacher and tutor for 13 years. She gives courses and demonstrations in Germany and abroad. She specializes in wedding work and has won many awards throughout the world for her work. Contact:
• Wally Klett, Studio Florale Gestaltung,
  Albstrasse 43,
  72581 Dettingen-Erms.
  Fax: 7123-88401.

Holland

Leo Koolen is a highly respected freelance designer and flower ambassador for Holland. He designs stands, flower parades, presentations of fruit and vegetables, and exhibitions. He gives flower demonstrations throughout the world. Contact:
• Leo Koolen,
  Madoerastraat 18,
  2022 ZM Haarlem.
  Fax: 023-5273285.
To join a flower club (NABS) contact:
• Daisy de Vries-Juncker,
  Tongerenseweg 8162 PP, Epe.
  Tel: 0578 612864
This club, founded in 1983, has 10 meetings each year. It holds occasional teaching demonstrations and workshops.

Indonesia

• Les Flori (Indonesian Art of Floral Design Institute),
  Jalan Citayem,
  1/2 Kobayorah Baru,
  Jaharte Seleton 12810.

International

A non-profit education service organization called the IDS or the International Design Symposium, based in Massachusetts. It is committed to advancing the knowledge and appreciation of design and horticulture world-wide and to bring awareness of design upon the lives of people. It offers numerous courses, workshops, demonstrations and seminars throughout the year. For further information contact:
• Kenn Stephens, International Design Symposium Ltd,
  PO Box 263,
  Westwood, Massachusetts 02090, USA.
  Fax: 001 617 329 8789.

Irish Republic

The objectives of the Association of Irish Flower Arrangers are to bring together for cultural and educational purposes all those clubs interested in flower arranging and to encourage the formation of new clubs. There are 98 affiliated clubs and many individual members from areas where there are no flower clubs. The association runs training courses of two-year duration followed by a test to qualify students as teachers, judges, demonstrators and speakers. National competitions are held every two years, and inter-club and flower arranger of the year competitions are also held – with the heats one year and finals the next year. For information on the Association of Irish Flower Arrangers, contact:
• Margaret Martin,
  13 Clareville Road,
  Kenilworth Park,
  Dublin 6W.

Israel

The Israeli Association of Flower Arrangers was started by Gina Eting in 1983 and its membership consists of both amateur and professional flower arrangers. The Association holds three national and three regional meetings annually. The regional meetings are small workshops, five similar meetings being held in different parts of the country so that all members can attend. As a group they have participated in setting up flower shows and charity events. Contact:
• Gina Eting FSF, NDSF,
  10/5 Emer Ayalon B.D.B. 2271,
  Shoham 73142.

Italy

The Italian Institute of Flower Arranging Decoration for Amateurs (Istituto Italiano Decoraziano Floreale per Amatori), founded in 1967 by Rosnella Cajello Fazio, has schools called EDFAs throughout Italy, which hold classes, exhibitions, competitions, meetings and seminars. The Institute periodically holds examinations for awarding diplomas to teachers and demonstrators and also supervises the selection of judges for national and international shows. It is greatly appreciated abroad, because the modern Italian style, which is still evolving, is seen to influence the world. Contact:
• Carla Barbaglia
  Via N. Sauro 132
  17027 Pietra Ligure, or:
• Instituto Italiano Decoraziano Floreale per Amatori (IIDFA).
  PO Box 229,
  18038 San Remo

Jamaica

For the Jamaican Panel of Floral Art Judges and the St Andrews Flower Arrangement and Garden Club contact:
• Mrs C. Moss-Soloman,
  PO Box 203,
  Kingston.

Japan

Ikebana is becoming increasingly popular outside Japan, being taught, demonstrated and exhibited all over the world. This is mainly thanks to Ellen Gordon Allen, who founded Ikebana International in 1956. There are now 1,247 chapters, very many of them in the USA and Europe, but there are also a growing number in almost all parts of the globe. Regional conferences are held every three years in different continents and a World Convention takes place every five years in Japan. 1996 is their 40th anniversary.

There are nine chapters in Great Britain, of which London is the oldest and was founded by Stella Coe and student friends in 1958. Thanks to her active hard work and enthusiasm, many of the other European chapters were formed. Stella also started the Ikebana Teachers' Association which is still very active in London and the North. Contact:
- UK:
  Tineke Robertson,
  16 Heath View,
  East Horsley,
  Surrey KT24 5ED
- Japan:
  Ikebana International,
  CPO Box 1262,
  Tokyo 100-91.

In Japan itself are many fine flower schools which have courses in Western flower arranging and Ikebana. Two of the most prestigious are:
- Manako Flower Academy,
  Roppong City Building 3-1-25,
  Roppong: Minato-ku,Tokyo 106,
  President: Yasuko Manako.
- Nippon Flower Designers Association (members of WAFA),
  4 – 5 – 6 Takanawa, Minato-ku,
  Tokyo 108.
  President: Sadao Kasahara.

Kenya

- The Secretary, Kenya Floral Arrangement Club,
  PO Box 45805,
  Nairobi.

Korea

- Korea International Floral Arts and Craft Development Association,
  Kyeong yang Blg. 201
  786–17 Yeoksam-dong, Kangnam-ku,
  Seoul (CPO Box 4078).

Malta

The Malta Floral Club, founded in 1965, celebrated its Pearl Anniversary in 1995. The club has 160 members who meet regularly in a large house in the heart of Sliema. The members have a full and varied programme of lessons, workshops, exhibitions and shows. Members also travel abroad every year to participate in international shows. At home, members do a lot of collage and craft work. Contact:
- The Malta Floral Club,
  57 Sir Luigi Camilleri Street,
  Sliema Slm 12.

Mexico

There are 17 garden clubs in Mexico City, all affiliated to the National Council of States Garden Club Inc., WAFA and NAFAS. There is also a chapter of Ikebana International. Throughout Mexico there are 100 clubs which are active in flower shows, with many judges and instructors affiliated to the National Council. The Flower Arrangement Club of Mexico City (Federación Mexicana de Jardineria y Arregio Floral AC) was founded in 1949. Contact:
- Isabel Ibarguen,
  Fuego 300, Pedregal de San Angel
  D.F. 01900 Mexico.

New Zealand

The Floral Society of New Zealand Inc. Contact:
- Margaret Morriss,
  Grinton, RVS Palmeston North.

Norway

Flower arranging clubs are not common in Norway, although there are gardening clubs. Floristry is regarded as being a respected profession with high standards of craftsmanship. Rolf Torhaug and Nils Norman Iversen are well-respected Norwegian florists with a stylish and creative florist's shop. They give demonstrations throughout the world. Contact:
- Rolf Torhaug and Nils Norman Iversen,
  Kreativ Flora,
  Nedre Slottsgt. 8, 0157 Oslo.

Pakistan

- Karachi:
  Karachi Floral Art Society of Pakistan,
  c/o Shahimah Sayeed,
  160c, Block 3, P.E.G.H.S.,
  Karachi.

Poland

Every year in Poznan there is a large flower show for the trade and public in the spring. In Gdansk there is an annual flower festival. For details contact the nearest Polish Embassy.

Russia

International Creative Association of Flower Arrangement Clubs, Art Flora is the central organization, comprising 52 clubs from 44 cities and towns of Russia and neighbouring republics. There are approximately 1,500 members. It is easy to join by taking a short course in flower arranging under Artflora. This association is now a member of WAFA. Festivals are held twice a year, and once a year for children, in different towns throughout Russia. The judges take account of recommendations by NAFAS. Arrangers from Artflora teach children, hold lessons in orphanages, and arrange festivals and exhibitions of flower arranging. They also work as floral decorators in theatres, exhibitions, cinemas, hospitals, museums, television studios and on sporting occasions. Contact:
- Nina A. Lozovaya,
  President Art Flora, Gen. Ermolov str. 12,28,
  Moscow 121293.

South Africa

The South African Flower Union (SAFU) is the official body representing flower arranging in all the Provinces. The flower clubs and associations within SAFU are committed to an 'Outreach' programme, which aims to reach out in friendship to all flower-lovers of South Africa and to reconcile all the differences in the wider section of the community. Contact:
- Rosemary Ladlau, President,
  Beverley Estate, PO Box 3,
  Umhlali 4390.

Spain

There are four flower arranging groups, all located on the Costa Blanca. They are the Costa Blanca Flower Club which meets at Benissa, which was founded in 1985, the Torre Vieja, the Marina Alta and The Penon. In 1995 they held their first competitive flower show, which was a great success. Contact:
• Dori Tiley,
  13a Avenida Valencia
  Valencia
  Calpe 3710
  Alicante.

Switzerland

The Swiss Association of Flower Arrangers (SAFA) is now a member of WAFA. Contact:
• Mrs Susan Hasner,
  88 Chemin de Ruth,
  1223 Cologny-Genéve 2.

Thailand

The SUPPORT Foundation (The Foundation for the Promotion of Supplementary Occupations and Related Techniques) oversees a nationwide network of crafts, including classic crafts and new ones developed from the old. It kindly supplied the photographs for this book. The headquarters are located in the royal family[sc]s Bangkok residence, where the Foundation receives the patronage of the Queen of Thailand. Throughout Thailand the art of flower arranging is encouraged in schools and colleges. Contact:
• 'Support Foundation', of Her Majesty the Queen,
  Chitralada Villa, Dusit Palace,
  Bangkok 10300.
The Susita Flower Academy has ben established by Miss Sunan Wongcharoen in order to raise the career standard of flower arrangement in Thailand. She runs many and varied courses. Contact:
• Susita Flower Academy,
  94726 Bangna Complex,
  Bangna Trad Road,
  Prakanong,
  Bangkok, 10260.
  Fax (662) 361-8835-40.

United Kingdom

The National Association of Flower Arrangement Societies (NAFAS) was founded in 1959 with much support from the Royal Horticultural Society. NAFAS was a leading force in setting up the World Association of Flower Arrangers (WAFA) in 1981. Most of the more than 100,000 members belong to one or more of nearly 1,500 clubs in the United Kingdom. There are also several hundred members overseas. There is a publications department where visitors are welcome and may purchase a wide variety of books, pamphlets, cards and gifts. Contact:
• NAFAS,
  21 Denbigh Street,
  London SW1V 2HF.
  Tel: 0171-828 5145. Fax: 0171-821 0587.

The United States of America

Two flower arranging movements in the USA have worked together for this book. The National Council of State Garden Clubs, Inc. was founded in 1929, and is the largest volunteer gardening organization in the world. It promotes conservation of natural resources and environ-mental awareness. It sponsors courses and promotes community service projects. In the area of flower arranging its aim is to promote creativity and artistic advancement. It looks forward to the new century and the challenges posed by new developments in materials, art works, electronics, etc. Based on the organization's flower arranging heritage, its members search the present for inspiration, which serves as a spring-board for the challenges of the future in floral art. 'It is a force for good, helping people grow.' Contact:
• National Council of State Garden Clubs, Inc.,
  4401 Magnolia Avenue,
  St Louis,
  Missouri 63110-3492.
The second movement is the Garden Club of America, which was founded in 1913 and has 16,000 members in 190 clubs spread across the United States. 'The purpose of the Garden Club of America is to stimulate the knowledge and love of gardening, to share the advantages of association by means of educational meetings, conferences, correspondence and publications, and to restore, improve and protect the quality of the environment through educational programmes and action in the fields of conservation and civic improvement.' Each year an average of 30 of these clubs have flower shows, which are open to the public and offer Garden Club of America Awards. Many more clubs have shows with their own clubs.
Contact:
• Garden Club of America,
  598 Madison Avenue,
  New York, NY 10022.
  Tel: 212-753 8287.
The Flower Arranging Study Group is the educational arm of the Garden Club of America. The Flower Arranging Study Group of the Garden Club of America is now a member of WAFA. Contact:
• Lucinda S. Sealey,
  805 Prince St, Alexandra,
  Virginia 22314.

Uruguay

The Garden Clubs of Uruguay, contact:
• Mrs Audrey Taylor de Gonzales,
  Ramble Tomas Berreta, 6725
  Montevideo, 11500.

Zimbabwe

In 1961 the then Rhodesian Association of Garden Clubs was formed which is now known as the National Association of Garden Clubs of Zimbabwe. It is a strong, flourishing concern.

The Association is affiliated to the RHS and NAFAS and is a member of WAFA. The objective is to encourage, establish and maintain a system of co-operation and mutual assistance for the benefit of members in the art and science of horticulture, floral art and allied interests; also to encourage judges to qualify and to further the objectives of the Association.

There is an Annual Congress, a stimulating get together, where business and entertainment are presented over the weekend. Every year a National Floral Art 'Team' Competition is held and every second year a Floral Art School takes place over five days.

Zimbabwe is twinned to a couple of clubs overseas and anyone wishing to join NAGC should contact:
• Patricia West,
  c/o Box 3067,
  Harare,
  Zimbabwe.

USEFUL ADDRESSES

• *Eucalyptus and other foliage:*
Strongs Greenery,
South Littleton,
Evesham WR11 5TR.

• *Flower Dry and sealant:*
Moira Clinch at
The Greenhouse Studio,
10 The Green, Mountsorrel,
Leics LE12 7AF.
Tel: 01162–375046.

• *Flower dyes:*
Carters of Blackburn,
29 Carham Road,
Blackburn,
Lancs BB1 8NX.

• *Fresh noble pine (blue spruce) and*
other foliage:
Deran Foliage,
Cilmeri, Pontrhydygroes,
Ystrad Meurig,
Dyfed SY25 6DJ.

• *Glycerine:*
Flowercraft,
18 High Street,
Chapel-en-le-Frith, Stockport,
Cheshire SK12 6HD.

• *Magazines available internationally:*
Flora International is available in
many countries throughout the
world, or directly from:

Fishing Lodge Studio,
77 Bulbridge Road,
Wilton, Salisbury,
Wilts SP2 0LE.
Tel: 01722-743207;

The Flower Arranger magazine is
available through Flower Clubs
affiliated to NAFAS,
or direct from:

Taylor Bloxham Ltd,
Nugent Street,
Leicester LE3 5HH.

• *Mistletoe:*
Mr & Mrs C.T. Adams,
Lower Doddenhill Farm,
Newnham Bridge, Tenbury Wells,
Worcs WR15 8NU.

• *Orchids and exotic foliage:*
Just Orchids,
Brookside Nursery,
Church Road, Swallowfield,
Berks RG7 1TH.
Tel/Fax: 01734-886481.

• *Ready-pressed flowers:*
Ann Stringer,
Poole Farm,
Raddington, Taunton,
Somerset TA4 2QN
(send s.a.e. for information).

• *Silica gel and sealant:*
Maureen Foster's Flower
Preserving Crystals,
77 Bulbridge Road,
Wilton, Salisbury,
Wilts SP2 0LE.

• *Flower Schools:*
Judith Blacklock
52 Suffolk Road,
London SW13 9NR (courses designed for
individual groups).

Michael Bowyer,
Flower Cellar Day School,
161 Wilton Road,
Salisbury SP2 7JQ.

Craig Bullock,
Montford Cottage,
Cuckstool Lane,
Fence, Burnley,
Lancashire BB12 9NZ.

• *Flower arranging sundries*
The Flower Cellar
2b Nursery Road
Salisbury
Wilts SP2 7HX

INDEX